W9-BTH-981

In Great Decades : Three

In Great Decades : Three

TRIAL BY TELEVISION

AND OTHER ENCOUNTERS

Michael Straight
With Illustrations by Robert Osborn

Devon Press : New York/Berkeley : 1979

The author wishes to acknowledge that certain of these pieces originally appeared in (and are copyrighted by) *The New Republic* in somewhat different versions.

LIBRARY OF CONGRESS CATALOGING IN PUBLICATION DATA

Straight, Michael Whitney.
    Trial by television (and other encounters).

    (His In great decades ; book 3)
    1. McCarthy-Army controversy, 1954. 2. United States—Politics and government—1945-1953. 3. United States—Politics and government—1953-1961. 4. Right and left (Political science) I. Title. II. Series.
UB23.S79   320.9'73'092   79-17889
ISBN 0-934160-03-1

Trial by Television is volume three of the set, *In Great Decades*, by Michael Straight. The other volumes are:

I   *Happy and Hopeless* (a novel)
II   *Caravaggio* (a play).
IV *Twigs for an Eagle's Nest: Government and the Arts: 1965-1978*

Contents

I: On the Eve

Introduction 11
On the Eve 12

II: You're in the Air Force Now

Introduction 19
So Long, Tex 22
The Ones that Make the World Go Around 27
Hot Pilot 30
Needle and Ball 34
The Koala Bear 42

III: Working for *The New Republic*

Introduction 51
Henry 53
Stassen and Taft: 1948 73
Adlai 78
With Eisenhower at the Summit 85
The Ghost at the Banquet 105

IV: Trial by Television

Introduction 123
The Collapse of Chairman Mundt 125
The Power of Private Schine 140
The Credulity of Mr. Jenkins 151
The Education of Secretary Stevens 160
The Art of Mr. Welch 179

The Employment of Mr. Adams 196
The Sanctimony of Senator Dirksen 207
The Pacifism of President Eisenhower 217
The Integrity of Senator McClellan 233
The Fear of Mrs. Driscoll 247
The Ambivalence of Mr. Cohn 253
"Thanks for the Marvellous Cheese" 272
The Conscience of Senator Symington 275
The Reluctance of Mr. Carr 288
The Fanaticism of Senator McCarthy 298
The Curtain Falls 316

I
On the Eve

Introduction

At two, I dressed up in a soldier suit to be photographed with my brother Whitney. Our sister Biddy stood between us, holding an American flag.

It was the summer of 1918. Our mother was engaged in war work. Our father had gone to France to fight.

He did not come back. In time, our mother remarried a young Englishman. Together, they founded a community in Devonshire, Dartington Hall. Farming and handicrafts were integral parts of the community; so were the arts, and a progressive school. We were a part of the student body—one fifth of it, in fact—when the school began.

I went on to Cambridge. Its dominant figure in the world of thought was John Maynard Keynes and I was fortunate in being a member of his circle. But, for students like myself, character was expressed not in thought, but in action. The decisive events for us were the rise of Hitler and the Spanish Civil War.

I traveled to the Spanish border in July, 1936, making the most of my freedom. A month later my closest friend, John Cornford, enlisted in the armies of the Republic, the first British volunteer. He was killed on his twenty-first birthday; I told his father in Cambridge; then I drove to Birmingham to tell his girl.

On the Eve

In early July festivals were held in the Basque country. The villages were bright with flags. We stopped many times on the road that led inland from St.-Jean-de-Luz to watch the dancing and the games of *pelota*. Then, as we climbed, the Pyrenees reared up on the horizon, blue, with the snow still on their summits, blinding white. Beneath them the green hills rolled in powerful rhythms beside us, and on the sides of the road corn fields lay, tawny and golden, and occasionally harvested.

Suddenly, on the road to Carcassonne, we were hailed by a girl with a knapsack on her shoulder. We drew in; as she ran toward us, a man rose wearily from the roadside grass. They told us that they were Austrian students, on their way to Spain. They had walked eighteen miles that day; they were very tired.

We had no room in our open car, but we buried the man under the luggage in the back seat, so that all we could see of him was his sunburnt face. We wedged the girl into the front seat with us, and we set off again.

We questioned them as we drove; they were guarded and vague. The secret police were everywhere in Austria they said; militarism was being revived in the schools; the Social Democratic Party and the Communist Party were illegal; the Chancellor, Kurt Schuschnigg was a dictator in everything but name. It seemed clear where their sympathies lay. I whistled the *Moorsoldaten*, watching the girl in the mirror of the car. She glanced toward me and looked away. For a hundred miles we talked of other things.

In the evening we came to the tiny town of Foix. We had dinner by lamplight on a hotel terrace overlooking a dark, rapid river. By then, they could see that we meant no harm. They told us that they were members of the outlawed Communist Party of Austria. They said that it was strong and growing; that it was organized in units of four; and that it was working closely with remnants of the Social Democrats. They were going to Spain on some mission; they would not say what it was.

At eleven we began a search for lodgings. We went first to the cafes since they had the cheapest rooms. At the entrance of one cafe in the town square a heavyset man sat at a table alone. He seemed to be drunken or asleep, his body slouched over the table, his head low. Hearing us talking in German, he jerked his head up, straining to listen.

We found no rooms in the cafe. We wandered on until we heard a cry behind us. We turned and saw the man, lurching beneath the lamplight like a dancing bear. He staggered up to us, muttering. He thrust out his hand to the girl, saying in German that he had known her in Saarbrucken. She insisted that she had never been there, but he swayed toward her: "You look just like Kathe from Saarbrucken," he said.

"Kathe? Which Kathe?" said the student.

"I knew a Kathe in Saarbrucken."

"So. You are from Saarbrucken," the student said.

"*Ja, ja; Ich bin Saarbruckener*," the man cried.

"In that case," said the student, "you must know Paula."

"Paula . . . Paula . . . There are lots of Paulas . . . What's her other name?"

"Paula has no other name. Paula is big and strong."

"No . . . I don't know Paula. . . . But if my friend were here . . ." the man shook his head to clear it; "It's just that I can't remember names."

There was a pause.

"So . . . you're from Saarbrucken," the student said. "Very interesting! Perhaps the political wind has blown you this way."

"*Ja, ja,*" said the man. "I left after Hitler moved in."

"Would you go back?"

"Perhaps. If I could."

"But you can't; is that it? You're a Communist, I suppose."

The Saarlander grinned again in his drunken way. "*Ja,*" he muttered, "*Ich bin Kommunistisch.*"

"Then why are you down here?"

"The Red Aid," said the man; "the Red Aid sent me." He drew himself upright. "I'm a mechanic," he said, "a skilled man."

"I'd like to go back," he added, "in a way. But here . . . I have a good job here; at good wages . . . I can do what I like here," he cried, his voice resounding in the silent square, "I can say what I like!" He spread his arms wide, embracing the empty town. "*Hier,*" he shouted, "*hier bin ich frei!*"

He stood there listening, as if his challenge might evoke an answer. "Yes," he said, "and here, I earn my living by honest means."

"So," said the student with bitter irony, "you are an honest man."

"Yes, I'm honest."

"You think you're honest! You call yourself honest, because you can say what you like!" The student turned to his girl. "*Wie ihnen der schnabel gewachsen ist!*" (How the moss has grown!) he said.

There was a long silence. The Saarlander stood grinning and swaying. Then he leaned toward the student. "And you," he said, "what are you doing down here?"

"Holidays."

"From Berlin?"

"Yes," said the student after a pause, "from Berlin."

"Why did you have to think so long about it?"

"Did I think so long about it?"

"You thought for too long!"

"Did I? Why shouldn't I tell you if I'm from Berlin?"

"Of course . . . of course . . ." Then, with sudden cunning, the Saarlander said, "But you wouldn't be down here, just for that!"

The student ignored him. "Tell me," he said, "where can we get some cheap rooms for the night?"

For a moment the Saarlander was sullen. Then he laughed. "Oh, there are plenty of cheap ones; but, you won't get out of them alive. The bedbugs are as bad as Social Democrats here, for pestering you!"

At that, we said good night and walked back to the hotel.

"A pity!" said the student, as we walked across the square. "He was in the underground all right. He cracked up, and they sent him here for a rest. Now he's been demoralized by too much freedom. He's no use to anyone."

We drove on together the next morning under the brilliant sun and the deep sky. Fifty miles from Foix, we came to a crossroads. There, we stopped and said good-bye; the two Austrians hoisting their packs onto their shoulders, and setting off down the slow road that led to Spain; the two of us driving on to Carcassonne and Cezanne's country.

Twelve days later, the Spanish Civil War began.

II
You're in the Air Force Now

Introduction

The recruits in the troop train were right out of high school. Their comments were often clichés, drawn from radio programs. Their conversation centered on sports.

We went to Miami Beach for basic training, and from there to Marietta College in Ohio. Our Commanding Officer called the roll on our first day, and demanded to know our religious affiliations.

"Catholic!" ... "Catholic!" ... "Lutheran!" ... "Methodist!" ... Then: "No religious affiliation," said one cadet.

There was an ominous pause. Then, "I'm sorry for you," said our Commanding Officer, "and you'll be sorry, before you're through." He delivered a short version of the prevailing doctrine: that in the foxholes there were no atheists.

I listened in alarm. I had found lodgings with an English professor for my wife and our infant son. I was planning to spend my Sunday mornings with them. I made some quick calculations, and affiliated myself with the church least likely to be found in Marietta. "Straight!" the Commanding Officer shouted. "Unitarian!" I shouted back. He paused at that; then he said: "All right."

The next morning, I was lying in my bunk when the student orderly woke me. "There's someone to see you downstairs," he said.

I followed him down, wondering who on earth would know me in Marietta. There, waiting for me, was a little man with bright eyes. "I'm your minister," he said with a smile; "My name is Mort."

He had, I learned, inherited a very large congregation. He lived alone in the loft of his very large church, where, on week days, he blew on a tenor saxophone.

I thought it best to reveal at once the circumstances of my conversion. Mort was unmoved. We were the first detachment of soldiers to be posted in Marietta. It was a matter of pride for each congregation to have its cadet, and to make him feel at home. Mort summoned me to church that Sunday and presented me to his congregation. Unitarians by the hundreds came up and embraced me. From then on my life wasn't my own.

In flight training we lived in fear of being washed out. So, when a Captain came by to recruit French-speaking pilots, I volunteered for an interview. The examination was not all that hard. "*Ouvrez la fenêtre.*" said the Captain. I started for the window, and he cried: "You're in!"

The French Squadron in Montgomery was surely one of the strangest collections of misfits ever assembled under the banners of the Air Force. We sorted ourselves out after the war: a few went into Democratic Party politics, a few into the CIA. Quite a few of our number became alcoholics, and one, Charlie Engelhard, won the Derby. But all that was still to come; at the time, we were simply strange.

We worked hard with our French cadets. Between classes we flew off on excursions, since the Training Manual stated excursions were good for squadron morale. On one such excursion we headed for the Gulf Coast. I was piloting a fighter-trainer; the Captain, hung over, was asleep in the back seat. We were over the piney wastes of south Alabama when, for a moment, he stirred himself. "Where are we?" he asked. I wasn't too sure but I saw one landmark ahead. "We're coming to a railroad line," I said. "When you come to a railroad," said the Captain drowsily, "always look to the left and the right. There may be a Navy pilot who's lost, coming down the line." I looked to the right, then to the left. I hit the stick hard, so that the Captain's head struck the canopy. As we dove, the Navy plane flashed over us.

It took Tom Corcoran, my old boss, and Senator Lister Hill to get me out of the French Squadron and into combat training. I went on to B-17s, a plane beyond any other in its capacity to take punishment. The sketches that follow were written at the time.

So Long, Tex

We were two days on the troop train going to Miami. We got there at three in the morning. We lay on the concrete platform until the bus came to take us to the Beach. They took us to the old Nash Hotel; we sat in the patio. The palm trees waved above us, and after a winter in Washington the sun felt good. Every once in a while a detachment of cadets would march past on their way to the drill field. We'd get up and watch them, wishing we could get out of our civilian clothes and into uniform, so that we wouldn't be laughed at any more.

All of a sudden, two privates and a Pfc. marched in. I mean, we sprang to our feet. We stood there, stiff as pokers, as if they were three generals and we were standing at attention. The Pfc. looked at us and grinned. "At ease!" he said, only we didn't know what that meant. "Stand easy, men," he said.

He was sunburned, real dapper, with his shirt and his pants all pressed and tight, and his flight cap tilted down over one eyebrow. He wasn't big, but he had a flash in his eye.

"My name is Joe Gordon," he says, "same as the ball player. These here are Privates Shimalewski and Turcowicz. On the drill field, you call me instructor, and them private. If you don't, you'll pull a detail cleaning out a hundred commodes. And they'll be full, if I have to fill them myself.

"Off the field," he goes on, "you call me Tex, and them Shimmy and Red. If you don't the beer is on you.

"I'll be honest with you, men," he says. "You're new to this; so am I. You're my first Flight; that's why I want you to be good. A lot of instructors on the Beach are chicken. I want to show them I can turn out the best, another way. That's what I'm going to do," Tex says, "and by Christ you'd better cooperate! You may think I've got a kind face—like the Topkick said, the kind you want to throw shit at! But, believe me, I can be the meanest son-of-a-bitch you ever saw!

"Understood?" he said, and we shouted, "Understood!" "All right!" he said, "but remember, being cadets, you got to behave.

"When I hit the Beach," Tex said, "They told me three things: I couldn't drink, I couldn't go into town, and I couldn't mess with the girls. Half an hour after taps, the first night, I was in a dive in Miami, with a barrel of beer on the table, and a girl on each knee.

"Men," Tex said, "it doesn't pay. It's too hot to drink, and in Miami it's eighty percent VD."

That evening, Tex took us out in an alley where no one could see us. He lined us up and gave us Position of the Soldier, Parade Rest and Facing Movements, by the numbers. He let us know that he was proud of us, even then. When we got our uniforms, he spent a whole evening fixing our belts and ties and caps. After the lectures he'd march us to a delicatessen to get some ice cream, and in the evenings we'd go for a beer, down at Sam's Place.

This'll show you how smart Tex was. One day during break, some cadets start talking about combat. "I reckon the real guy is the tail gunner," says a dumb guy called Big Stoop, who was coming to realize that he wasn't going to get through. "Hell, no!" says another. "Every time a bomber comes back, it comes back for more bombs, more gas, and more tail gunners. They wash them out with a hose." Then Swig says: "They say the average life of a pilot in combat is two missions." There was a little runt called Sparrow, looked like he was sixteen and never been away from home. "Christ," Sparrow says, "an awful lot of us have got to die, so as one can live."

I could see that Tex was frowning. He cut in real quick. "I never learned mathematics," he says, "but how about some football?" Just like a monkey, he shimmies up a palm tree and throws a coconut down. In half a second the boys are tearing in and out of the palm grove. I saw Tex smile.

Sometimes Tex was rugged, like the first day we went to the drill field. "Dress it up! Thumbs in! Elbows locked! Six to the front and three to the rear!" He kept it up, all the way down Collins Avenue. He must have shouted "Sound off!" a dozen times. You should have heard us! All the way down the avenue, you could see old soldiers turn and stare at us. You could hear instructors shouting to those raunchy draftees, "Look at them cadets! Why can't you march like that!"

We hit the drill field singing the Air Corps song with Tex shouting: "Chins up! Suck in those guts! Eyes straight ahead!" Then he said in a low voice: "Men, you're looking great." That was all we needed. We went past the Colonel like West Pointers; we felt that way.

After chow that evening, Tex comes in and lays down on Swig's bed. We lay on the floor around him. "Men," he says, "It looks like my idea was the right one after all. The Colonel said you were the best flight on the field today. He says you're going to carry the squadron colors in the parade." We let out a great cheer.

We had a real bull session that night. First we talked about sports, then about girls. Then we talked about after the war. Some wanted to be test pilots. Swig said he was going to be a cop. Then everyone wants to know what Tex is going to do. Stay in the Army, we reckoned. "Hell no!" he said. "I'm going back to my brother's farm, near Sweetwater," he says. "Pretty soon I'll save enough to buy me a farm of my own. I'll get me a nigger and a mule, and I'll be happy. And if my son ever says he wants to be a soldier, I'll shoot him dead."

That didn't sound quite right to Swig and to me. But we didn't say anything.

The next morning we tore out when the whistle blew. We lined up, real eager. Then Tex comes up and we can see there's something wrong.

"Men," he says, "I've got bad news. The Captain told me this flight is being broken up. You'll go to Flight M, down by the Fairmont. There's nothing I can do."

Flight M was a pack of rebels, really gross. The instructor was mean. When we got back from drill that day, we were ready to weep. We lay down to rest, then the word spreads around: Tex has got a room at Sam's, we're going to meet.

We all got tipsy that night—it didn't take much. Swig sang a song or two; then we all sang the old ones. We gave Tex a forty-dollar watch. We each put in a dollar for it. Tex put the watch on his wrist; he wiped his eyes. Then he stood up and made a speech. Said he'd never met a bunch like us; and never would again. Said he wanted our addresses, so he could keep in touch with us. He said he'd never forget us, even if we forgot him.

He sat down again, and this little guy Sparrow jumps up. He says: to hell with the Air Corps; the Air Corps can stuff it. If this is the way we're going to be treated, he doesn't want to fly.

Tex is shaking his head; he heaves himself up again. "You can't talk that way," he says. "You're in this, all of you, just like me. You know I'm broken up," he says, "hell, I'm all cut to pieces. But men, that's the way it is, in the U.S. Army. You move from base to base; you're broken up and put back, and broken up again. Learn to take it," he told us, "then you'll all be soldiers."

What could we say? We stood up and sang Auld Lang Syne. Then we stumbled outside. It was a clear night and cold. The moon was out, and thousands of stars. We stumbled around, making plenty of noise. The MPs were patrolling the streets, and Tex was afraid we'd be arrested. So he shouts out: "Flight L, fall in!" Just like the first time. We formed ranks and marched off. "Heads up! Guts in!" Tex shouted. As if we were on the drill field. The streets were dark and silent; you could hear his voice echo far away. "Chins out! Eyes straight ahead! Look proud men!" he shouted. "That's the way I want you to look, always!"

Back at the Fairmont, we shook hands and said so long to Tex. It was long after taps by then. We snuck in and undressed in the dark. I was half asleep when someone shook me. It was Swig. "Get dressed" he whispered. "Tex is back at Sam's, and he said for you and me to meet him there."

We worked our way back there, dodging the MPs. Inside there was so much smoke that for a while we couldn't see anything. Then we saw Tex and Shimmy at a table. We were close by them when we stopped.

Tex was lying across the table. I never saw anyone so drunk. "Crazy," he was muttering; "I'm going crazy."

Shimmy was shaking him. "Tex," he was saying, "Tex, sober up. You know what you are," Shimmy was saying, "a fool. You're a fool to let a bunch of kids do this to you. A bunch of raw kids. They'll forget you inside a month; you know that. All you got to show for it is a lousy watch. And you'll pawn that inside a week to pay your rent."

"Going crazy. By the numbers," Tex says.

"Damn fool," says Shimmy. "Best damn instructor on the Beach, you are, and look at you."

"By the numbers," Tex says.

"A Pfc.," says Shimmy. "You're nothing but a lousy Pfc."

Tex just lays there. Shimmy looks up, as if he'd remembered about us. We turned and made our way out before he could see us.

We stole back, keeping in the shadows. I was shivering; so was Swig. We slid into bed, as if we'd never been gone. We never said anything to the others.

We worked hard in Flight M. It got better. Our new instructor was a sergeant, strictly military. He was proud of his stripes.

We didn't see Tex for a week. Then one night Swig says to me: "Tex is down at Sam's Place. He's dead drunk and the watch is gone, like Shimmy said." We were all disgusted with him after that. We'd see him in the street sometimes and he'd try to speak to us. We'd nod, and move on. We were close to shipping out by that time, and we could see ourselves as officers. Tex had been busted back to private; he looked sort of cheap.

It was a funny thing, he seemed like a stranger. Maybe we had become soldiers, like Tex said.

The Ones that
Make the World Go Around

When the dishes were stacked we went back to the other end of the sitting room. "You'll excuse me, Joe," Ace said, "I got some letters to write." He sat down in an armchair and started chewing on his pen.

"Isn't that just like a mail sergeant?" said Mrs. Ace, when she came back. "All day long he sorts out letters and gives them to you cadets; then he comes back and writes letters all night. Here, Joe," she said. "Have some cheese blintzes I just made—you boys love them."

Mrs. Ace turned up the gas flame and we drew our chairs close to it. "You know, Joe, what's wrong with you and all the fellows we bring here? You ought to be married.

"Three years ago," she said, "if you'd told me I was going to marry Ace, I'd have said you were crazy. Now I think I must have been crazy not to marry him the first time I met him.

"You remember The Great Thurston, Joe? Me and my twin sister handled the props for him and did a tap routine in the intermission, The Polly Twins. All the men were after us. Then one night Ace came to the show. He looked at my sister and said, 'That's the girl I'm going to marry.'"

"It was you," Ace said, writing.

"How do you know?" said Mrs. Ace. "He couldn't tell us

apart, even when she let him kiss her—anyway he pretended he couldn't.

"Then the war came. One night Ace came backstage. 'Honey,' he said, 'I'm a private now, but pretty soon I'll be a staff sergeant. Will you marry me?' 'I'll marry you when you're a staff sergeant,' I said. Afterwards I was scared. I thought it would take Ace twenty years. But a year later a telegram came. He said:

> *Roses are red, violets are blue,*
> *I'm a staff sergeant, how about you?*

"What could I do, Joe?" Mrs. Ace said. "Even when we were getting married, he kept looking sideways at me. He wasn't sure whether he was marrying me or my sister."

"I'm still not sure," said Ace, reading his letter over.

Mrs. Ace came over and sat on the arm of my chair. "You're like an old friend, Joe," she said in a low voice. "I'm going to tell you a secret. No one but the captain knows about it.

"You know how the boys crowd into the mailroom," she said. "They're so far from home, and getting a letter means so much to them. They wait there half an hour every day, just to get one letter.

"You know, there isn't one among the six hundred of you that Ace can't call by his first name," Mrs. Ace said. "At night sometimes, it's almost as if he talks in his sleep; he says—'Kreamer, Ktsanes, Kivi, Krulewitz.' He knows all of them, and when one of them waits at the window day after day, Ace worries about it until he can't sleep. It got so bad once that I said to him, 'Ace, why don't you write letters to them?'" She looked around; Ace was completely absorbed—"That's what he's doing now—writing letters to the cadets."

Mrs. Ace walked over to his chair, read one of the letters, and brought it back. "Listen," she said:

Dear Ernest
    You will be surprised to get this letter, but don't be surprised. You look as though you worry a lot about your flying and I know how much you want to get through. You look depressed,

and maybe I can help. I've watched you around the post and you seem like the finest type of American who will soon be flying for all of us. I'd like to get to know you better.

I know what it means to you to hear from home when you're far away. By accident I overheard some of your friends say that you weren't getting many letters. Ernest, maybe the reason you don't get more letters from home is that you don't write enough. Why don't you write home more often and see what happens?

Your friend

Mrs. Ace folded the paper. "Isn't that a nice letter," she said. "Usually he signs them 'an unknown friend' or 'a silent admirer.' Sometimes we sit down and write them together in the evenings. The boys are so glad to get them Ace says, and they never guess who the friend is.

"You know the captain, Joe, he's a lonely man. He doesn't get many letters either. I wanted Ace to start writing to him, but Ace was embarrassed. He said he couldn't write to an educated man. So I told the captain about Ace anyway—you know what the captain said?"

She looked at Ace—his head was bent over his letters. Then she said softly: "He told me, 'You're the ones that make the world go around.'"

Hot Pilot

As the storm approached, the planes on the flight line trembled. The few that were left in the air came bouncing in. The red warning flag snapped like a pistol shot up in the control tower. We waited in the ready room, watching the darkening sky.

At the cry of "Attention!" we stiffened. Our captain came in. "Flying is off for the day," he said. We waited to be dismissed, but he sat on a table and lit a cigarette.

"You're just about through," he said, when his cigarette was glowing. "And some of you are beginning to think that you're pretty hot pilots.

"There are two kinds of hot pilots," he went on. "Those who are dead, and those who will soon be dead.

"Last week," the captain said, "I ferried a B-25 up to Nashville. I took the night train back. There wasn't a berth on the train, so I had to sit up all night. I sat beside another man. The lights were dim and I couldn't see him clearly. I had the impression that he was sort of worn out and old.

"The train was rocking along, and I was dozing when this old man spoke to me. 'Excuse me,' he said, 'but I see that you're in the Air Corps.' I nodded. 'I was wondering,' he said, 'if you could tell me where you took your training and what class you

were in.' I told him. Then he said: 'I was wondering if you knew
a cadet who was in your class, name of Jim Gordon.'

"At that I whipped around. 'Knew him!' I said, 'Jim and I
were together from pre-flight till the day he was killed.'

"'I never knew what happened,' said this old man. 'I wish
you'd tell me.'

"'I'll tell you what happened,' I said. 'He was a hot pilot.'

"'You mean he was no good?' the old man asked. 'That's
not what I mean,' I said.

"'Look,' I said to him, 'most of us worked hard to become
pilots; a few were lucky. One in a thousand of us is born with
wings. That one was Jim.

"'The rest of us struggled with our slow rolls,' I told him.
'For Jim, they came naturally. We fell out of our Immelmans;
whatever he did was perfect. I remember the morning we so-
loed,' I told him, 'Jim after seven hours, me after fifteen.' 'Just
remember, I won't be there to save you,' said our instructor,
when he sent me up. He told Jim, 'I'm checking you out, but it's
you who should be checking out me.'

"'Go on,' the old man said.

"'It was at basic that Jim began to heat up,' I said.

"First a story went the rounds that a Vultee had landed on a
cotton patch and taken up the cotton pickers for rides. Then
someone told about a stampede out of an outhouse at an infantry base, when a plane rolled its wheels on the roof. Jim didn't
say anything, and we weren't about to turn him in. But someone called him Flash Gordon, and the name stuck to him.'

"'Go on,' this old man said to me, so I told him about
advanced. 'It was at advanced,' I said, 'that Jim really started to
burn. You couldn't tell him that an AT-10 couldn't do an outside loop; he'd looped it. No use in warning him that it was
redlined at two-twenty; he'd pushed one to two-fifty in a verti-
cal dive.

"'They made us instructors,' I said; 'and for a while it
looked as if Jim might settle down; but he was a boundary
pusher. A bunch of hotrocks flew in one day on a ferrying job.
They started to joke about the single-width turn boys, and Jim
came in. He said he'd show them some single-width turns. He

winked at me as he said it, and I winked back.

"'That was on a Sunday morning. Around lunch time Jim helped the first of his passengers out of his plane and called for another. He and another instructor took off in tight formation with two of those hotrocks. We watched them climb up and out of sight.

"'I was sitting in the ready room,' I told the old man, 'when the major came charging in.' 'Who the hell has been flying this morning?' he wanted to know. 'Flash Gordon,' I told him and I asked him why. 'I'll tell you why,' he shouted, 'there's a rip a yard long in the belly of his plane!' I didn't say anything, but I guessed: he'd been chasing after alligators in the Okefenokee, and there were some stumps sticking up out of that swamp. 'Where is he now?' the major wanted to know. 'Flying tight formation,' I said. 'He'll kill himself,' said the major; 'I'm going to call him down.'

"'We were climbing the stairs in the tower when I heard Jim on the radio, talking to the other pilot. 'We'll roll to the right and split S down,' he said. 'Holy Christ, they'll never make it,' we heard the officer in the tower say. Then he cried out, 'They're locked together!' We tried to see them; we couldn't at first. They were way way up there, and we were looking into the sun. Then we saw them, falling. The whole tower shook when they hit the ground.'

"'They told me he died in service,' said the old man.

"'Service, hell!' I said. 'He broke every regulation in the book! Threw his own life away, and the lives of three others. And he wrecked two good planes.'

"The old man didn't say anything for a time. Then he said: 'What was left of him, when they found him?'

"'His dog tags and some bridge work' I said. 'He was killed and cremated, all at the same time.'

"'That's what I figured,' the old man said.

"I didn't say anything. But, I thought to myself: that's queer. 'How did you figure that?' I asked him.

"'There were four of us carrying the coffin,' he said, 'and it was easy to carry. Jim weighed a hundred and eighty pounds, but the coffin was light.'

"It was hot in that train," said the captain, "but I was cold all over. I put out my hand. 'My name is Miller,' I told him, 'I didn't catch yours.'

"'Gordon,' he said, as he put out his hand to me. 'I heard about you from Jim.'

"Well," said our captain, "a word to the wise. The regulations were written for a reason; remember that. And stick within them, if you want to come out of this war alive."

He nodded to a cadet; the cadet shouted, "Attention!" We all sprang up and stood there. He kept us standing for a minute. Then: "Dismissed!" He walked out of the ready room, and we filed out after him. By then, at the end of the runway dark rain was driving in.

In tight formation we marched back to our barracks, leaning against the wind. We weren't supposed to talk in formation, but a few cadets were talking. "What did he tell us that for?" "To scare us, of course!" "What did he want to scare us for?" "So as we won't go out and kill ourselves." "Sheeit, man! Who's going to do that?"

As for me, I was thinking about what the captain had said. *Born with wings . . . a boundary pusher . . .* and *everything he did was perfect.* Like that Greek who flew too high and fell . . . Maybe if you gain perfection, there's nothing left. That's what I was thinking. "Why did the guy take all those chances?" said Krulewitz, marching beside me. I said, "Search me."

Needle and Ball

The fields twisted around and around in front of us as the spiral tightened. It was as if we were in a paper boat entering a whirlpool.

I kept on talking in French. "We are in a spiral to the right. Look at the needle and ball, Duran. You have permitted the needle to go all the way to the right."

As our airspeed built up, toward the red line, the engine began to groan.

"To recover from the spiral, bring the needle back to the center of the instrument. Center the stick, then press upon the left rudder."

No response. I felt the controls; he was clutching them like a drowning man.

"Center the stick, Duran . . . CENTER THE STICK!"

No response at all. The fields were coming up fast, towards us. "I've got it," I said. I wrenched the controls out of his hands, and hauled the plane back, through the horizon and up into the sun. I held it, hanging on its prop, until it started to shake in a stall. And that trainer could shake. The Vultee Corporation was pleased to call it the *Valiant*. We called it the *Vibrator*.

We leveled off. I told Duran to come out from under the black instrument hood. I glanced in my mirror. He was hunched up in the rear cockpit, gasping for breath.

"Look, Duran," I said. "A spiral is the worst killer in instrument flying. It kills more pilots than the Nazis. They enter the spiral so slowly they don't know they're in it. Their instruments tell them they're spiraling; they don't believe it."

"Suppose you make it," I said "Suppose you get your B-26. You'll fly at night, and one night your gyros will tumble. That little needle and ball is all that you'll have left. If you can't keep that needle centered, you and your crew are going to go into a spiral. And no American instructor is going to be there to pull you out."

Well, that's about what I said. I was pissed off, and I kept getting my French verbs fouled up.

The sky seems brilliant, almost blinding, when you come out from under the hood. For a time we fooled around, following the contours of the clouds. I gave him the textbook lecture on the needle and ball for the twentieth time. Then, I switched over from intercom to radio. The control tower was calling all the planes in, first in English, then in French:

"Mike Dog Six Two to all planes . . . *Marcel Denise Six Deux, à tous les avions Français* . . ."

I sent Duran back under the hood. I said: "We'll try it, one more time."

Duran shook the stick to signal that he was taking over. For a few moments he held the needle in the center. Then he lost fifty feet. As he regained it, the right wing of the plane began to sink. The Alabama landscape rose toward us; the airspeed began to build up.

"The needle, Duran; look at the needle! Bring it back . . . bring it back! . . ."

One hundred and eighty, one hundred and ninety . . .

"Bring it back, Duran . . .

Once again, the fields were coming up fast. I took over and went in for a landing.

It was almost evening. Deschamps, Dufour, Duchatel, my other students, were waiting for us at the flight line. They knew that Duran was failing in his instrument flying. They glanced at him for some sign as I filled out the Form One. We walked back to the ready room and they followed in silence.

"I'm sorry Duran," I said. "I know that the graduation party is only three days away. That makes it tough to get washed out now. But you're washed out. You fly contact like a real fighter pilot. You're okay on full panel. But you just can't fly needle and ball."

I kept staring at the cement as I talked, and hoisting my parachute up on my rear. Duran kept looking right at me and saying, "Yes, my lieutenant," and, "I understand, my lieutenant." His voice never broke.

*   *   *

The knives and the forks began to twist around in front of me. It's the sauterne, I thought; I'm stewed on sauterne.

Deschamps was trying to slip some gin into my sauterne. Dufour was complaining that in France, soldiers were treated no better than Negroes in America. Duchatel, who came from Algiers, was chanting some song in Arabic. Duran was somewhere down the long table. He'd left us, for fear that he'd dampen our spirits.

We had a lot to make up for in one evening, after two months of flying night and day. The back room of the Elite Cafe was all lit up and decorated for the party. Every instructor had a menu, with the signatures of all fifty French cadets on it. And a little present—a ladies comb for the major with his shaven head, a chess set for me.

Everyone was laughing and shouting. I was telling Deschamps to keep the hell away from my drink, when someone started pulling on my shoulder. It was Prevost, the commandant of the French detachment.

"Look, look at Duran, my lieutenant," he said in English. "He appears gay, but, in effect he is sad. *Il a le vin triste.*"

"That's tough," I said.

"Is a marvelous boy," Prevost said. "I rest on him."

"You *what?*"

"I lean on him?"

"You lean on him! You rely on him, you mean. Why don't

you speak English, Prevost!"

Before he could answer the speeches began. Someone helped the major up onto a chair. He began his usual harangue about how this was the best damn class of cadets ever trained by the United States Air Force. Everyone knew the speech by heart. We stood up and gave him the *Banc des Aviateurs,* a kind of fight-team-fight cheer. The major went on for a while in his dreadful French. We kept up the *Banc.* Then someone yanked him down, and the captain climbed up in his place. We gave him the *Banc* a couple of times, and when that failed to shut him up, we shouted: *"Ta geule!"*

"Ta geule! Ta geule!" we shouted. And all the time, Prevost was shouting as well, with his mouth right against my ear. "Is a brave boy! . . . Was in the Underground! . . . Dieppe!"

"Stop shouting, Prevost!" I shouted. "Enjoy yourself! Here, have some sauterne!" He tasted it and his lips curled up in a grimace.

"Pilots!" Prevost shouted. "Were hundreds of RAF pilots shot down in France. Duran has met them. He accompanied them . . ."

At that moment, we started to sing. First, *Les Africains,* very loud. Then the *Lorraine,* everyone standing up; very grave. Then *Peestol Packin Mahmah* which the French always insisted on singing. Then the *Chevaliers.* It was my favorite and I sang as loudly as I could in Prevost's face, hoping to drive him away.

> *Chevaliers de la Table Ronde*
> *Goutons voir si le vin est bon*

Prevost paid no attention. He went right on shouting: "He accompanied them, disguised as peasants . . ."

> *Goutons voir oui oui oui*
> *Goutons voir non non non*

". . . under the noses of the Germans . . ."

> *Goutons voir si le vin est bon*

". . . from Paris to the Pyrenees."

We started the next verse:

> *S'il est bon, s'il est agréable*
> *J'en boirai jusqu'à mon plaisir*

"No food. Was cold. Was hunted by the Gestapo. . . ."

J'en boirai oui oui oui
J'en boirai non non non
J'en boirai jusqu'à mon plaisir

"Was dancing on a string."

"Dancing on a string?"

"Yes. Was caught, by Vichy. Was given to the Gestapo. Was tortured." Prevost touched his finger nails. "These have not returned." I remembered Duran's odd use of his hands.

"Was put on a train to Berlin. To finish him. The RAF shot up the train. Was too weak to jump. He fell out. A peasant has saved him."

Dancing on a string. What in the hell, I wondered, does he mean by that? I started to sing again, a little uneasily.

Si je meurs, je veux qu'on m'enterre
Dans la cave où il'y a du bon vin

"Was told he had fought enough," Prevost said. "Duran said *no!* He waited for some Americans to abandon their plane. He has accompanied them to Spain."

Dancing on a string, I thought, *dancing on a string.*

"Was caught. Was in prison. In Barcelona. Was horrible. No food. One latrine for thousands. Were animals with claws. In one day, Prevost and his companions in the cell have killed one thousand such animals."

"Dancing on a string!" I said. "You mean walking on a tightrope! Why the hell don't you speak French, Prevost!"

"Was befriended by his comrades. Was hid, until he could find a sailing boat. He has sailed to Africa, alone."

"All right!" I said. "He can fight. He can sail. He can dance on a string. But, he can't fly needle and ball!"

The party was breaking up. Prevost glanced around, as I finished my last drink. He began to speak faster and his English got worse. "French Africa. Was Vichy. They have arrested him. He will be shot! One told him he would be pardoned. If he joined them. Duran have said *No!* Was cast in prison. Was almost gone, when de Gaulle have arrived in Algiers. Was found. Was liberated. General de Gaulle have said: what is your wish? He said: to bomb the Nazis, in a bomber of my own."

By then, we were almost alone.

"If you wash him now," said Prevost, "was all for nothing. For him it will be a great disgrace."

If I wash him! "Look, Prevost!" I said. "It's the regulations, not me! The regulations say that if he can't fly needle and ball, then he can't be a pilot. I didn't write the Goddam regulations, I just carry them out. So, if you want to . . ."

"Impossible," said Prevost. "Is impossible that such a one should be vanquished by a needle and a ball."

A needle and a ball. That did it; that, and the wine.

"All right, Prevost," I said, "I'll take him up one more time. Only, it means altering the Form One. And I'm warning you. If the Major ever finds out about this, he'll have a shit hemorrhage."

"A what?"

"*Une effervescence de merde.*"

"Ah!"

*   *   *

We climbed to our altitude; I talked all the way. I told Duran I knew all about his work in the underground. "It was like dancing on a string, right?" I said. He nodded, as if he understood.

"You can't be tense on the string," I said; "you must be supple. You must move with small movements. You must anticipate. You must have a light touch."

He nodded.

"All right," I said. "The needle is the string. The ball in the center is you. You stayed on the string for two years, in the underground. You can stay on it for two minutes now."

It sounded silly, I know. But it helped. Maybe it was the tone of my voice that made him let go, and not what I said. In any case, he nodded. He went back under the hood, and when he shook the stick to take over, I could feel that it wasn't so rigid in his grip.

I laid the wings level on the horizon for him. He kept them there for a minute. Well, it seemed like a minute; it was a

definite improvement anyway over the time before. The right
wing began to dip; I nudged it back. It dipped again; I nudged it
back, and held it level, until I could sense that it was balanced
in his grip.

All right; I shouldn't have done it, but I did. I was thinking
of what I'd said to Prevost: *it's the regulations, not me.* I didn't
like the sound of myself saying that; not after he'd told me
what this boy had done. Well, frig the regulations, I said to
myself; so what if it's cheating. Doesn't everyone cheat, one
way or another? For their own advantage mostly, but this boy
wants to fight. I thought to myself, I've lived by the regulations
since the day I joined the Air Corps. And for once, between the
lad in the back seat and the bomber that he wants to fly, it
won't be the regulations that matter; it'll be me.

I checked to make certain that the radio was on intercom.
Then I said: "Look, Duran, you're doing fine. I think that in
time you can manage the needle and ball, so I'm going to pass
you. I'm going to write *passed* on your test sheet. So you don't
have to be tense any more."

I couldn't see his face as I was talking; he was still under
the hood. But I felt the stick go limp in his grip. That's fine, I
thought. Because it's freezing up on the controls that takes
pilots down to their deaths. I thought: just keep it that way.

I shook the stick to tell him I was taking over. I flew the
Vibrator around in slow circles while he sat there in the dark.
After a while, he signaled that he was ready. He laid the wings
dead level on the horizon; he kept them there by himself. I gave
him some patterns to fly, when I was sure that he could handle
them; then some steep turns. He brought the needle back to
dead center every time.

After a while, I switched from intercom to radio. It was the
end of the day, and the tower was calling all the planes in.

"Come on out from under the hood," I said to Duran. I
grinned at him in my mirror. "Well," I said, "it looks as if you'll
get your B-26 after all."

Some smartass was in the tower. "Plane giving away
B-26s," he said, "get back onto your intercom."

I'd forgot to flip the switch. I looked at Duran in the mirror. We began to laugh.

"Hey! Marcel Denise!" I shouted, "I'm dancing, on a string!"

"Plane calling Marcel Denise, repeat your message," said the tower, "repeat your message, over."

"Dancing on a string, Marcel Denise. I said I'm dancing on a string."

That tripped him up. "I do not read you clearly, plane calling Marcel Denise," he said, "Say again, say again, over."

"I'll do better than that; I'll sing it for you," I said. And I began to sing:

> *On a string, oui oui oui*
> *On a string, non non non . . .*

At that, everyone got into the act. "Get that hyena off the air!" some senior officer shouted; the other names they called me made *hyena* sound polite. Marcel Denise kept asking for my call letters; as if I'd be enough of a fool to give them; a couple of cadets were asking solemnly for landing instructions; Mike Dog was yelling to everyone to shut up; you could hear English and French, and a mixture of the two all jumbled up. As for me, I went on singing the *Chevaliers* on radio. Hell, there was no way they could catch me; there must have been fifty planes in the air.

The Koala Bear

Scared? Listen, the only time I wasn't scared in the Pacific was when I was stewed. And it was plenty hard to get stewed on Aussie liquor. I got stewed all right. I raised plenty of hell. But I never did get in trouble, not until just at the end.

Sure I shot my mouth off. I made sergeant when I went to my captain and said I'd never fly another mission as a corporal. Then there was a major, a real mean one. One day he said to me, "Corporal, do you think I'm chicken?" "Yes sir, I do," I said. He couldn't do nothing. They needed us too bad.

I never did get in trouble until I was on my way home. And then it was over a little son-of-a-gun of a koala bear!

Listen, I was never supposed to be a waist gunner in a B-17 to start off with. I was an armorer at Clark Field when the Nips hit Pearl Harbor. I was asleep in the tail of my plane when someone run in and yelled "Nips!" I started for the door and a blast blew me clean out of the hangar. When the fires were out and we were heading for Port Moresby, the colonel told me and Tracy, "You're waist gunners."

Waist gunners! What a laugh that was! They talk about mils and rads and deflection and aircraft recognition now—hell, we blazed away at anything that turned in toward us, from P-40s on down. It didn't make no difference anyway. I must have fired 20,000 rounds and I never hit a plane. That's the way it was all the way through the old 19th Bombardment Group.

Look, one night we went on a raid over Bougainville. The captain was flying. Me and Tracy were in the waist with some green kid in the tail. We had an Aussie fighter pilot for navigator, and a yardbird second lieutenant—a mess officer—for bombardier.

It was black and freezing cold. Twenty minutes from the bomb run we could see tracers coming up like firecrackers in the night around us. The Nips found our range and we started to shake and bounce as they hit us. It was bad.

When we got close to the target and the flak was really thick, the yardbird took over the plane. He started fidgeting with the bombsight. We flew right up to the target and he pulled a couple of levers and yelled, "Bombs away!" Only the plane didn't leap upwards like it should and there weren't any bomb-bursts. We looked through to the bay—the bombs were still sitting there!

The captain called for everyone to take it easy. We went on out, and circled and came back. They nailed us in a searchlight and followed us all the way in. The flak was worse than ever.

The yardbird worked away at the bombardier's panel like a crazy man. When we crossed the target he pulled a lot more levers and yelled again, "Bombs away!" The bombs just sat in the bomb bay.

Tracy looked at me. He picked up a gun barrel and went up front. He stood over the yardbird, crouching in the bombardier's seat.

"You son-of-a-bitch!" Tracy said, "if you yell 'Bombs away!' once more and those bombs still sit there, so help me I'll crack you over the head with this gun!"

"You wouldn't do that," the yardbird says.

"You see if I won't," shouted Tracy. He stood there. We went on out again, and circled, and headed back in. The yardbird was throwing every switch in the nose from the electric heating pad to the anti-icing wipers. He followed the target in and hit the last switch. He yelled out, "Bombs away!"

The bombs sat in the bay. The yardbird ducked as Tracy

swung, and the gun barrel caught him on the side of the head. Then Tracy sat down and salvoed the bombs in the sea. We started home, but the Aussie spent so much time patching up the yardbird and telling him to put in for the Purple Heart that he lost us. We landed with thirty gallons of gas.

It was the same way on the ground. We lived in tents. It was hot as hellfire back in the bush. We had malaria and dysentery. The flies were terrible. Once a week we'd fly up to the sub-depot at Charleyville for supplies. You could tell when a crew had been to Charleyville. They'd go on slapping at their faces and necks for days after.

We lived on spam—spam and a slice of bread. When the spam ran low, we'd eat twice a day. We'd get real hungry. When we weren't flying there was nothing to do but sit and think how hungry we were.

One time the chaplain fixed up a boxing match for something to do. Only no one would fight. So the Chaplain said, "Tomorrow we'll have another match, and anyone who fights will get a good square meal." Man, I was sick of that spam. I climbed into the ring the next day and slugged it out with a huge colored mess boy till we couldn't stand. Then we went down to the mess tent for our good square meal. They gave us two slices of bread and some spam.

The Aussies loved us. Once in a while we'd get leave and go down to Sydney. The Aussie soldiers were away then, in Africa. We'd go out with their sisters, their girls and their wives. When they got back there wasn't a Yank in Sydney dared walk down the streets alone at night.

I was alone one night when a real good-looking girl passed me. I whistled and she stopped. "Are you free tonight?" I said. "No, but I'll be reasonable," she said. She was kidding. We laughed, and from then on nothing could keep us apart.

That was where this little koala bear came in.

She lived in the Hotel Australia—Room 318. She kept the bear in her room for company. She used to feed him bunches of shiny leaves. He was real little and furry, just like a kid's teddy bear, with round ears and a kind of sullen little face. At night, when all the lights were out, she and I would be together and,

after a while, this little bear would uncurl and shuffle around
the room, chewing on the leaves. She'd pick him up, and he'd
put his arms around her and cling to her, tight.

We had great times together. I knew it would be tough
when my last leave was up. She cried for a while that night and
we didn't talk at all. As I was leaving, she stopped me and gave
me the bear. She wanted me to keep it—for good luck.

I didn't want no bear. I took it because I couldn't stand to
hear her cry no more. All the way home that little bear clung to
me. I knew the boys would laugh at me. So when I stepped in
the hut I said, "Hey, look! Fifteen bucks' worth of fur for my
mother's winter coat!"

No kidding, I thought those boys would kill me. Someone
slugged me and Tracy grabbed the bear. He wouldn't give it
back till I swore not to hurt it. Pretty soon we took the bear up
in the plane. He slept. Before long the crew wouldn't go on a
raid unless that little cuss came along. He used to curl up in a
corner of the radio room where it was warm, and no Jap flak
ever woke him.

Our last raid, and the worst one, was Rabaul.

It was always rough there. When they told us in the briefing that we were going over the target at 8,000 feet, we knew it
would be plenty rough. I was glad we had our old crew on that
day.

We came in low over the mountains. We could see the
ships in the harbor ahead of us. The flak in the sky around us
was as thick as freckles on a boy's face. They had us spotted.
They hit us all the way in. We pitched and rolled. We lost an
engine. I thought we were gone. We sunk a Jap tanker and we
pulled out. Tracy was lying on the floor beside me. When we
were clear, the captain started calling over the intercom. I was
the only one who answered the call.

I started up front. There was a great tear in the radio room,
and the radio operator was bent across his table. He was gone. I
crawled up into the nose. It was all smashed. The Aussie
navigator was killed outright, and the bombardier was choking
to death. I slapped some engine grease on his face where it was
torn. I ripped off his shirt and stuffed it into a big hole in his

chest. But he was breathing through his chest and after a while he started to choke again so I'd pull out the shirt and let him breathe, and then stuff it back to stop the blood.

The tail gunner had a foot blown off. I gave him two shots of morphine and left him alone. Tracy had caught some flak in the rear. All I could figure to do was to make him lie down and to sit on him. All the way home I went forward and back, sitting on Tracy when I had the chance. I don't know yet how we made it.

It was evening when I thought of that little bear, back in the plane. I went back for him and son-of-a-gun if he wasn't still asleep in his corner. He never was worried at all.

Pretty soon after that things changed. A bunch of B-24s came in to replace the old 19th. We got our orders to ship home. I was leaving by boat when the colonel saw me. He remembered me from the time he decorated me. He flew me back as part of his crew.

That was a break. I got a great bunch of leaves, and I stuck the bear in the radio room. We took off from Port Moresby for the last time.

Up at Hawaii the colonel left me to guard the plane while he filed our clearance. It was hot, and I was half asleep when I heard someone climb aboard. It was a little warrant officer with a waxed mustache. "I'm the customs inspector," he said, "making a routine check." I watched him as he poked around the plane. After a while he found the leaves. "What do you call these?" he said. "Shrubs for my old man," I said, "he's a great gardener."

"They probably contain harmful insects," the warrant officer said, "they'll have to be declared."

He stood there in the radio room, looking at his papers. I wasn't worrying. I never did think much of the bear. He'd slept through fifty-two missions without ever leaving his corner.

Suddenly there was a scratching noise under the table. I looked down. That little son-of-a-gun was crawling out onto the floor.

He grasped the inspector around the ankle and started climbing up his leg. The inspector yelled and managed to shake him off. I picked him up and he clung to me.

"What in hell is that?" said the inspector.

"An Australian bush dog," I said. "I'm taking him back to my mother."

"Too bad for your mother," he said, "it's staying right here."

"Supposing I take him with me?" I said. I was getting sore.

"You will violate Clause 8-A, Article 4-B, Part II-C, of the Foreign Diseases Control Act of 1938 governing the importation into the United States of certain live insects, birds, animals and other vertebrates," he said.

"No kidding?" I said. "Supposing I kill him and just take the skin?" I wanted to see what he'd say.

"Then you will violate Sub-paragraph 9, Paragraph 3, Subsection 2, Section 5 of the Customs and Revenue Act of 1937 as amended," he said. He reached out and grabbed the bear. He started out with it.

I got up.

"What will I violate if I smack you on the kisser?" I said.

He smiled. He said:

"You will violate Article 64 of the Articles of War."

"It's a deal!" I said. I let him have it.

. . . Boy, what a jail they have at Hawaii! I'd be there yet if the colonel hadn't found me. He laughed when I told him what had happened. He told the commanding officer there that he couldn't leave without me, and they let me go. The next day we looked down over good old San Francisco.

The captain was lost later on. They sent Tracy to a base hospital and then back to the States. I never did hear from him. I stopped writing to the girl in Sydney, but she still writes to me. She says she loves me, and she wants to know how the bear is.

They kept that little cuss at Hawaii. But, hell—they hadn't any leaves for him. They couldn't feed him right.

I sure do wish I knew what happened to that little bear.

III
Working for *The New Republic*

Introduction

The Promise of American Life was published in 1910. T.R. gave a copy of it to my mother and father. I doubt if he read it through, but they did. Then they tracked down the author, Herbert Croly. They asked him how the concepts of *The Promise* could best be advanced. He answered: through a weekly journal of opinion.

They worked together, from then on, to found the journal. It was to be called *The Republic*. But, that name proved to be the property of a Boston politician named John F. Fitzgerald and known as "Honey Fitz." My father took him to lunch and suggested that he give up the name in the higher interest of a national magazine. Honey Fitz replied that there was no higher interest than the distribution of his sheet to the party faithful. My father returned to New York, amused but defeated. The journal had to be called *The New Republic*.

I never read it until I returned to America in 1937. In 1940, when the fall of France seemed imminent, I left the State Department to become the Washington editor of the *New Republic*. I wrote for it until I joined the Air Corps; I went back to it in 1945.

By then, it seemed as if the best chance of survival for the *New Republic* lay in expansion. Ignorant of the precedent of

T.R.'s brief career in journalism, I made the mistake of trying to build a magazine around the image of a public man.

The pieces that follow relate to that decade, starting in 1946 and ending in 1955, when we turned the *New Republic* over to a close friend, Gil Harrison.

Henry

1978

Henry Wallace was Secretary of Commerce in the Administration of President Truman. He resigned, at Truman's insistence, on September 12, 1946.

One week later I stood at the door of his apartment in the Wardman Park Hotel in Washington, rehearsing the short speech that I had come to deliver. It ended with a proposal: that he become the editor of the *New Republic*, the journal of opinion that my parents had founded in 1914.

The door opened. A grey poodle sniffed my trousers. Its owner, Mrs. Wallace, led me through the dark apartment to the terrace that overlooked Rock Creek Park. There in the autumn sunlight the familiar, unkempt figure sat, sorting out telegrams and letters with his principal advisor, a meaty Texan named Harold Young.

I had never met Wallace, but he had written many articles for the *New Republic*. In company with the editors, and with most liberals, I looked up to him as Roosevelt's heir-apparent who had been deprived of his heritage. I had cheered, sitting by a radio on an Air Force base when he shouted to the Democratic Convention of 1944: "The poll tax must go!" I had felt cheated when he was denied renomination as Vice President. I had shared his concerns when, in 1946, the wartime alliance crumbled. As for his speech to the Stop Dewey Rally in Madison Square Garden—the cause of his dismissal from the Cabinet—I knew that Truman had read the speech in draft and, at first, had seen nothing wrong with it. The Communists in the audience had tried to howl Wallace down in the course of that speech. The *New Republic* had commented: "In attempting to expel Wallace from the progressive movement, the Communist Party will succeed only in expelling itself."

I handed Wallace the comment. He read it in silence and handed it to Harold Young. I hurried through my little speech. Wallace listened, staring at his shoes. Harold fingered the telegrams and letters that contained prior offers of employment. Newspaper publishers were offering a syndicated column; lecture agencies, a national tour. There was also an offer of collaboration in a continuing political campaign from the National Citizens Political Action Committee, whose director, Beanie Baldwin, had worked for Wallace in establishing the Farm Security Administration.

To Harold, the *New Republic* was a prospect about as inviting as exile to Siberia. Wallace, in contrast, recalled that at moments of personal crisis his father and his grandfather had turned to publishing. He weighed all his offers, and chose the *New Republic*. So one week later we wrote out on a grubby piece of paper the terms of our association. Wallace would be editor of the *New Republic*; I would be publisher; he would devote himself to the magazine; I would push its circulation up five-fold, to one hundred thousand or more.

With the paper in my pocket, I hurried back to New York. We cleaned out a corner room in our offices for our new editor. We bought, borrowed or stole every mailing list that we could find. We raided the fortified empire of Henry Luce and made off with some of his ablest men. We hired Edward Bernays to stage our press announcement. Sitting in a New York skyscraper, Bernays decreed that it should come from the town in Iowa where Wallace was born.

The Wallaces moved to a farm in South Salem, New York. One Sunday, Bruce Bliven and I drove up to have lunch with them. They laid out a splendid meal made up of produce they had grown. They were especially proud of their tomatoes. "My these tomatoes are delicious!" said Bruce to Mrs. Wallace. "What did Henry do to make them so tasty?" "He fed them with radioactive fertilizer," said Mrs. Wallace, smiling. Bruce turned pale.

As Editor, Henry advocated many innovative programs. He called for an international authority to provide power and irrigation for the Jordan Valley. He proposed massive economic aid for Europe eight months before Secretary Marshall delivered his Harvard address. At times however, he seemed to be insensitive to the impact of his words. He would seem to be evasive when he thought that he was being outspoken; he would give offense when he intended to give praise. Did he shield himself against the unwelcome aspects of reality? At times we would press our ideas upon him, only to realize that nothing was getting through to him; he was there and not there; he was far off and out of reach.

We brought in an urbane intellectual, James Newman, to work with Wallace on his editorials. The three of us would meet once a week to talk over the subject of the editorial; then Jim would prepare a first draft. We would take our places on the sofa in Wallace's office; he would sit between us, jingling the keys that he carried in a pants pocket. Jim would read aloud a paragraph or two; Henry's eyelids would narrow and his head would sink inch by inch, until it came to rest upon his chest. The jingling would stop; Jim and I would glance at each other. Then Jim would read the editorial on to its end. We would wait and, after a moment or two of silence, the jingling would start up again. Henry's head would jerk up; his eyelids would flutter and part. "Fine," he would murmur, "that's fine."

As for the rest of the magazine, Wallace rarely read it through. The articles were not commissioned by him; the reviews, he found of little interest. We worked past midnight to improve the magazine and to generate income to match our soaring costs. Henry did not come to our staff conferences. He was not sure of the names of our staff. He would walk forty blocks from his apartment to our offices. Once there, he entered a world of his own.

The organizers of the Stop Dewey Rally complained with
some justification that we had stolen Wallace from them. We
managed to keep them out of our offices, but we could not keep
Henry in. One day a shapeless figure appeared and closeted
himself with our Editor in the corner room. After an hour they
went out together. They went out a good many times together
from then on. Perplexed, we tried to discover the identity of
Henry's companion. All that we could discover was that he
came from Brooklyn and that his name was Max. Much later,
we learned how they spent their days. Max would lead Henry
down the streets of the East Side, stopping at one delicatessen
after another. "Mister Iushewitz," Max would say, "meet my
good friend, Henry Wallace. Mister Wallace, meet my dear
friend Eli Iushewitz." Henry would return from these excursions, his pockets bulging with tins of gefilte fish and bottles of
borscht. In the cold and alien city, he found warmth in these
men who venerated him.

Week after week, the pages of the *New Republic* were
filled with cries of alarm. Governments were collapsing in
Europe; a third world war seemed close at hand. The trade
unions were raging against Harry Truman; the leaders of the
Democratic Party were searching for a candidate to replace him
in 1948. Anxious liberals were sending handwritten pleas to
Wallace: give us hope again. More to the point, the National
Citizens Political Action Committee was being hard pressed
by its creditors. So was the Independent Citizens Committee of
the Arts, Sciences and Professions, an organization chaired by
James Roosevelt and Harold Ickes and run by Hannah Dorner
with the support of some undercover leaders of the Communist Party who held positions of power in the Congress of
Industrial Organizations.

The two organizations merged in December, 1946, becoming the Progressive Citizens of America. For chairman, those
who controlled the PCA chose Jo Davidson, an uncompromising artist, but a pliant man. He called me one morning in
March, 1947. "We're having a little party this evening," he said,
"for Henry Wallace. We'd like you to come."

So, once again I rang a doorbell and waited. After a time

the door opened and a heavyset woman, Jo's wife, let me in. The dimly-lit studio was filled with disembodied heads. At its far end a group stood; evidently they had been there for some time. Jo, short and bearded, gave me a bear hug although we'd never met; Henry looked ill at ease; I shook hands with Harold Young, Beanie Baldwin, and with a stranger who announced herself as Hannah Dorner. I said to myself: *ouch!*

We ate many Mexican dishes, prepared for Henry's benefit. We drank several bottles of burgundy. Jo called me *amigo* and spoke of his early days with Gertrude Whitney, my Uncle Harry's wife. Then, at some signal, there was silence. I waited; Harold cleared his throat. "Mike," he said, "you've been keeping Henry to yourself for long enough. We've decided that it's time that he got out and met the people again."

I glanced at Wallace. Once again, he had fallen asleep.

To Hannah and to Beanie, "meeting the people" meant stumping the country for the PCA. To Harold it meant speaking to Democrats; that is, if it meant anything at all. It was hard at that moment, even for wise men, to look ahead.

Far off in Europe, the Greek state was crumbling under the pressures of civil war. In order to offer weapons to that tiny country, Truman found it necessary to make an open-ended commitment, to intervene wherever communism seemed to pose a threat. On March 9, he proclaimed the Truman Doctrine. On March 14, Wallace replied, attacking the Doctrine in a broadcast carried by NBC. Five thousand Americans wrote to Wallace, thanking him, and urging him on. So the issue was joined.

Wallace was ready to stump the country in opposition to the Truman Doctrine. He could not set out at once. He had accepted an invitation to visit England, under the auspices of the *New Statesman and Nation*. His itinerary had been extended to Scandinavia and France.

It was agreed that Wallace should tour the United States on his return. But under whose sponsorship? I argued that the *New Republic* should sponsor the tour; Beanie insisted that it should be organized by the PCA. There was no time to settle our dispute. I left Helen Fuller, the Washington Editor of the *New*

Republic, to fight it out with Beanie, and flew off to England to be with my family for a few days before Wallace arrived.

By then, the Truman Doctrine was before the Congress. The President had called upon the House and Senate to vote for military aid for Greece and Turkey. The Congress was unhappy, and passage of the bill was far from assured. In England the Labour Party was in power. In turn, it was deeply divided by the Truman Doctrine. Many Cabinet Members sided with Wallace, and more than fifty Labour M.P.s signed a telegram, welcoming him to London. To them Wallace represented a challenge, not only to President Truman, but to Ernest Bevin, Britain's hard-pressed Foreign Secretary.

Once in England, I must have sensed the perils in this situation. The Wallace archives in the University of Iowa contain a telegram from me to Henry, urging him to be constructive in his comments in England, and not to criticize Truman or the Truman Doctrine.

That proved to be impossible. Wallace was led into a press conference at the Savoy. There, under the glare of kleig lights and with the cameras grinding, reporters shouted questions to him about his stand. He had never before been in a foreign country as an opposition leader. He had many times been scorned for ambiguity and evasiveness. He chose to answer all questions as he would have done at home. But he was not at home, and his charge that his country was turning to "ruthless imperialism" caused a furor in Washington.

On the floors of the House and Senate, men rose to denounce Wallace. One Senator demanded that his passport be withdrawn—a safeguard which the *New York Times* condemned as foolish; Walter Lippmann called Wallace's action "uncouth." Then, as Frederick Kuh reported in *The Chicago Sun,* "When U.S. Senators, Congressmen and the press began to storm against Wallace, this was the signal for British conservative papers to start criticizing him too." Speaking to a Conservative Party rally in the Albert Hall, Winston Churchill attacked Wallace as a crypto-Communist who was seeking "to separate Great Britain from the United States and to weave her into a vast system of Communist intrigue." This was false and slanderous, and Churchill knew it. He disowned his own statement, claiming that he had been misquoted by the press. Nonetheless, Wallace served a purpose, not his own. The *New York Times* on April 19, pointed to "an obvious trend among many who had formerly sat indecisively on the fence to throw their weight behind the Administration's program." The *Times* added: "It has seemed that they needed some such stimulus as Mr. Wallace's espousal of the negative side of the debate to make up their minds to vote 'yea'."

Wallace, to his credit, was not deterred by the abuse that was heaped upon him. He spoke to one-third of the British nation over the BBC, advocating his own doctrine of economic collaboration to raise the world's living standards. Before immense audiences, he waved copies of *Life*, with its maps of an American Empire stretched across the world. In place of Luce's vision of The American Century, he offered his vision, of the Century of the Common Man.

We took a night train to the Midlands. We were met in the morning at Preston by the local M.P. We drove through the morning fog to Blackpool for the first of many receptions by gold-braided lord mayors. We drove on through Lancashire and Cheshire to North Staffordshire and the Black country; we had a fine feast at Stoke-on-Trent. The city was engaged at that moment in trying to gobble up its little neighbor, Newcastle-under-Tyne, and between the little Lord Mayor of Newcastle-under-Tyne and the large Lord Mayor of Stoke-on-Trent, there was a good deal of jousting. The large Lord Mayor neglected to say grace at his banquet; a blooper which the little Lord Mayor was quick to note in some witty word-play. Much embarrassed, the large Lord Mayor rose at the end of the feast and drew his splendid robes about his middle. "For all that we have received," he intoned, "may we be truly thankful." "About time, too!" said the little Lord Mayor. "Aye," said the large Lord Mayor, "but I couldn't say it before because I didn't know what a splendid feast we were going to have." He turned then to Wallace. "We may not always agree," he said, "but it takes a man to speak his mind, and we love you for it." "Aye," said the little Lord Mayor," and in North Staffordshire when we love a

man we call him by his first name." So, for the rest of that
evening it was "Henry" and "Mike". I learned later that both
mayors had lost their only sons in the war.

It was hard to believe in those hours that much mattered
besides the struggle we were engaged in. But other battles
proved to be in doubt. A British contender was challenging the
American holder of the Heavyweight Boxing Crown, and he
apparently was first in the hearts of his countrymen. We
stopped at a red light in Manchester; and seeing the American
flag flying on the bonnet of our rented car, a workman came
running up to us. He poked his head into the car. "Yanks, are
you," he shouted to the startled Wallace. "Who's going to win
the fight?"

On balance Kuh concluded, Wallace's visit to England was
well received. "Millions of Britons," he reported, "were pleased
to learn that there are still prominent Americans who see
Britain's destiny as something other than that of an atom
absorber in a future U.S.-Soviet war."

In Norway and in Sweden, as the *New York Times* reported, Wallace's visit was sponsored "by a coalition committee of all local political parties, from the extreme Right to the
extreme Left." Speaking to an audience of 3,000 in the Social
Democratic Workers Hall, Wallace, the *Times* added, "drew
applause with just about every second remark."

In Sweden before the same broad audiences, Wallace drew
equal applause by declaring that, in criticizing the imperialist
course that his own country was embarking upon, he was
speaking as a world citizen and honoring the charters of the
United Nations and of UNESCO. We flew on to Paris. A large
crowd had gathered at the airport. Looking down, as we disem-
barked, I recognized two leaders of the French Communist
Party, Marcel Cachin and Jacques Duclos. I held myself at
fault, and I was heartsick. But reading through the Wallace
archives thirty years later, it appears that I was not to blame.
Two friends of Wallace's, Alfred and Martha Stern, led him to
entrust his Paris visit to a former Air Minister, Pierre Cot. In
time, apparently, they moved to Czechoslovakia.

Our largest meeting in Paris was at the Sorbonne. The

French Communist Party, in its businesslike manner, saw to it that the immense hall was filled by giving each student who attended a sandwich and a bottle of wine. The aged Leon Jouhaux slumbered in the Chair. Henry read out a tactful and blameless address. Duclos, sitting beside me on the platform, nodded benignly as each paragraph was translated. "Very nice; very moderate," he said.

I was, in those days, an elected leader of the American Veterans Committee. The meeting sponsored by its Paris Chapter in the Crillon became an occasion for Wallace to present a reasoned statement defining his own, independent position. His speech was printed in full in the *Herald Tribune*. In general the press treated Henry with fairness and restraint.

One other event on our European journey stands out in my memory. In Copenhagen the American Ambassador, an old friend of Henry's, had refused to receive him; an action which added a grain to Henry's store of bitterness. We were welcomed however by Ole Cavling, the owner of the daily newspaper *Extrabladet* who gave a large luncheon in his apartment in Henry's honor.

Cavling proved to be a hearty host. Insisting that whenever anyone said something pretentious the rest of us should stroke our imaginary whiskers, he initiated us into the International Society of the Long Golden Beards. The initiation ceremony was simple; it consisted in swallowing one drink after another. An hour passed. Then at a call from Cavling, we headed in the general direction of the dining room. The dining table was set for thirty places. At each place were four plates, stacked on top of each other. On the top plate lay one small anchovy.

Food, apparently, was still scarce in Denmark. Liquor, which had been hidden from the Germans, was plentiful. Around the stacks of plates were grouped six glasses filled with aquavit, slivovits, schnapps, and three other colorless but fiery liquids. The glasses ascended in height to a centerpiece: a silver tankard filled to the brim with Danish beer. To drink each one in turn was a fearful prospect; there was no escaping it. Every time I looked up a Dane would be holding up one of the glasses and waiting for me to join him in a private toast. I sat there, stiff as a board, with the room whirling around me. At the other end of the table, no doubt, was Henry. Poor Henry! He was, as far as I knew, a teetotaler, but I was beyond caring. Henry, I thought to myself, this time you're on your own.

Toward the end of the meal, Cavling stood up and proposed a toast to the President of the United States. We all managed to rise and cry: "To the President!" We sat down again and there was a long silence while the Danes waited for our response. I sensed after a minute or two that it was up to me. I heaved myself up and shouted: "To the King!" We all drank to the King and I sat down, wondering if I was going to be sick. A few blessed minutes passed in which no toasts were offered. Then at the far end of the table, I heard a chair scraping the floor. Henry was standing, his silver tankard in his hand. "Gentlemen," he said, "gentlemen, let us rise for one more toast." We rose, not knowing what might follow. "Let us drink," said Henry, "let us drink . . . to the great state of Texas!" I stared into my tankard, wondering if I could manage one sip. Then I heard Cavling's impressive bass. "Fellow members of the International Society!" he cried, "I remind you! When we drink to the great state of Texas, we must drain our tankards dry!"

We landed back in New York at four in the morning. The reporters were waiting. Two days later we set out on the promised tour of the United States.

Helen had done what she could to keep the tour under broad and independent auspices; it was no use. The left wing unions and their allies had the organization and the will. They were locked in local power struggles with leaders such as Mayor Hubert Humphrey in Minneapolis. They looked on Wallace as one to be used. And he was willing. The left wing was committed, as he was, to fight against the Truman Doctrine; the liberals were vacillating, unsure.

We traveled from city to city; the meetings were always the same. Local leaders would work up the audience. Paul Robeson would sing *Old Man River*—in his own version, which ended "Keep on fightin' until I'm dyin'." Then, prompted by cheerleaders, a chant would start up: "Wallace for President!

Wallace for President!" It would gain and gain in force; then Robeson's great voice would roll over the crowd: "Yes! The people want Wallace for President! And if they can't have him as a Democrat, they'll know where to go!" A money-raising pitch would follow, and at last Henry would step forward to stand, blinking and waving in the floodlights. By then, many farmers and working men who had driven for hours to hear him had gone home.

Listening and looking on, night after night from the back of the halls, I became more and more disturbed. By day, while Harold and Beanie called on Democratic politicians, I worked on Henry's speeches. By night, I sat alone. In time my disaffection became apparent. One morning in Chicago a succession of visitors came by my hotel room: Harold Young, Clark Foreman, Paul Robeson whom I had revered as a boy when my mother brought him to England to play *Othello* to Peggy Ashcroft's *Desdemona*. The last visitor was Beanie, the soft-spoken Virginian. He was, I believed, committed to working within the two party system. He was doing his best to persuade unhappy Democrats to vote for Wallace in the Democratic Convention of 1948. I reminded him of the refrain that we were hearing at meeting after meeting: *if the people can't have Wallace as a Democrat, they'll know where to go.* He nodded. "Without that threat," he said, "we haven't a chance." I agreed to that. I added that it would be very hard on Wallace and everyone else to allow the momentum of a Third Party to build up and then to cut it off. Beanie looked at me and smiled.

When the trip was over and we were back in the *New Republic* offices, it was possible for me, for the first time, to sit down with Wallace and to talk about our trip. I went over the meetings one by one.

"What did you think of Cleveland?"

"It was fair."

"That was a broad meeting, supported by the ADA. What about Chicago?"

"Much better."

"There were twenty thousand in the Chicago meeting. It was organized by unions that are Communist-led.

"What about Los Angeles?" I asked.

"It was a great rally," said Henry and he was right. There were film stars by the dozen on the platform and twenty-eight thousand people in the Bowl.

"Once again," I told him, "it was Communist-led."

"Can you prove that?"

"No," I said; and I went on down the list.

"What did you think of Seattle?"

"Fair."

"And San Francisco?"

"About the same."

"Those were meetings that started with broad sponsorship and ended up under left wing control. What about Portland?"

"Very good."

"Communist-organized again. And Olympia?" I went on through the list of meetings. At the end, I asked: "What do you think of what I'm saying?"

He shrugged his shoulders. "They get out the crowds," he said.

That was in late May. In the three months that followed we seemed to be becalmed: "a painted ship upon a painted ocean." Wallace spent the summer on his farm in South Salem; Harold answered mail in the Washington office financed by Mrs. Anita McCormick Blaine; Beanie soldiered on in the forlorn task of lining up delegates for the 1948 Democratic Convention; I returned to the *New Republic,* which by then was incurring unmanageable losses. In my innocence, I'd believed the advertisers who'd assured us that, once we'd reached a circulation of a hundred thousand, we could count on them. We reached it at great cost, but they were nowhere to be found.

Publishing the *New Republic* AND barnstorming with Wallace was too much for me. In a moment of exhaustion in Detroit I asked Lew Frank, the son of a prosperous businessman, to join the staff as an aide to Henry. We'd worked together in the American Veterans Committee—or rather, against each other since he was on the left wing and I was on the right wing of that embattled organization. I knew that we disagreed; I felt that he was able, earnest and sincere at heart. He was glad to come. He became an invaluable aide to Wallace—and a barrier, isolating Wallace from liberals like myself. I wondered in time where his allegiance lay and blamed myself for bringing him into Wallace's inner circle.

At the time—the late summer of 1947—the conflicts between us were masked. The Communist line had still to harden at three separate levels of authority.

In New York the primary concern of the Communist leaders was the Labor Party—a powerful organization in which they shared authority with the Amalgamated Clothing Workers Union. The heirs of Sidney Hillman in the Union were opposed to a Third Party, and Robert Thompson, the leader of the Communists promised that there would be no Third Party if it would cause a split.

Nationally, I learned later, the Communist Party was divided; the old-time party officials opposing a Third Party for fear that they could not control it; the young, undercover leaders, such as Lee Pressman, seeing the Third Party as a means of perpetuating the substantial power they had gained in the CIO.

In the Soviet Union the Politburo itself was shaken by the Marshall Plan. Should it support the Plan as a means of acquiring the capital equipment which it desperately needed? Or should it denounce the Plan as an imperialist trick? One course pointed toward collaboration with the Truman Administration; the other to an onslaught against it with every weapon at hand. Only when that bridge was crossed, it seemed to me, could we assess the pressures that would be brought to bear on Wallace to lead a Third Party.

In October the leaders of the Communist International met in Warsaw. The Manifesto which ended the meeting denounced the United States for seeking "to subjugate the world." "The greatest danger to the international working class," said Soviet spokesman Andrei Zhdanov, "is the underestimation of its own power." I read his statement in the *New York Times;* I telephoned Harold Young and told him that there was going to be a Third Party. "You're crazy!" he said.

Henry was away that week, driving through the New England countryside. When he returned to New York, a meeting was held to plan his schedule in 1948. We met in my sitting room: Henry, Harold, Beanie, Lew, Mike Nisselson, a businessman who was Treasurer of the PCA, and myself. Beanie laid out his proposal for a January rally in Madison Square Garden. Who would chair the meeting? He agreed that it had to be a trade union official. He spoke of many, starting with Phil Murray, but he could only promise the participation of one: Albert Fitzgerald. Then better no rally, said Mike and I. We turned to Henry for support; he was fast asleep.

I lay awake that night, wondering what to do next. It occurred to me that the best course would be to get Henry out of the country. Palestine, I decided, would be the place to go. There were some protests, but Henry liked the idea, and our schedule was set.

It was up to me to get Henry aside and to confront him with the dangers that he was being drawn into. I knew that; but I kept putting the moment off. The plane, I thought to myself; there will be no interruptions on the plane. So I left Henry and went instead to see Beanie. "I think that there's going to be a Third Party," I told him. "I agree" he said.

"I want to say this to you," I told him. "You won't get the liberals. Some of them will leave you because of the pressures that will be brought to bear upon them; some out of conviction. I'd like to be counted now in that second group. So don't count on the *New Republic* or on me."

Beanie listened. He said: "I wish you would go and tell that to John Abt."

John Abt was General Counsel of the Amalgamated Clothing Workers. I had barely heard of him. I went down to the Union headquarters near Washington Square and introduced myself. He was a quiet man, and he listened quietly to what I had to say. When I'd finished he said only: "Thank you for telling me."

"What are you going to do?" I asked him. He said: "We'll go through with our plan, no matter how small the movement is. Any protest is better than none. The world must know that not all Americans have given up hope of peace."

A few days later we climbed aboard the bus for Idlewild.

Lew came along, since Beanie and his friends did not trust me; so did Gerold Frank, since the Zionists did not trust either of us. Henry took his seat in the Constellation; Lew crowded into the seat beside him. I sat with Gerry. When the plane takes off I said to myself; then I'll ask Lew to change seats with me. The plane took off; as it climbed I unstrapped my safety belt. I started to get up and Gerry nudged me. "I brought along a chess set," he said. He held out two fists; I tapped one and drew white. By the time the Connie leveled off, our pieces were well deployed.

We had many memorable days in Palestine and in Rome. Henry described them in his weekly column in the *New Republic*, but there was one incident that did not see its way into print.

The Stern Gang was an armed force in British-ruled Palestine, bombing, burning, capturing British soldiers and executing them. Through an American reporter, the head of the Stern Gang sent a message to Wallace, proposing a meeting. We agreed that Wallace should say no, but that Lew and I would meet Stern and would tell Wallace what he had to say. So, late one night we walked up and down a back alley in Haifa. At the appointed hour in the best Hollywood manner, an ancient cab lurched around the corner. It swerved toward us and stopped; we were hauled inside it and blindfolded. Still blindfolded, we were led into a building, up in an elevator, through a guarded door. We were thrust onto two chairs; our blindfolds were taken off. We sat for a time in darkness; then the lights came on. We were seated at a dining table, covered with salami and sausages—as if we wanted to eat. Across the table, staring at us, was a man whose hair was dyed black and whose dead-white skin was drawn across a smooth, remodeled face—Stern. He described his objectives and urged us to support him. We mumbled some weak disclaimers. After an hour his guards stepped forward. We were blindfolded again, led back to the cab, and dumped out where we had been picked up.

We saw everyone, from the Pope to Togliatti in Rome. Then we flew back to New York. From then on, Henry's corner room in the *New Republic* was guarded as well as Stern's.

Visitors who presented themselves as union officials brought petitions from their members urging Wallace to lead a new party. The people wanted peace, they told him. If Philip Murray, Walter Reuther and James Carey opposed a Third Party, they no longer spoke for the rank and file. It was hard to get to Wallace with another view. I brought in Max Lerner for lunch, and he denounced the Third Party preparations. Wallace listened in stony silence. I took him out to Long Island for an evening with Charles Bolte, who described to him our struggles with the Communist Party in the American Veterans Committee. Wallace sat, jingling his keys. "You can't build a movement on the principle of opposition to Communism," he said. "Nor on the basis of subordination to Soviet policy," Charles answered. He tried to explain, but Wallace cut him off. "The issue," he said, "is peace."

Helen Fuller came up from Washington to see Wallace. "Would you lead a Third Party if the liberals were against you?" she asked. "Most of them are for me," he said. "Are you sure?" she asked him. "Do you mind if I urge them to get in touch with you?" "If you want to," he said. She enlisted Mrs. Roosevelt, Charlotte Carr, Helen Gahagan, Aubrey Williams and many more old friends of Henry's in a telephone campaign. He would stand at the doorway of my office, never coming in. "Tell Helen," he would say, "that another of her friends called today."

Wallace himself made no decisions. He was carried in the current, and by then the current was strong. The Executive Committee of the PCA met in December. Howard Fast and John Abt moved a resolution calling on Wallace to lead a people's party; Ray Walsh, Frank Kingdon and Charlotte Carr spoke against it. A bitter argument followed; at its height Helen Fuller moved that the resolution be referred to the National Committee of the PCA. John Abt, in his quiet voice, ruled her motion out of order. So, the Progressive Party was born.

Henry understood that he could not be a candidate and an editor. He wrote his last editorial in the January 5 issue of the *New Republic*. "Stand Up and Be Counted," it was called. It was an eloquent statement. Embedded in it was a carefully worded, revealing comment on who would control the new party he had agreed to lead. "Many of the friends who have supported my decision argued in advance that it was dangerous because the Communists want it. But I have never believed in turning from a principled position because it happened to win the support of others. . . ." A sad delusion; for the issue was not *support*, but *control*. Henry would never understand that, because he was not interested in organization. Harold Young had fallen off somewhere down the line. Beanie saw himself as the James Farley of a new party. I think he believed that, like John L. Lewis, he could use the communist organizers as shock troops and then send them to the rear.

The *New Republic* did not denounce the Progressive Party. We were too close to Wallace to do that. We gave him a page for a signed column, and for a few months that seemed to work. But we were moving apart and in the nation tensions were rising. I realized that, sitting in the Boston hall where the Steelworkers were holding their annual convention, and listening to Phil Murray. Murray had followed in Lewis's footsteps, relying on Lee Pressman, and denouncing Walter Reuther as a Red-baiter. At last, in a towering passion he denounced the Communists in his union. After his third outburst a Communist delegate stood up and called him a tool of the bosses. At Murray's signal, a band of strong-arm men rushed in and seized the man. They punched him and kicked him as they dragged him from the hall. They dumped him outside, more dead than alive.

I saw very little of Wallace after January. I wrote to him three times. The first letter was to tell him that the *New Republic* would oppose the stand that he had taken against the Marshall Plan; the second was to tell him that we could no longer run his column; the third, written after the Democratic Convention, was to tell him that we were about to endorse Harry Truman for the Presidency. All three must have wounded Henry, but his replies were gentle. His final column was a model of grace.

The November election was, of course, a disaster for the Progressive Party. It struggled on. In the Spring of 1949, I went to Rutgers to speak. Four people came to the meeting—it turned out that the Progressive Party was holding a mammoth rally in a movie house in Jersey City. We adjourned our meeting and went to the mammoth rally. It was a dispirited affair. A British M.P. delivered a dreary address. The fund-raiser flogged the inert audience with weary clichés. Ingrid Bergman had been having marital troubles, and they had filled the tabloids. "Ingrid Bergman and her husband have met!" screamed the fund-raiser at the peak of his frenzy; "why can't Truman and Stalin?" Held until the end, as always, Henry sat hunched over on the platform. I hoped that he was asleep.

I was reading at home one day in the autumn of 1953, when the telephone rang. It was Henry. He was in Washington, he said; he wondered if I could join him and his family for dinner.

He had left the Progressive Party by then. He had acknowledged his errors in a widely syndicated article; he had defended the liberals who had broken with him, saying that they were right. He had made his peace with Harry Truman and Dwight Eisenhower; he was living in retirement on his farm. Nonetheless, he was being hounded.

A Senate Subcommittee, headed by William Jenner, was looking into Communist infiltration of the federal government. It had centered its investigation on the cell organized with the Department of Agriculture in the Thirties to which, according to sworn testimony, Lee Pressman, Nathan Witt, John Abt and Alger Hiss, among others, had belonged. It had tracked down two former officials of the Department and taken their testimony. They had described themselves as advisers to Henry Wallace in the days when he was Secretary of Agriculture. In response to further questions, they had cited the Fifth Amendment and refused to speak.

The Subcommittee had summoned Wallace to testify on what he knew about the cell. That, in itself, was legitimate and his answer would be: *nothing*. But the national climate had been poisoned by Joseph McCarthy. In what was described to reporters as an effort to take McCarthyism away from McCarthy, the Attorney General, Herbert Brownell, had accused

Harry Truman of knowingly promoting a Communist spy.

If Truman was vulnerable to that accusation, how could Wallace be spared? A number of right wing commentators led by Fulton Lewis, Jr. repeated, again and again, that Wallace was the knowing associate of traitors to the United States.

The charge had angered me. Digging into some wartime documents, I'd come upon some dispatches that linked Lewis to the Government of Adolf Hitler. Word of my discovery had reached Wallace, who had come to Washington to defend himself before a Congressional committee. I was glad to tell him all that I knew.

We went into dinner. He sat in silence and the gloom that exuded from him spread around the table. No one had any light comments to make; I did my best. I'd been in Europe and I described the places that I'd visited. It sufficed for five minutes or so, then Henry broke in. "Where would you live," he demanded, "if you couldn't live in America?"

I tried to treat his question casually. "There's a village on the Lake of Lucerne where Mark Twain lived . . ." I began, ". . . there are some lovely old houses in the Cotswolds, not far from Oxford. . . ." I wandered on through Tuscany and Provence. Then once again Henry broke in. He burst out, in a bitter denunciation of the charges that were being pressed against him. "Do you think," he demanded, "that the American people believe all of those lies?" No, no, of course not, we all mumbled. "That's why I asked you the question," he cried. "Because, if they do, I don't want to live in America any more!"

It was a sad ending to one of the sadder chapters in Wallace's life. But the chapter was not all sad. There was the sunlit day when we sailed around the Sea of Galilee in a tiny steamboat, piloted by Teddy Kollek. There was another day in the North of England, when we drove to Freckleton. There, in 1944, an American bomber, struggling to reach its base, had crashed onto the playground of the village school killing all of its crew and all but two of the children who were playing there. The men at the base had rebuilt the shattered playground, fashioning seesaws and slides and a merry-go-round from the twisted beams of the wreck. They had placed a plaque on a wall: *This playground presented to the children of Freckleton by their American neighbors . . . in recognition and remembrance of their common loss.*

The two children who had survived the disaster were brought up to Wallace, to curtsey and to shake his hand. They were horribly scarred, and they were shivering in the cold wind. Wallace put his arms around them and, his grey hair blowing, spoke about the issue that mattered most to him: peace. The fathers and mothers nodded in silence, and all the time a new batch of kids, too young for speeches, were playing on the slides and breaking across his phrases with their discordant cries.

Harold Stassen; Mister Taft

APRIL 1948

It's springtime, sweet and mild, in the Midwest as Taft and Stassen battle for Ohio's delegates. Dogwood and redbud fill the woods in southwestern Ohio, where Stassen has pushed his way into Taft's political heartland. Fruit blossoms, white and lovely, cover the hills of the northeast, where Taft has countered. As far as the battle of ideas, promised by Stassen, is concerned, spring in its mildness has won. Stassen has said little that Taft hadn't said, and Taft has said little that McKinley didn't say.

Touring through McKinley country, Taft told schoolchildren how as a little boy he had sat on the great man's knee, and added, "I have been trying for eight years to reestablish some of the principles of liberty in which McKinley believed." He lectured the children on the details of the Taft-Hartley Act.

Moving southward, Taft took off his hat and spoke from the steps of the Lisbon courthouse. The spring breeze stirred the few strands of hair combed over the dome of his head. One hundred people listened quietly, half of them county clerks brought out from the old building and glad of a chance to stand in the morning sunshine and watch the elms and maples budding into leaves.

The day grew warmer. At Carrollton, in the public square, the high-school band, dressed in black and gold, perspired as it played "I'm Forever Blowing Bubbles" and "Put on Your Old Gray Bonnet." Old men sitting on the public benches leaned on their canes and spat. In the courthouse, facing the A & P, there were notices, "Win with Taft," in every window. And Taft, standing on the yellow wagon of the Farmers Exchange, repeated his lecture to silent farmers and children let out of school.

At Cadiz, the courthouse from which his father once expressed similar views to larger crowds was done up in flags and bunting. Excited children and a few loyal supporters surrounded Taft, but across the street stood a line of frowning miners, still on strike and smarting. "Son-of-a-bitch," they muttered. "Shoulda been hung before he was born! Shouldn't have stuck his nose into organized labor." They shouted interruptions, and typically, Taft repeated his defense of every detail of his law without altering a phrase.

Miners aside, on that spring day it was hard to believe that this courteous, didactic man was a hard-pressed candidate for the presidency, fighting to hold his own. The references of local politicians to "our next President" seemed unkind, even grotesque. Taft was the benevolent squire moving among his dependents with an easy handshake, a benign smile, a casual word, a handsome insistence on greeting the humblest and poorest.

His speech in spirit sounded like one lifted from a trunk in his father's attic: decent and honest and exactly as lifelike as the fine old cannon mounted in the courthouse squares. He attacked communism and defended the rights of Communists; attacked universal military training and called for a large air force; attacked the wickedness of federal intervention and defended the Taft-Hartley Act. But most of all he belabored the New Deal, blowing up dry dust around a long-laid ghost.

Of Stassen, Taft spoke with obvious horror and pain. His own policies, Taft said, were exactly those of the Republican Party. If Stassen disagreed with Taft's views, then he disagreed with the views of the Republican Party. That meant, Taft said, that he must be a New Dealer. "It ill behooves Stassen," said Taft, "to criticize the Republicans who have been fighting in the front-line trenches." Where was Stassen during the battle against the New Deal? he asked, and answering his own question, he added that Stassen was AWOL, gallivanting around campaigning for the presidency and mouthing fine-sounding generalities.

Taft moved through Ohio with the outworn grace of a coach and four, Stassen with the brutal force of an armored car.

Stassen's much publicized modernism lay in his technique alone. His meetings were packed with young and cheering crowds. His one speech was up-to-date and persuasive. His manner in handling questions was smooth. "First the lady with the red hat; then you, sir, in the back of the hall."

As if having a presidential candidate visit each little town to answer questions was not flattering enough, the chairman ended with, "Now Governor Stassen will be glad to shake everyone's hand." Stassen, springing down from the platform, rushed each time to the entrance. There he took a firm stance, grabbed the hand of each nervous and surprised Ohioan, flashed a glassy smile, and with a wrench of his forearm down and back, propelled them along with the force of an Indian wrestler throwing his opponent. In this way Stassen shook hands with fifty people a minute, filling hotel foyers, hall entrances and crowded streets with beaming faces and delighted cries of "Shake the hand that shook the hand . . ." and "Strong as an ox, ain't he?"

Shocked and embittered, Taft kept asking, "Where does he disagree with me?" Stassen, who declared that the battle was one of issues, never answered. He had no program. His strongest demand was for the prompt outlawing of the Communist Party, not only in America but in all free countries.

This demand—delivered in a crescendo of oratory—was greeted with tremendous applause, loud laughter and resounding cheers. Communists he defined for skeptical questioners as people who "deny the fatherhood of God," and who "seek to further the foreign policy of the Kremlin." Outlawing the Communist Party, he immediately added, was no violation of free speech.

Stassen did question the most extreme provisions of the
Taft-Hartley Act. He did favor World Federation. He did express the belief that ultimately the USSR and the U.S. might
live in friendship. On UMT he hedged: he had been for it because Eisenhower was for it. Now, he said, he was inclined to
oppose it because the overwhelming majority of the people are
not for it. He proposed a "selective service and training act"
administered by Congress, in accordance with "the American
way." Like most of his programs, it was, as one journalist said,
"More than nothing and less than something."

Everyone who heard Stassen agreed with all that he said
and no one knew quite what he meant. Every one of his tory
demands was clothed in liberal language. Every liberal suggestion was qualified at once, and wrapped in tory winding sheets.
In a state ridden by machine corruption he never mentioned
boss rule. In a region governed by giant corporations, and in a
nation threatened with militarization and intolerance, he
made no mention of the powerful forces which dominate his
party and our lives.

No issue has been stated in Ohio; yet an issue has been
drawn. Ohioans know what Taft stands for: a nation governed
by initiative fittingly rewarded, kept in balance by self-interest,
holding in tight rein an alien and remote national government,
and correcting its excesses of misery through bounties dis-
tributed by the wealthy and the benevolent among the grate-
ful and indigent.

In a state that is conservative by nature, and prosperous by
effort, this viewpoint corresponds to deep-laid prejudices: dis-
like of interference, resentment against taxes levied to aid
slackers, suspicion of the faraway, fear of the unknown. Yet
here Taft's appeal stops, and beyond this there are other feelings that he cannot bring himself to express: powerful frustra-
tion, real want, deep insecurity, all creating an urgent desire for
change. Stassen, voicing all the contradictions and some of the
virtues of the middle class, expresses also its unnamed rest-
lessness, its latent idealism and its incoherent desire to move
on.

All this emerges in the two campaigns. Taft is the face on

the poster in the courthouse window—the machine's man. Stassen is the man who made opposition to Taft respectable. Taft's slate of delegates is the machine slate: lawyers made great by patronage and judges grown old and sour. Stassen's delegates are a diverse crowd of amateurs: young veterans; businessmen; civic leaders; crusading ministers; AFL business agents, and one official of the Rubber Workers, CIO.

These various individuals are bucking the machine, bucking the favorite son sentiment, bucking tradition. But they are working under expert direction and with plenty of money, in the industrial districts where the ferment is greatest. They are banking on Taft's unpopularity in Ohio; on labor's hatred for the author of the Taft-Hartley Act and on labor's willingness, already shown in Wisconsin, to cross over to the Republican side for the primary.

A further source of strength and inspiration among his backers is Stassen's momentum, which, if it continues in Ohio, can carry him past Oregon to his goal at Philadelphia. Sure, Stassen is straddling and backsliding, they say he has to in order to win the Republican nomination. After that he will show himself as the liberal that he really is. This secret seems to be shared by many voters. They have a sneaking feeling that their Senator would make an awful President. If they vote against him it will be because of a general sense that Stassen belongs to today's world and that Taft does not.

How it will come out on May 4 is anybody's guess. At Lisbon, Walter Kay, running for sheriff in the Republican primaries on the simple slogan "Abolish Crime," moved among the little crowd, handing out match boxes to the men and nail files to the women.

"How will it come out?" he said. "I ain't predicting; but on May 4 I'll know how many liars there are in Columbiana County."

Adlai

NOVEMBER 1955

Of all the riddles that make up American politics, the greatest today is Adlai Stevenson. He is a cautious man with great appeal in the expansive West; a spokesman for civil rights whom the South accepts as a friend; a conservative among Democrats who is the first choice of the trade unionists; the favorite of professional politicians who dislikes the game of politics. Stevenson is complicated, aloof and physically unimposing; in no sense the traditional image of the successful politician. And yet he commands more loyalty and devotion than any man in our political life save one.

To these riddles there are, of course, answers. Westerners see Stevenson as a self-willed man, a respected figure in states notoriously free from party discipline. Southerners cast him in the Wilsonian tradition of the scholar in politics—one again which is their own. Trade unionists prefer to work with an established candidate rather than undergoing the expense, the labor and the risks of introducing a new man to the voters. As for the professional Democrats: "The time has passed," says James Finnegan, Secretary of State of Pennsylvania, "when a precinct captain could swing his precinct by favors or the force of his own personality. The people look at television now; they vote for the face they trust."

And, with some reservations, they trust Adlai Stevenson. He comes through as the man he is; he can do no other. Stevenson cannot, as Eisenhower did, take another man's work and read it off as his own. He would regard this as intellectual dishonesty. It is an act of faith with him to disappear for two days in order to work on a minor speech. Thousands of votes may have been lost in 1952 because Stevenson was polishing the style of his speeches when he should have been polishing political apples. His absorption with his own drafts added to his reputation for aloofness, which is still a serious political liability. In exchange, as the nation suffers with him while he wrestles with the farm program, or rises with him in his eloquence, it knows that it is seeing the candidate himself, and not the processed package of a public relations firm. An unknowing audience, given an Eisenhower speech to identify, may name a hundred different orators. Stevenson's whistle-stop speeches, his best, could only have been given by one man. Only one man could have spoken as Stevenson did, for example, on November 4, 1952, when he encountered a band of children in a school yard used as a polling place:

> ... I think you are going to remember today for one thing only, that you got a half-day off from school. I am sure I have enjoyed this as much as you have and I would like to spend the recess this morning playing with you in the school yard. But I don't know what we would play. What would we play?
> (Shouts, "Baseball! Football!")
> The same old fight between the cattlemen and the sheepmen. Wouldn't anybody like to have a little mock game of politics?
> (A little boy: "We don't like mud fights")
> Well! I never saw a kid who didn't like a mud fight! ...

Nor could any ghost writer match the grace of his extemporaneous speech of farewell of August 14, 1952, at the Illinois State Fair:

> ... Before I leave I want to say to you shamelessly and sentimentally that my heart will always be here in Illinois. Here five generations of my family have lived and prospered. My roots are deep in our prairies and I owe Illinois a great debt. I have tried

my best to discharge that debt honorably and well. But in the
process I have only increased my obligations.

A President must be able to give vitality to his projects, to
mobilize his party behind them in the Congress and, when the
Congress balks, to bring public opinion to bear on the Congress
on behalf of his aims.

As Governor of Illinois, Stevenson demonstrated those
qualities. And yet, among Democrats, a doubt persists that he
possesses a feeling for people, an ability to communicate, a
human warmth, a common touch of the kind that made Harry
Truman President in 1948.

One kind of reservation points to the contrast between
Stevenson and Truman, and holds Stevenson at fault. "In
1952," one Democrat recalls, "we were driving across the fields
to the farm rally in Kasson. We were urging Stevenson to make
a real give-'em-hell-Harry speech. About then a weatherbeaten
old farmer runs out of the crowd. 'Give 'em—give 'em heck,
Adlai!' he cries."

But if this quality is a liability with some voters, others are
drawn to Stevenson by his reverence for restraint.

A second reservation concerns Stevenson's unwillingness
to generate mass support. "Slum clearance is a crying need for
America," the critic argues. "Tell me when Adlai Stevenson
last visited a slum? Automation is causing layoffs by the hundreds of thousands; when did Adlai last talk to the men on an
assembly line? Farmers are going bankrupt by the thousands
right now. When they listen to Adlai wrestling with himself on
the subject of parity, do they feel he's on their side? When
Emmett Till was murdered down in Mississippi, every colored
man in the country and every decent white man wanted to
protest. Where was the leader of the party of justice then?"

A third reservation, often heard, concerns Stevenson's use
of unfamiliar images, abstract arguments, involved sentences
and polysyllabic words. "The people don't think he talks above
them," Stevenson's advisers insist. "The heck they don't!" a
labor leader replies. He continues:

I was speaking to a trade union conference not long ago, and I said, "How many of you here understand Stevenson?" "Oh, we all understand him," they answered, "it's just that the other guys don't." A woman came up to me afterwards. "They don't understand him either," she whispered. "They're ashamed to admit it, that's all."

A further reservation concerns Stevenson's unwillingness to undertake the political chores demanded both of a successful candidate and of a President who keeps in close touch with his supporters. "Of course Stevenson is our first choice," agrees a trade union official. "And yet," he adds, "I scratch labor and I find indifference. Walter Reuther is for him, of course, and so are Jacob Potofsky and Dave Dubinsky. So is George Meany, I suppose. The rest are lukewarm to cold. Do you know why? It's because Stevenson has never called them up, never said 'come on over for a chat.' He assumes that they must be interested in what he has to say. But he's never indicated that *he's* interested in *their* point of view."

There is a final reservation concerning Stevenson as a President who can carry the people with him—it is that, at heart, he really doesn't like politicians or politics. In this, there is certainly some truth. It is said of Senator Hubert Humphrey that he can return to Minnesota ashen-faced and exhausted after months in Washington, set out on tour, speak ten times a day for a week, and sleep four hours a night and then return to Washington as fresh as a daisy. Stevenson, in contrast, is more enervated than nourished by adulation. Franklin Roosevelt was a great President in part because he loved to hold the federal power. For Stevenson, again, power is more headache than aspirin.

This last reservation is perhaps the most serious of all in assessing Stevenson's qualifications for the Presidency. For Americans do not want as their President a man who does not want to be President. They remember that in his acceptance speech in 1952 Stevenson referred to the "dread responsibility" of the Presidency. They recall that he added, "I have not sought the nomination. . . . I would not seek it in honest self-appraisal. . . ." They wonder if his self-appraisal has altered since then. The death of Franklin Roosevelt and the disability of Dwight

Eisenhower have convinced them that today the Presidency is a killing job. They realize that it demands a man who is mentally, emotionally, and physically prepared. They believe that self-doubt and hesitation in a candidate may lead to paralyzing indecision in a President once he is subjected to the Presidency's fearful strains. They see in Richard Nixon a man who entertains no shred of doubt that he would make one whale of a President. And in this, at least, they find respect for Nixon.

Some of these criticisms of Stevenson relate to the past. Others concern traits of his personality that are not likely to change radically. For these traits are part, not only of a steadfast personality, but of a well-founded attitude towards politics.

Stevenson, when he travels overseas, will not send postcards by the thousands to precinct workers back home in the manner of the indefatigable Estes Kefauver. His refusal to do so reflects the fact that winning is not his highest goal.

It is probable moreover that Stevenson will always prefer the company of a Harvard historian or a Chicago North Shore squire to that of an official of the International Brotherhood of Teamsters, or a convention delegate who claims to control five votes. He may be told a thousand times that a leader of the people, in these days of press and television, is a wholly public personality whose every movement the people must watch and approve. He will stand fast on his conviction that the right of privacy is fundamental and that, just as he respects it in the public, so the public must respect it in him.

Stevenson will not oversimplify issues nor limit himself to words of three syllables. He will resist making promises that he cannot fulfill. He will not change his public personality in search of votes, as the public personality of the Vice President appears to be changing these days from partisan to statesman. Stevenson respects the American people and treats them as his equals. He is available for leadership, but on his own terms.

Stevenson is opportuned every day now by advisers who beg him to build his campaign around an emotional appeal. He will do no such thing. He dislikes emotionalism; he has no wish to stir up further feeling where feeling already runs deep.

To reduce the point to the grotesque, it is as unthinkable that
Stevenson could wind up a television appearance by daring his
enemies to deprive him of his cocker spaniel, as it is that
Nixon could tell a Republican rally, "Better we lose the election than mislead the people."

Stevenson's distaste for emotionalism derives from the
heart of his political faith. It is contained in the testament of
William James that serves as the frontispiece of his volume of
1952 speeches, and until it is read, Stevenson cannot be understood.

> Reason [James wrote] is one of the very feeblest of Nature's
> forces, if you take it at any one spot and moment. It is only in
> the very long run that its effects become perceptible. Reason
> assumes to settle things by weighing them against one another
> without prejudice, partiality, or excitement; but what affairs in
> the concrete are settled by is and always will be just prejudices,
> partialities, cupidities, and excitements. Appealing to reason as
> we do, we are in a sort of forlorn hope situation, like a small
> sandbank in the midst of a hungry sea ready to wash it out of
> existence. But sandbanks grow when the conditions favor; and
> weak as reason is, it has the unique advantage over its antagon-
> ists that its activity never lets up and that it presses always in
> one direction, while men's prejudices vary, their passions ebb
> and flow, and their excitements are intermittent. Our sandbank,
> I absolutely believe, is bound to grow—bit by bit it will get
> dyked and breakwatered.

Stevenson went into politics because "the governorship of
Illinois was a great dramatic opportunity to demonstrate to all
and sundry ... that ... 'our sandbank is bound to grow.'"·
Again, it was his concern with the sandbank that led him in
the 1952 campaign to warn Legionnaires that he would not
succumb to pressure groups, to tell trade unionists that the
nation came before labor's interest, to inform farmers that
they would get no special treatment from him, to insist to
European-Americans that "Even if votes could be won by it, I
would not say one reckless thing [on the liberation of Eastern
Europe] during this campaign." The same faith in reason led
Stevenson to warn the electorate that his term of office as
President would be one of "strife, dissension and ruthless, un-

controllable and hostile power abroad." Eisenhower, in contrast, made it clear that once the party of patriotism was elected to power, then under the warmth of his sunny personality, the hardships of high taxes and the threats of world Communism would recede.

Stevenson lost in 1952, for a powerful vision of a better time is at any time more appealing than the promise to preside over grim and bloody years. And yet Stevenson's faith in the power of reason was unaltered. "It is only in the very long run that its effects become perceptible."

With Eisenhower at the Summit

JULY 1955

I: IN THE WARMTH OF HIS PERSONALITY

Throughout the final day at the Geneva Conference, the chiefs of state struggled to write their Directive. At five o'clock they agreed upon its ambiguous wording. And that evening they returned for what should have been a round of friendly generalities spoken in farewell. "In our Directive," declared Sir Anthony Eden, who spoke first, "we have included the essentials of a comprehensive settlement." It was then up to Marshal Bulganin to second this moderately hopeful view. Instead the Marshal read an unyielding repetition of his original demands. He spoke in a low voice, and as he spoke the Soviet delegates gripped the sides of their chairs and stared at the floor. These things must be spoken for the record, they were sorry.

Bulganin was followed by President Eisenhower. In a few dignified phrases he passed over Bulganin's challenge. He recorded once more "my lasting faith in the decent instincts and good sense of all peoples," including the Russians. Then, when the conference ended, he went over once more to embrace and to reassure the Soviet leaders. The final impression that the

American experts brought away was of Bulganin, Khrushchev and Zhukov, beaming and basking in the warmth of the President's personality.

Whether the Russians needed more time to consider the proposals made at Geneva, whether they were offended by their defeats at the propaganda level, or whether they had to end on a strong note in order to bolster the satellite regimes no one knew for sure. Two things alone seemed certain on that Saturday night: the first was that the personal impact of President Eisenhower was tremendous in Geneva; the second, that the meaning of the conference would turn, as the President concluded, on the follow-through. And if it was not certain, it seemed reasonably sure that in the five days from July 18 to July 23, 1955, the world moved a short but measurable distance toward peace.

The American approach to the Geneva Conference was summarized by President Eisenhower in his opening address. ". . . We cannot expect here," he said, "to solve all of the problems of the world . . . It is out of the question in the short time available to the heads of governments meeting here to trace out the causes and origins of these problems and to devise agreements that could, with complete fairness to all, eliminate them. Nevertheless we can perhaps create a new spirit that will make possible future solutions."

In this key passage the President reconciled the irreconcilables of Geneva: the bitterness of its origins and the necessity of overcoming bitterness; the impossibilities of real agreement and the public demand that the impossible be attempted; the pessimism of Dulles and the President's view that "pessimism never won a war."

Because of its origins the Geneva Conference seemed doomed at first to fail. It was, it is worth remembering, brought into being as a means of inducing the French Assembly to ratify the German Accords. The French supposed that a conference at the Summit would lessen tensions and make German rearmament superfluous, but the reverse seemed a more likely result. The Soviet Government, after all, had warned over and over that ratification would increase tensions and end all hopes of negotiation in Europe. And while the Soviet leaders could not afford the political penalties of refusing to attend a conference dedicated to peace, they were under no compulsion to be generous at Geneva, least of all in payment for what they had described as an act of treachery.

The negative approach to Geneva was reinforced by the personal pessimism of Secretary Dulles. For twenty years the Secretary had followed each maneuver of Soviet diplomacy. He had learned to be suspicious of overtures from Russia, scornful of generalities, skeptical of agreements and doubtful about apparent changes of heart. He dreamed that his lifetime of diplomacy would be crowned with a peace settlement. But his dreams had a way of ending in nightmares dominated by Senator Knowland. He felt that in the period of Western strength that would follow the German Accords, a year of hard Yankee trading might begin to show results. And he anticipated this trading with the grim pleasure of a lawyer trying a criminal case. He granted and then appraised the propaganda advantages of making the first play for public opinion in any conference. He weighed them against the bargaining advantage in forcing his adversary to make the first move. The canny trader in him chose the second course. Above all, Mr. Dulles remembered that, thanks in part to his own talents, the good names of Franklin Roosevelt and Harry Truman had been blackened before history with the brushes of Yalta and Potsdam. With his lawyer's concern for his client and his preoccupation with domestic politics, Mr. Dulles was determined that Geneva would never serve as a brush for Democrats to blacken Eisenhower. So, at Mr. Dulles' direction, negativism was the American watchword before Geneva.

The primary objective at Geneva, as Mr. Dulles interpreted it, was not to reach a settlement with the Russians but to preserve the unity of the allies. With this approach the working parties of the Foreign Office, the Quai d'Orsay and the Bonn Government agreed.

And yet public opinion, taught over lean years to believe in negotiation through strength, pressed for proposals that the Russians might accept. The pressure mounted sharply after January.

Le Degel is the French title of Ilya Ehrenburg's novel *The Thaw*. And *le degel* was the phrase used with some irony by the French to describe the months that led up to Geneva. During those months the Soviet leaders thawed not only in the sunshine of garden parties but in the shadows of conference rooms. Even the coldest of Soviet officials, Mr. Molotov, thawed out enough to apologize to Secretary Dulles for repeating the old Soviet line at San Francisco. "This anniversary celebration," Mr. Molotov explained, "is neither the time nor the place for serious talks."

The foreign ministers and their experts were content to ignore the thaw until it proved to be real. Their chosen approach to the Geneva conference remained unchanged. But the chiefs of state, unlike their servants, are public figures. They are political leaders, spokesmen of the national purpose and custodians of the national morale. The public may be moved by illusions, but chiefs of state cannot rough-hew these illusions.

The world's hopes for Geneva mounted following the thaw. And, thaw or no thaw, the three chiefs of state understood that it was for them to give expression to these hopes.

Edgar Faure was the weakest of the three and also the least involved. In France, where foreign policy is peripheral, premiers are not made and broken by their record on world affairs. Faure nonetheless felt impelled to establish France's independence and his own role as an innovator in statesmanship. He lacked the political power to undertake a man-to-man appeal to Marshal Bulganin. He could not, like Eden, propose further concessions on Germany; since, as an advocate of German unification, his neck was already well extended on that issue. He chose therefore the Mendesian course of an ambitious scheme relating disarmament to economic benefits through budgetary controls which, no doubt, would create fascinating problems in the case of France alone. His proposal certainly caused little loss of sleep among the Russians, but Frenchmen seemed well satisfied.

Sir Anthony Eden was also thinking largely in political terms. Superficially his leadership was unchallenged in his own country. In fact, as Prime Minister and as party leader, he was still on probation. Eden was not, like Churchill, the beer and bread of England. In a nation where foreign affairs are important, he had staked his place in history on his record beyond England's shores. In approaching Geneva, Eden shunned, of course, the rococo presentation of Mr. Faure. His long record in the Foreign Office taught him further to distrust the American instinct for personal contact with the Russians. The only serious program for German unification, the Eden Plan, was his own creation. So he elaborated it and set out to make it more acceptable for the Russians in a series of proposals on partial neutrality for Germany. These he listed as "examples" in deference to Mr. Dulles' distrust of the specific. "We will lay them on the table at Geneva," said one of his aides, "and watch closely to see when Russian eyes light up."

Eisenhower, in contrast, cast aside the subtleties and the complexities of the Eden proposals, sensing in his unerring way that when chiefs of state meet, only great and simple gestures are deeply felt and long remembered. In this spirit he resolved to act on his own. Earlier delegations of the Presidential powers to Admiral Radford and Secretary Dulles had, on more than one occasion, landed Eisenhower close to disaster. So in Geneva he determined that he would play the President's part. Lacking Roosevelt's jaunty conviction that he could charm the buttons off Stalin's vest, Eisenhower had enough of Roosevelt in him to believe that he could redirect the course of world diplomacy by the force of his personal impact on the Soviet leaders. And on the one issue of disarmament on which he trusted his own judgment, the President worked alone, without the knowledge of his own delegation.

So the final preparations were made for Geneva. In inspired editorials of the *London Times*, through quiet briefings of the American reporters, and in the spirited debate which Premier Faure staged with French journalists, the outlines of the Western position became clearer. The Russians, in turn, matched every dramatic development with one of their own. Two senior Soviet advisers on Germany were added to the Russian delegation. Then Marshal Zhukov's participation was

announced in a plain bid for direct talks with Eisenhower.
Next Khrushchev said that he was coming. The reason, American experts supposed, was that Khrushchev was anxious to
share the credit for any success that might be registered at
Geneva, while all the other Soviet leaders wanted to be quite
sure that in the event of failure Khrushchev would share the
blame.

So, in Paris the sense of excitement mounted, despite the
warnings of old timers that nothing could take place. "We're
dealing with three mavericks in our chiefs of state," said one
expert. "Who knows," he added, "the conference may amount
to something after all."

From then on, of course, the outcome of the Conference
turned on the Russians. If their purpose at Geneva was propaganda, they would endorse the Faure Plan and blame the
United States for withholding from the masses its immediate
fruits. If instead they wanted rapid progress toward a real settlement, even at some cost to themselves, then they would
advance to a detailed examination of the Eden proposals. But if
their main objective was to create a better international atmosphere without giving up anything of significance, then
Eisenhower's appeal for a new spirit would be the one to which
the Soviet leaders would respond.

It was the third course that the Russians chose at Geneva.
They showed a new spirit of friendliness from the moment that
they walked down the ramp of their plane. They demonstrated
in particular an ardent desire to please the Americans and a
touching capacity to be pleased by the Americans in return.
But they did not relate the new spirit to any new plans for
peace. They advanced over the five days of the conference a
series of detailed proposals. But all of these proved on close
examination to be repetitions of familiar propositions with
only minor modifications. Bulganin and Molotov, in other
words, came to Geneva with precisely the same thought as
Eisenhower and Dulles: the Conference should create a new
spirit, but one not sustained by any new ideas.

It was on the opening day of the Conference that the Russians scored their great success. They arrived at the Palais des

Nations in an open car in obvious contrast to President Eisenhower who roared by encased in a bulletproof limousine es-
corted by motorcycle policemen and surrounded by armed
guards. In further contrast, the leader of the free peoples hurried unsmiling up the steps of the Palais while the heirs of
Stalin paused with a wave and a smile on each step. The President spoke first in the morning and, in homage to his party,
voiced his concern over the enslavement of the satellite states.
In the first of many rumors started in the Maison de la Presse,
French journalists reported that the Russians were upset. The
polemics of the President, they felt, made it hard for them not
to engage in counter-polemics, and yet they had no desire to
see the Conference start on a sour note. But, if the Soviet delegates felt the temptation to argue, they resisted it. Marshal
Bulganin, it seemed, had chosen as his model for Geneva the
prior success of his side at Bandung. There Chou En-lai had
brilliantly countered rudeness with courtesy, and extremism
with moderation. The Russians were determined to appear
even more mature. In one mild word "inappropriate" Marshal
Bulganin passed over the President's unkind phrases. "The purpose of this conference," Bulganin stated in an exact paraphrase
of the President's main point, "is not to indulge in recrimina-
tion but to . . . create an atmosphere of confidence in relations
between nations."

So the new spirit survived. "If we can preserve this spirit of
friendship," declared the President at the close of the first day,
"then . . . this conference will be a great success."

With equal determination the Soviet and American delegates generated the new spirit throughout a trying week. The
Marshal demonstrated that he was truly moved. The President
appealed to Marshal Bulganin to believe in his peaceful inten-
tions. Marshal Bulganin replied that indeed he did. Mr. Dulles,
who once relished his bitter encounters with Mr. Molotov,
joked about their past exchanges and approached the Soviet
Foreign Minister with courtesy and respect. Mr. Molotov also
joked and appeared to be open to reason. "You may be right, of
course," said Mr. Molotov. "No doubt I may be mistaken. . . . I
quite see your point. . . ." The veterans of ten years looked at
each other in total disbelief.

In the buffet luncheons and the elaborate dinners the new spirit was maintained. The President kidded Zhukov about his many colored uniforms and Bulganin about his non-military suits. The Marshal in turn kidded Eisenhower about his new-found civilian status. Even the most cynical of diplomats was impressed. The Soviet leaders had always trusted and admired Eisenhower in the same wholehearted way in which they distrusted and feared Dulles. They are, in addition, sober students of protocol who respect rank with the same intensity as they revere power. Quite apart from personality there is a majesty that surrounds a President in Soviet eyes. To this majesty Eisenhower added human warmth. He was riding a crest of self-confidence at Geneva, passionately believing in his mission and at the same time thoroughly enjoying himself. His earnestness and friendliness were pressed upon Bulganin and Khrushchev who had barely met an American, and the impression was apparently profound.

There were, however, iron boundaries where the excursion of personal diplomacy came to a halt. They were reached on the second day when German unification dominated the agenda. The allied leaders had pressed hard for unification during the first day's discussions. Marshal Bulganin had spoken in rather vague and encouraging phrases. He agreed that German unification was the goal. He maintained only that it must be accomplished step by step, which was a position that German spokesmen themselves advanced in private conversation.

This view was not beyond reconciliation with allied demands. For the allies agreed in private that a period of lowered tensions would necessarily precede a solution in Germany. They feared principally that the Russians would look on this period not as an interval of relaxation but as an opportunity for active intrigue to extract West Germany from NATO. Lacking any evidence that the Soviet thaw extended beyond smiles to minds and hearts, they pressed the Soviet delegation on the second day for prompt assurances on specific points. Thus cornered, Marshal Bulganin chose to be frank. He declared that the time for unification had not come and could not be fixed.

So Eden was brushed aside. It remained for Eisenhower to

try his alternative approach. The President fixed his eyes on
Zhukov and declared that the Russians had nothing to fear
from NATO. But an impression is less than a conversion, and
conversion required a greater figure than Eisenhower at Geneva. Bulganin closed the day with finality, declaring that his
statement reflected the well-considered view of the Soviet
Government and that he would say no more.

On the third day the Conference turned to security. To Mr.
Dulles the issue was very clear. Seen as an abstraction, he
believed European security was a meaningless effort to join six
or twenty-six nations in the common illusion that there was
some safety in paper promises.

Seen instead as a means of limiting the dangers attendant
upon German unification, a security system moved into focus
as a set of well-defined and well-enforced guarantees. These
guarantees would concern the frontiers, the alliances and the
armed forces of a unified Germany and therefore, Dulles argued, security for Europe could be considered only in the con-
text of German unification.

But unification had been set aside by Bulganin, and on
security the Russians had a plan apart. A new and realistic
proposal on security might have recovered for the Russians the
ground lost on the previous day. But their proposal proved in all
essentials to be the plan presented in Berlin eighteen months
before. It did offer participation in the security system to the
United States, but this concession had long been discounted.
And while the plan moved toward realism in proposing two
stages, the Valhalla of unification lay in the second stage and,
on the farther side, of the destruction of NATO.

The United States insisted on unification before security,
the Russians on security before unification. The French hinted
at a plan for linking security systems which the Germans indignantly vetoed as an unacknowledged acquiescence in the
status quo. There the deadlock continued until Eden proposed
that unification and security be considered together. On that
basis the Foreign Ministers were sent off to work up a directive.
Their constructive act in turn nearly wrecked the Conference.

For in dispatching the Ministers, Eisenhower seemed to tell them to follow the Soviet stand. A near-panic followed in the German press, and usually responsible British journalists enlivened their nation's newsstands with preposterous stories of an American surrender to the Kremlin. But Mr. Molotov, still gracious, saved the President from further embarrassment on the following morning by remarking that everyone understood that unification and security were linked together. This however, appeared to be the last point on which the Foreign Ministers could agree.

The chiefs of state moved on to the great issue of disarmament. Here the Russians were on their most favorable ground. Their major proposals of May 10 stood unanswered after ten weeks, and no well-prepared answer was available on the allied side. In his last press conference, however, and in his opening address at Geneva the President had moved a substantial distance in the direction of the Soviet plan. The distance that remained in principle was not too far to prohibit a detailed directive to the UN experts to start over in the preparation of a modest and realizable program for early warning and selective inspection.

"The United States," the President stated in Thursday's session, "is prepared to enter into a sound and reasonable agreement." He defined this agreement as one based on adequate inspection and reporting. "I propose," he said, "that we instruct our representatives on the subcommittee on disarmament . . . to give priority effort to the study of inspection and reporting." This was perhaps the most important recommendation of the entire conference, but it was wholly lost. The President apparently had been brooding in secret upon a much more dramatic idea, and some remark of Bulganin's prompted him to bring it forth. Setting aside his glasses and speaking "from my heart," the President proposed to exchange "immediately" the complete blueprint of our military establishments and "to provide within our countries facilities for aerial photography to the other country." The Russians said nothing. Faure regretted only that all his countrymen could not have witnessed the President's great act. Eden was a little more reserved. The

French and Swiss papers called the proposal "audacious." "*Grossartig*..." exclaimed the admiring observers from Bonn. The American journalists in contrast, were inclined to be resentful, feeling that they had been misled.

The President's offer certainly could scarcely have been designed to be more unacceptable to the cautious and suspicious Russians. And a good many observers, when they recovered from the first shock, concluded that the President's purpose was not to give a start to new discussions but to put an end to the Soviet boasts that his country could not match the courage and boldness of the May 10 plan. It is more charitable to accept the President's own explanation. "I have been searching in my heart and mind" he declared, "for something I could say here that would convince everyone of the great sincerity of the United States in approaching the problem of disarmament."

Eisenhower presumably was still endeavoring to convert the Russians to his own belief that they had nothing to fear but fear itself, and so to salvage some great achievement from the ruins of the earlier discussion on Germany. But well-meaning and daring almost to the point of recklessness as this intervention was, it seemed probable that it would do more harm than good.

The risks most certainly were very great. For the Russians are allergic to all theatrics except their own. If now they decided that the President's action was not a generous impulse but a well-prepared plan, contrived to look like an impulse, then they would be driven toward the conclusion that Ike's other acts of impulse were also contrived. And if this idea took hold in inherently suspicious minds, then the greatest of Geneva's assets—the Russian belief in Eisenhower's personal integrity—might be sacrificed on the altar of one propaganda blow. In either event the Soviet reaction was unlikely to find expression at Geneva. For by Thursday evening the conference was moving toward its end. As the Foreign Ministers struggled with the final communiqués, a few conclusions could be drawn.

The Soviet government came to Geneva with well-established positions. And neither the limited offers of Eden nor the personal assurances of Eisenhower could work any substantial change in these positions in the course of five days. Nor was this a cause for gloom. It was, after all, Mr. Dulles' emphatic view that a long period of study, of reflection and of verification in subsequent meetings would be necessary before any new position would emerge. And the Soviet leaders, as I have indicated, shared Mr. Dulles' opinion to a startling degree.

Only great weakness within the Soviet Union could have led the Soviet Union to yield on Germany. And if the conference served no other purpose, it demonstrated that the Soviet state is not, as Mr. Dulles maintained, on the point of collapse.

Far from showing weakness at Geneva the Russians demonstrated that their ambitions as well as their defensive positions are unchanged. "Do not imagine," said an influential and sophisticated Russian to me, "that there has been a revolution within the Soviet Union. Mr. Khrushchev, I assure you, is following the Stalin line."

The Stalin line as last laid down at the 19th Party Congress, was that, given the right tactics by the Kremlin, wars between the capitalist countries were still as probable as capitalist war upon the Soviet world.

For the present Soviet ambitions are unaltered. And yet the new spirit is also real. It survives because both sides have need of it; the West, because free societies need hope for nourishment; the East, because the immense tasks of internal consolidation require a period of *detente,* relaxation in strained relations between nations.

The Russians insist on a period of *detente* before yielding on the great sources of tension. The West will accept the *detente* because it has no choice.

In terms of concrete agreements, the immediate gains from a relaxation are likely to be meager. But the significance of agreements can be enormously overrated today. On the great issue of disarmament, for example, we have come down to the technicalities of early warning. And yet they are far less significant than political and psychological storm signals. In Russia today, as in China, months of telltale psychological preparation must precede an aggressive war.

Wise men, the experts recall here, have argued that the semi-myth of foreign hostility is indispensable in justifying the repressive instruments of the Soviet state. How far, they wonder now, can economic exploitation and police terror be maintained during a *detente*? If the relaxation should long continue, then the thaw may truly melt more than the hard resolve of the allies.

In that event, as President Eisenhower prophesied, our problems may become manageable.

II: IN THE GIGANTESQUE MÊLÉE

The radio was playing the saddest *Sinfonia Concertante* of Mozart as I packed my bags.

Overcome with nostalgia at the end of a week without sleep, I wandered back to the *Hotel du Rhone* for a last look around. There the swans rode still upon the blue torrent where Lac Leman emptied into the headwaters of the river. And there, in the dining room, was the red leather chair on which the immaculate Billy Graham came to rest in the mornings, to masticate prunes and review with his manager the financial details of his latest contract. These monuments remained, but all else was gone. The heavyset FBI youths no longer strolled outside in their open shirts. And William Randolph Hearst, Jr. no longer held his customary corner at the bar. In place of the familiar figures a new crowd of tourists crowded around American Express, already well established and demanding from its weary clerks the latest routes onward from Geneva to Zurich and Lucerne. It was hard to believe that until today the American contingent at the Conference—nine delegates, seven assistants, fifty reporters and 450 bodyguards and secretaries—had during one memorable week at the *Hotel du Rhone,* kept the rumors flying and the gin-and-tonics flowing.

Don't kill it, let it grow was the password at the *du Rhone.* And the rumors grew in the lustiest way. Sitting on the porch you could whip up a sensational dispatch from Geneva, based upon what French sources reported to be Soviet intelligence on the German reaction to a proposal that the British Prime Minister had not yet made. And more than one such dispatch, raised to full stature at the *du Rhone*, went rattling around the world on the white tape of Press Wireless.

At midnight at the *du Rhone* the bar closed, the lights went out, the rumors began to sink of their own weight. Then wise correspondents wandered up to bed. Soon the time came for the mile walk down the lake front to my own hotel. It was a mile ambushed with sidewalk cafes, where the reporters of other nations lay in wait, heavily armed with new rumors, and eager to argue until the morning's coffee and croissants arrived. They varied from Indonesians fired by logical positivism to Bevanites prophesying doom, and they shared a common compulsion to talk. In the rare moments when they paused for breath a small sound intruded on the sudden stillness—the faint pecking noise of typewriters from rooms far up in the night, where reporters with early deadlines worked on until dawn.

The French reporters were briefed continually and with dramatic gestures by Jacques Duhamel, Secretary to the cabinet of Premier Faure. They seemed better informed than the Foreign Ministers themselves. The British reporters were not reporters at all, but Our Diplomatic Correspondents and Our Special Representatives, as far as the great institutions of British publishing were concerned. They were, of course, treated by the Foreign Office with the respect that their status deserved. It was the American Government, ironically, which remained faithful to Sir Winston Churchill's view that newspapermen should be prohibited from swarming all over the Summit. Accordingly the American journalists, with the most to report, had the leanest time of all. Charles Bohlen and Llewellyn Thompson, the two senior diplomats in the American delegation, wisely begged off the burden of briefing the reporters on the grounds that it would be inconsistent with their ambassadorial roles. James Hagerty, on whom the burden descended, was a good police reporter who conceded that in the labyrinth of Geneva he was lost from the start. There were, of course, midnight sessions with more experienced advisers. But from these, the American reporters emerged more frequently exasperated than enlightened. Between the sessions and the evening feasts, and once again between the feasts and the early hours spent in dictating reports to Washington, the wise men of the American delegation paused briefly under the parasols on the porch of the *Hotel du Rhone.* But the hints that they dropped among the small talk were of the most cryptic kind.

Under these circumstances the American press struggled along as best it could. The old timers, Frederick Kuh and Edgar Mowrer mixed with Pertinax, Madame Tabouis and other specters risen from the thirties. Less experienced international reporters: Fred Collins of the *Providence Journal,* Martin Hayden of the *Detroit News,* Nat Finney of the *Buffalo Evening News,* Arthur Sylvester of the *Newark News* and Richard Wilson of the Cowles papers compared notes on the separate briefings with painstaking concern for details. Drew Pearson resorted to a series of flashbacks from the past. The well-knit staff of the *New York Times* combined boldness and responsibility. The *Herald Tribune,* true to its objective of scooping the *Times* on the week's big event, sent a far larger staff and frequently tripped over itself. Paul Ward sent a series of masterly reports to the *Baltimore Sun* and Westbrook Pegler, who signed in on the opening day was never seen again.

At mid-mornings with many sighs, the working press left the *du Rhone* for the *Maison de la Presse,* the old stone parliament now lined with yellow Celotex, whose central features were a bulletin board and a bar. There the reporters drank *Canadas* and *Cocas* and worse, until, at 1:30 and 7:30, the briefings by the few press officers began.

The American briefings were in the basement of the old building, where faded photographs of the Swiss national guard hung on the walls. There, with engaging frankness, Hagerty told all that he knew and that did not take very long. There was in fact one memorable moment on the first day, when Hagerty referred to a meeting by "Bulganin, Zhukov and ... ah, what's-his-name ... you know the one I mean ... yes! ... that's the fellow! ... Khrushchev!"

On the other side of the cellar, Sir George Young of the
Foreign Office tapped a cigarette on an ash tray and answered
wearily, "I suppose they'll have to," when reporters asked if the
Big Four would soon meet again. "What of the jolly old atmos-
phere?" cried one of Our Diplomatic Correspondents, close to
despair when all other attempts to draw confidences from Sir
George proved unavailing. "It was jolly," said Sir George drily.
He then withdrew his remark describing it as "facetious."
"Cordial," he said would be a better approximation.

Upstairs, in a cold stone chamber, Leonid Ilychev, the
Soviet briefing officer, presented his report. He was a
candidate-member of the Central Committee of the Communist Party of the USSR, a hard and chunky man. His two
assistants scribbled nervously as he spoke and then presented
translations, of which the English was, if anything, harder to
follow than the Russian. Ilychev did not move the single microphone toward them, but allowed them to lean across him
until their heads were almost lying upon the table. He listened,
cocking his head with a wry smile, mopping the sweat from his
forehead and stroking the underside of his nose with his
thumb.

The opening day of the conference was the longest, the
hottest, the most newsworthy. By 8:30 that evening, the text of
all the opening speeches save Bulganin's were in the hands of
the reporters, and deadlines were closing in with the approaching nightfall. In well-stacked piles the translations of Bulganin's speech were brought to Ilychev's briefing and held, well
guarded, while he spoke. The reporters, wilting in the heat and
more desperate with each passing minute, stared at the platform like famished dogs. The burning floodlights added to the
heat of the day. But Ilychev droned on. He spoke one long and
cumbrous sentence after another, and each was translated into
English and French. He paused to pour himself a glass of water,
holding it up against the floodlights before he sipped it. He
seemed, in his grim way, to be enjoying his encounter with the
capitalist press. Only a few of us, very close to him, could see
the tremble in his hands as he lit one cigarette after another,
and the tightness of his throat.

At last he came to an end and the roomful of a thousand reporters pressed forward. But Ilychev held them back. He spoke again in Russian, and the nervous translator announced that Mr. Ilychev had expected questions and hearing none, found himself surprised and even shocked. There was a low groan in the crowd of reporters and then to everyone's horror a Byronic figure in an open shirt arose in the middle of the room. "I have a question!" the young man announced pleasantly, in response to Mr. Ilychev's invitation and when the murmur rose he shouted, "I HAVE A QUESTION!" Mr. Ilychev nodded approvingly, and with a fixed smile, the young man first explained his question. "It is a friendly question to my friend Mr. Ilychev," he said. "Forcrissake," the crowd growled, and the young man's smile became a little agonized. "I am a friend of many languages!" he cried, "But I should like on this important matter to inquire of my friend Mr. Ilychev whether he does not agree with me that one international language would be better. You see I . . ."

But no more was heard of this constructive contribution to the Geneva conference. Starting in the back of the room pandemonium broke out. The crowd became a mob and the mob rushed the platform in what *France-Soir* on the next day called *une gigantesque mêlée de Rugby*. Mr. Ilychev was pushed half through a Celotex wall. He fought his way back, shouting something, and heard his dutiful translator mutter ". . . civilized men!" My one desire was to get as far from the platform as possible, but this was as absurd an ambition as endeavoring to clamber onto it. My shirt was torn, my foot was trampled by a maddened journalist. I protested weakly and he cried in an interesting accent, "Whose foot do you think that is—your own?"

From these *gigantesques mêlées*, the survivors sorted themselves out at last and went their ways. French and Italian journalists rushed for telephones. Our Diplomatic Correspondents walked hurriedly after them. Asian and Yugoslav reporters resumed their unhurried task of spreading out the previous day's newspapers and carefully underlining certain phrases in blue ink. The Americans dashed out to the taxicabs that looked like little beetles and crammed into them shouting *"du Rhone!"*

Here we learned once more that the citizens of Geneva were unmoved by the great events that gripped us. The taxi drivers felt no pressure from deadlines in Minneapolis. They accelerated only when pedestrians appeared at street crossings; they paused alongside other taxi drivers to pass the time of day.

To the Swiss, the Summit meeting was one more conference. When Bulganin caused a deadlock, headlines in other nations were blackened. The billboards of Swiss papers posed more lasting questions such as: *Parents, are you to blame?* and *The Church; why does it oppose artificial insemination?* In the same manner, the waiters in restaurants held with Molotovian tenacity to their own pace. They constituted a major hazard for reporters like Michel Gordey of *France-Soir,* compelled to satisfy the endless appetite for copy of his publisher, Pierre Lazareff. Gordey and I sat in Landolts, the restaurant whose upper-stories had been the headquarters of the Bolsheviks during Lenin's exile in Switzerland; the waiter ambled around, deaf to his pleas. "The Swiss are a clever race!" cried Gordey. "They enslave the world with their watches and they themselves don't know the meaning of time!"

For myself, free of deadlines, the slow pace of the waiters came as a blessing, for it enabled me to sit for two hours at Landolts with Georgy Zhukov whom I found to be intelligent, informal, sophisticated and well informed. He spoke easily of the limited role of the military in the Soviet regime. He chided me gently for the articles written by the newspapermen who had been given the first passports to journey through the USSR. "They lectured us on the evils of Communism," he said. "It never occurred to them that, right or wrong, it is our system to which we have given our lives." "Did they really suppose," he added, "that we would get down on our knees and agree that we'd made a dreadful mistake!"

I was distrustful at Geneva of the view that the H-bomb had brought about the change in Soviet attitudes. For this implied a kind of conversion that I could not picture in doctrinaire Marxist minds. With this the Editor of *Pravda* agreed.

"There is no change," he reflected, "only a bilateral development which results from the ending of two wars, and which on your side includes the decline of your excessive and somewhat stupid fears."

"In 1946," he continued, "Stalin declared that we needed sixteen years to build our coal, our iron, our steel. Aha! your journalists cried, Stalin is saying that in sixteen years a plane will take off one night and drop a bomb on Washington! Their reaction is one that we cannot comprehend. Why should we work all-out for sixteen years in order to have another war, and more destruction followed by sixteen more years of working our way back?"

We spoke of our common problems as editors, in filing stories to our papers. I mentioned my chagrin on learning that my first story had been cut. Zhukov was dumbfounded. "But . . . *you* are the *Editor!*" he kept repeating. It seemed clear that, if he were the Editor of the *New Republic,* the Managing Editor would soon find himself in jail.

Throughout the first three days of the Conference, the Russians showed great amiableness. On Thursday at the *Maison de la Presse,* however, the Russians were seen no more. Kosov developed stomach trouble; Zhukov and his aides were overcome by deadlines; even Ilychev failed to turn up to brief us, for reasons that were never explained. Presumably they had to do with the Soviet delegation's concern over its defeats in the limited war of propaganda, and its reluctance to talk until new instructions from Moscow might be received. This left only Andrew Rothstein, an old Bolshevik who at that moment was travelling under Czech papers, to answer for the Kremlin, and on the matter of Ike's fly-over proposal Rothstein was speechless. That was a pity, for elsewhere reactions were surprising and strong. Traditional internationalists among the American reporters were suspicious of the plan. Paul Ward, who probably knew more about the background of the problem than Eisenhower, pointed out in the *Baltimore Sun* that it was old hat at the UN. But Mr. Hearst, after an uneasy moment, rallied strongly and endorsed the plan. And Fulton Lewis, Jr.

thought it was terrific. "It's like a hand in poker," he explained, "in which you've got deuces back to back and three aces showing while the other man has nothing at all!"

At last on Saturday, the Russians reappeared. It was Ilychev, in fact, on whom the honor of speaking the last word at Geneva fell. The hard-boiled candidate-member of the Central Committee repeated in his usual way the closing speech of Marshal Bulganin. Then he became soft spoken. "Happy landings!" he cried to the departing journalists in Russian and, in the manner of the romantic lead in a French play, he added, "May this be *au revoir* and not *adieu.*" That at least was how it was translated for me by Alex Kendrick. Ilychev's own man failed more dismally than ever to translate these novel sentiments. But the journalists sensed the point and responded with a smattering of applause.

There followed the usual stampede to obtain copies of Bulganin's speech. Swept along in the mob I found myself pressed against Mayevsky, *Pravda's* American expert. To him I protested that the final Directive of the Chiefs was ambiguous on Germany, and on disarmament, more ambiguous than the statements of the two sides now permitted. Mayevsky tried to shake his finger at me, but could not disentangle his arm. So he shook his head. "You are quite wrong," he said. "Great advances have been made here. We have agreed to go on talking and that is enough."

By then I was anxious to get away. I had bet a bottle of beer with Stewart Alsop that an agreement on substance would be reached at Geneva. I was thirsty, and ready therefore to argue that I had won. Stewart was unwilling to pay up, sure that no substantial agreement had resulted. And among all the reporters at Geneva, I could find none that evening who dared to act as referee.

The Ghost at the Banquet

NOVEMBER 1954

No banquet is complete without a ghost. One who will serve as well as any to haunt this issue, published in celebration of the *New Republic's* 40th anniversary, is Mr. Richard Crossman, a recent traveler in this country who has returned to inform the British readers of the *New Statesman and Nation* that freedom has vanished in America and the liberals are dead.

In freedom's place, Mr. Crossman declares, an authoritarian dogma called the New Loyalty governs a silent people. "According to this dogma," he says, "Communism is a terrible disease which threatens the American way of life and which can only be met by the elimination of Communists. Loyal Americans must therefore be constantly fearful of infection and ready to accept the most ruthless tests in order to defeat the epidemic—tests which may force you to denounce your best friend as a secret carrier owing to something he did or said twenty years ago."

"These loyalty tests," adds Mr. Crossman, "are as impracticable and morally corrupting as the Nuremberg Laws." Nine out of ten Americans are not concerned because "they have changed their views as they change their motor cars." Those who should be concerned, such as "Senator Humphries" and Paul Douglas, "are like the Germans in the late 1920s who tolerated Jew-baiting in order to preserve the Weimar Republic." The liberals are powerless to stay this nation's march toward fascism because "they are scared . . . of the FBI and the amateur witch-hunters." Liberals "have come to terms with the New Loyalty" and so "the liberal movement is conniving at its own destruction."

But there remains, in Mr. Crossman's view, a grain of hope in the United States. It is nurtured by "conservatives and non-party men and women who have no guilt about the past to inhibit their present indignation." Mr. Crossman concludes: "If I am asked whence the movement to restore American freedom will come, I would forget the professional liberals and put my faith in these men and women."

So the ghost speaks, and since the sepulchral voice is familiar, one's first impulse is to clasp its clammy hand. I once attended Mr. Crossman's apocalyptic school where each setback is presented as a crisis and each crisis must be the greatest and the last. I understand why Mr. Crossman must voice these views, for as one of his *New Statesman* co-editors recently explained, their political success is predicated on disaster. I gave up hope long ago in Mr. Crossman and his friends and concede his right to reciprocate today.

And yet on reflection Mr. Crossman's observations seem so superficial, and his conclusions so unsound, that it would be a disservice to permit them to intrude upon this celebration were it not that the half truths he voices serve to introduce legitimate doubts and questions worth asking.

Whether or not the present national mood is illiberal is hardly debatable. But it points toward the significant question of whether the mood is permanent or subject to change. Whether or not a passing generation of liberals is paralyzed by fear and guilt is not of lasting significance. The lasting issue is whether the liberal idea itself possesses validity, and how it is to be renewed so that it may summon to service succeeding generations.

In this sense the threat is no longer one which ravages the face of American liberty and leaves England unscathed. The sources of our liberal faith are common sources. The danger, internal and external, is one both nations face. The initial responses of both are far less dissimilar than Mr. Crossman would have his audience believe. The answers both peoples ultimately shape will not be far apart.

Our common liberal faith, now under siege, is the conviction that the collective interest of society is best determined when the individual's right to self-expression is most fully assured. That conviction in turn was an expression of the rationalist belief that every individual was intrinsically good and subject to the sway of reason. The belief was written into the Bill of Rights, but for us its immediate lineage lies in the generations that produced Brandeis, Dewey and Croly in this country; and in England, Russell, Scott and Maynard Keynes, whose views run like a binding thread through the eighty volumes of the *New Republic's* past.

Of his generation Keynes wrote:

> We were among the last of the Utopians, or meliorists as they are sometimes called, who believe in a continuing moral progress by virtue of which the human race already consists of reliable, rational, decent people, influenced by truth and objective standards, who can be safely released from the outward restraints of convention and traditional standards and inflexible rules of conduct and left from now onwards to their own sensible devices, pure motives and reliable intuitions of the good. . . .

The same rationalist faith inspired the exuberant men who founded the *New Republic*. To them (and to the founding fathers of the republic itself), Croly attributed one central vision:

> A vision of the latest goodness and regeneracy of human nature, a goodness which would surely come to the surface if only society would permit to the ordinary man and woman a fair and full chance of self-expression.

Croly continued:

> We can no longer honestly charge up to fate or Providence our own blunders. For the first time in history, the human spirit is the captain and the only possible captain of the ship upon which

the human race has embarked. . . . In so far as it has sincerely renounced these consoling yet none the less disabling illusions about its subordination to an anthropomorphic and imperative universe it has freed itself for a task which it is fitted to perform.

Mankind, reasonable and regenerate, freed from prior restraints, then proceeded to wage the bloodiest war in history followed by a blockade of the defeated and starving enemy. An unworkable peace treaty promised new wars to come. A new form of barbarism arose in Russia. Still worse, the reaction against the age of enlightenment set in within the West. "We are at the dead season of our fortunes," Keynes recorded in the autumn of 1919. "Never in the lifetime of men now living has the universal element in the soul of men burned so dimly." Similarly, in interpreting the "abominable election" of 1920, Croly noted that for the first time since 1896 neither candidate of the major parties considered the progressive vote worth bidding for.

On a larger scale, the present intolerance and anti-intellectualism repeat the pattern of the years that followed the First World War. And because a lack of historic sense is perhaps our gravest weakness, it is useful to review the contrasting interpretations that Keynes and Croly placed upon the growth of unreason after 1918, and the differing responses they believed it demanded.

Keynes granted at once that the society he had assumed to be permanent had been "unusual, unstable, complicated, unreliable and temporary." He accepted no responsibility for the breakdown and assessed no blame. The eclipse of the liberal spirit he attributed to "the reaction from the exertions, the fears and the sufferings of the past five years." He wrote simply: "We have been moved already beyond endurance and need rest."

So Keynes interpreted the growth of unreason as a passing phase. He did not conclude that night was eternal because the present was dark. He counseled patience and prepared for the siege. Keynes wrote in 1919:

> The events of the coming year will not be shaped by the deliberate acts of statesmen, but by the hidden currents flowing continually beneath the surface of political history of which no one can predict the outcome. In one way only can we influence these hidden currents—by setting in motion those forces of instruction and imagination which change *opinion.* The assertion of truth, the unveiling of illusion, the dissipation of hate, the enlargement and instruction of men's hearts and minds must be the means.

The closing lines of his *Economic Consequences* read:

> The true voice of the new generation has not yet spoken and silent opinion is not yet formed. To the formation of the general opinion of the future I dedicate this book.

Thus Keynes resigned himself to a rhythm of ebb and flow in human progress. Croly in contrast could not. In an editorial which preceded Mr. Crossman's verdict by 34 years Croly held that Harding's resurrection of pre-Roosevelt Republicanism, like Wilson's betrayal of the Fourteen Points and the New Freedom were "the natural result of the practically confessed political bankruptcy of every group of progressives. . . ."

Croly's cure was drastic change. Only by a new order, he believed, could order be restored. To redress the imbalance in American politics he set out at once to arouse the class consciousness of the workers. So, he seized a flag and marched in the Presidential parade of a Mr. P. P. Christiansen, candidate of the Farmer-Labor Party which he held to be the best hope of American politics.

Events since 1922 suggest that Keynes was right, and Croly wrong. Croly in 1922, like Crossman in 1954, gave in to the volatility, the manic-depressive cycle, the lack of steadfastness politically that party men complain of in the liberals. Croly's swing to the American left in 1920, like Crossman's swing to the American right in 1954, reflected a loss of confidence in the commitment of the majority to orderly progress, and its ability to discern and recover from occasional errors in political judgment. A single illustration of the flexibility and soundness of the majority stands to dispute Croly and

Crossman; beside the name of P. P. Christiansen on the 1920 ballot was the name of F. D. Roosevelt.

Nonetheless the central idea, voiced by Keynes and Croly in 1914, was under attack from trends more profound and permanent than the exhaustion and reaction of 1920. The attack was voiced even in 1914 by D. H. Lawrence who held that Keynes and his generation were "beetles," skimming the surface of life. They were without reverence, he concluded, and they were "done for." Keynes in 1938 granted that: "The attribution of rationality to human nature instead of enriching it, now seems to me to have impoverished it." So he conceded that there was "a grain of truth" *but no more than a grain*—in Lawrence's view.

Croly's doubts, in contrast, deepened. In 1922 he published the pamphlet, *The New Republic Idea*. It was written as a reaffirmation of the spirit of 1914. But it is less convincing in its affirmation than in its misgivings. The American ship whose launching on the unchartered seas of rationalism he had hailed in 1914 had drifted by 1922 "into dangerous waters." In fact the whole civilized world, in Croly's view, faced the greatest peril since the barbarian invasion. Expressing a notion that undermined his assumptions, Croly recorded that the peril "did not arise from accidental, easily distinguishable and obviously guilty sources but from sources which are themselves characteristic of the society which they are undermining and in some form indispensable to it." These included the "increasing concentration of economic power and the corresponding centralization of political power;" the cultural sterility caused by science and technology, and the "negative and unedifying" quality of liberty. All these conspired against the regeneracy and latent goodness of human nature and together in Croly's view, they constituted "the existing breach in civilization."

If Croly hoped that the breach could be closed, he could no longer be confident. Conflict, civil and international, was spreading and deepening; so was the conviction that it must be solved by violence. Croly recorded:

The chief obstacle to the solution of conflicts by specific adjustments is the disposition of the conflicting interests to insist upon the ultimate righteousness of their motives and objects, and it is this morally pugnacious disposition which has to be undermined. It is incompatible with the modesty, the flexibility and the hospitality of humanism. It forbids an honest experiment in the direction of realistic coordination of the interests of mankind.

Haunted by this new vision, Croly stood by the old. Rational discussion, he argued, might still absorb "a large part of the shock of the conflict" and thus render it unnecessary. And yet rational discussion was possible only among men who affirmed the goodness and regeneracy of human nature. Reason alone could no longer provide this unifying force. The affirmation, Croly concluded in *The New Republic Idea* "was essentially religious"—an assertion that would have been indignantly repudiated by the generation of 1914. "It means," said Croly, "the working of a God symbolized not as Power but as understanding and love."

By this extension of his faith, Croly encompassed realms of human experience beyond the limited field of aesthetic appreciation, and summoned new battalions to the service of the liberal idea. And yet this reconciliation of reason and religious feeling was still insufficient; for in the struggle of the 20s, 30s, and 40s, to which the dictators brought overbearing organization, Power was symbolized as God while God as understanding and love was denied a unifying role. Great regimes rose, based upon the irrational and negative in man's nature; his fear of freedom, his capacity for hatred; his yearning for authority; his vulnerability to psychological manipulation. To these regimes, hostility to the outside world was the necessary precondition of internal order, and violence was the natural and proper method of resolving conflicts beyond reconciliation.

The liberal mind had few reference points to turn to in meeting this onslaught. It had repudiated the doctrine of original sin. It had not assimilated Freud's new interpretations of the ambivalence of human nature. It had barely discerned how thin and brittle the crust of civilization had become. It met the challenge by developing a body of social reforms and while Roosevelt held together a coalition of Catholics, unions, city machines and low-income groups, it provided superb intellectual leadership. At the same time, it could not easily assess and counter anti-democratic trends. The inability of the rationalist mind to treat force as a necessary part of its framework in protecting essential values led to the wild swings that George Kennan has complained of: the adherence to pacifism and isolationism in years when the forces leading to war could still be checked, followed by an abandonment of restraints and reservations in time of war.

One ennobling and shattering experience, the Spanish Civil War, did work a transformation in the liberal mind. It resurrected the discarded but necessary reverence of heroism and sacrifice. It also caused some erosion of liberal values as all times must in which action outruns reflection. It left among liberals a capacity to feel deeply rather than to think clearly; a largely sterile prejudice against the Church; a willingness to see the sweet but not the bitter, a desire to believe that there were no conflicts of long-term interest with the needed allies of the day.

The Spanish struggle, and all the years of action in organizing labor, in overcoming depression, in waging war, led to an intermingling of tradition and revolution on the Left. The success of the Communist Party in recruiting intellectuals and the acceptance of its role by liberals reflected the loss of faith described here in the liberal idea, and the inability of the liberal mind to assess anti-democratic movements. And yet the new recruits of the Communist Party, like the fellow-travelers, supposed with some reason that they were advancing democratic objectives. The immediate objectives of Communists and liberals were often the same: for an end to discrimination against minority groups; for collective bargaining by workers through representatives of their own choosing; for opportunities for professional groups commensurate with their skills; and for collective resistance to aggression. The Communists worked skillfully and successfully for these objectives. Many of the bulwarks of democracy in the present contest stand as partial monuments to their outward endeavors.

The legitimate nature of the demands voiced by the Communists concealed for a time the illegitimacy of their basic design. For true collaboration was made impossible by the nature of the Soviet State. It became altogether intolerable when the Kremlin turned its overseas parties into training grounds for treason. From then on the liberals' ability to defend the Communists' rights rested on the liberals' denial of any common political front.

But, separate as they are now, the liberals are weak, and in Mr. Crossman's views dead. So the questions worth asking arise in terms of the present: is *the present mood passing or permanent* and: *is there vitality in the liberal movement, and validity in the liberal idea*?

Is the present mood permanent? Those who answer *yes* surely ignore the whole history of the United States and the constant flux that marks our political life. There was never a time when the Bill of Rights was not under attack. While the present onslaught on the First Amendment is more powerful than that of 1920, its domestic origins are equally identifiable and just as transitory. In *The True Believer* Eric Hoffer notes:

> When hopes and dreams are loose in the streets it is well for the timid to lock doors, shutter windows and lie low until the wrath has passed. For there is often a monstrous incongruity between the hopes, however noble and tender, and the actions which follow them. It is as if ivied maidens and garlanded youths were to herald the four horsemen of the Apocalypse.

We let loose hopes and dreams in the streets of America in prewar and wartime years. The ivied maidens and garlanded youths were the promises, as noble and as unrealizable *in the short term* as those that clothed The New Freedom with Croly's aid. In the grey dawn that broke in 1946, as in 1920, allies became enemies and enemies allies; democracy was sold as a universal panacea and yet $30 billion spent overseas could not secure it.

Communism was presented as the universal anti-Christ and yet vast areas passed easily under its rule while weapons we supposed we alone could develop appeared in its arsenal, threatening our homes. So dreams long oversold were shattered, while sacrifices accepted as final emerged as nothing more than rehearsals for greater sacrifices to come.

All this and much more gave an explosive character to the public's reaction to the revelations of treason that followed World War II. The prior intermingling of progressive and Communist movements, and the imprecision of the Truman Administration in meeting the problem of subversion opened the way for the Republican Party to exploit and magnify the issue until it became a lever for prying apart and overturning the coalition Roosevelt had built. The Republican decision turned politics into political warfare, and set in motion precedents, habits and attitudes that will haunt us for generations. Yet like all crusades, the onslaught has given rise to a counter-movement, a reawakening to the value and meaning of civil liberty among many who had taken it for granted and relinquished its defense to a very few courageous men. Late in 1954 the patient seems to be rising even while Mr. Crossman draws the winding sheet over an empty bed.

Nowhere certainly are liberal candidates running on the unequivocal platform that Jefferson once raised. But that proves little. Young Mr. Roosevelt, the associate of Mitchell Palmer, did not brighten the 1920 campaign with any stirring defense of the rights of dissenters. That did not prevent his leading, 12 years later, a reaffirmation of the liberal faith. Men raised in his image are on a thousand ballots this year. To take a static attitude towards American politics, to spot no philosopher in an army as it lumbers past, is to invite repudiation by American history. Each new contest is decided on a new set of issues; yesterday's enemies are today's allies; today's preoccupations are tomorrow's after-thoughts. If further ground for hope is required, it is worth remembering that civil liberty was only one of the four conditions Croly set in 1922 to sustain the promise of American life. The other three were full employment, fair distribution of wealth, and adequate public education. These three conditions have been built so far into our society over thirty years that the die-hard wing of the Republican Party has accepted Croly's assumptions, while the party itself has moved beyond the New Deal.

In one respect, of course, the present inroads on liberty are paved and durable: the problem to which they form a response is real. The decisive advantages that nuclear weapons confer on the aggressor, as much as the innate hostility of the Communist regimes compel us to adopt some aspects of the garrison state. We must develop secrets; we must guard them. We must punish and seek to forestall those who betray the secrets. The unprecedented nature of the problem is heightened by the character of the Communist Party. The military discipline its members accept undermines the prohibitions against guilt by association. The dedication it arouses among men, who may prepare for generations to commit treacherous acts, undermines further the doctrine that belief is no concern of government, whose concern must be limited to the commission of crimes. The problem is acute, but only in sensitive or strategically important positions. There it can be met by precise techniques. One would gather from Mr. Crossman that there is no security problem in Britain and no security check. The contrary is true. The British loyalty program is as vigorous and as effective as ours; it is also selective and silent. It does not undermine British liberty, and it is toward the British system that ours will evolve.

The security problem, then, is no mortal threat to the liberal idea. It has worked havoc on a generation of liberals that were drawn by depression and war into association with Communists. Succeeding generations, just as militant and radical, will not be tormented by the confusions of the past. In the brief space of five or ten years the problem will shrink to one of screening new recruits for government. For veterans of the thirties, as time passes the discount rate will rise on the associations of 20 years ago.

In the same way today's rash of Communist control legislation indicates no incurable disease. The accepted view that advocacy of the overthrow of government constitutes, in itself, a clear and present danger is obviously a menacing precedent. It is also unnecessary, as the country will discover. The United States Government is not easily overthrown, still less by advocacy and least of all by a group as isolated as the Communist Party. Even in its balmy days the enormous turnover in the Communist Party paid tribute to Croly's confidence in common sense. Today the Communist Party is barely good for a weary smatter of applause in a political peroration. The Communist control legislation may not be revoked; once popular bills seldom are. But short of a new catastrophe, the anti-Communist acts will inhibit dissenters no more than men who drink and swear on Sundays are curbed by blue laws.

I don't suggest of course that Croly's dream is in the ascendant—yet. The present trend is still against rationalism and back toward subordination to the "anthropomorphic and imperative universe" that is spelled out in words of one syllable by the new salesmen of popular religion. And yet the spirit voiced by Croly and Keynes is the only spirit which can reconcile the United States and its allies, and offer some means of adjusting the conflicts that otherwise will lead to the common destruction of adversaries in nuclear war.

Twice in the past two years the United States has confronted the opportunity for world war, in Korea and Indo-China. On both occasions it has repudiated the demand that we resolve our conflict with Communism by global war. These decisions have left in ruins the policies both of unconditional surrender and total victory that the conservatives have made their own. To that extent we may have won one victory. "There is," writes George Kennan, "no more dangerous delusion, none that has done us a greater disservice in the past, or that threatens to do us a greater disservice in the future than the concept of total victory." The precondition Kennan sets for the continued unity of the free nations and our continued coexistence with the Communist nations is precisely the repudiation of the "morally pugnacious disposition" that Croly deplored, and a new commitment to "the modesty, the flexibility and the hospitality of humanism" that Croly identified as *The*

New Republic Idea. In its general belief in human goodness, that idea affirms today that given containment of aggression, and acceptance of discussion, the Communist regimes in time will mellow or else be replaced. I know of no other alternative to an endorsement of preventive war.

The task is still to assert truth, to unveil illusion, to dissipate hatred, to set in motion those forces of instruction and imagination in which Keynes saw a shaft of light in 1919. The task is not only well-intentioned, but also practicable. It accords with the attitudes of a healthy minority in the rising generation.

Today's young men and women are committed neither to Croly's early optimism, nor to his later pessimism. They accept his religious conviction without concentrating their hopes upon it. They are prepared for a long and inconclusive struggle. They have encountered the Communist movement and they understand its evil. They have disciplined themselves in political organization and consciously traded some independence for the sake of steadfastness. They have gained the sophistication in matters of organization that Croly's generation lacked. They have overcome their initial reaction to aggression, which was that there was no accommodation with Communist nations. They have discerned the critical weakness in the conservative position, which is the gap between its insistence on unconditional surrender, and its inability to bring it to pass. They start with a framework of reference in the general welfare concerns of the New Deal and the Fair Deal. They have the experience and will to keep the heritage fresh and alive. They have little respect for voices such as *The Nation* magazine's, whose intellectual growth failed to advance beyond the rigid and now archaic patterns of the Popular Front. They have little more respect for voices such as Crossman who cannot distinguish between the security programs and the Nuremberg Laws. They see no easy return to a past free of conflict. They know that the days of careless rapture are gone and will not come again at least until time and pressure wear away the Communists' fighting faith. They grant that for the foreseeable future young conscripts will have to serve overseas, scientists will have to reconcile themselves to secrecy; government workers will have to give up a part of their civil rights. And yet they believe that the liberal spirit alone offers a basis for sound relations between the United States and the world. In overall terms it may be that as in 1919 "the true voice of the new generation has not spoken and silent opinion is not yet formed." But they are present, and they will be heard.

The problem is *how*? If Mr. Crossman is searching for reasons why dissent will decline he might spend less time on the Communist Party and more on the cost of newsprint. For the ability to dissent as much as the right to dissent is threatened today. The concentration of corporate power that works against independence of thought and action is fostered by every economic trend. The standardization of culture and opinion is furthered by the extension and concentration of mass communications. The centralization of power tends to make of politics the adjustment between giant pressure groups rather than the clarification of individual convictions. And yet any man with vital and important convictions can make himself heard. All these trends have advanced much further in Britain than in our nation. And they have done so without undermining her respect for nonconformism, her reverence for individualism, her insistence upon the privacy of mind and home.

So I don't believe in Mr. Crossman's vision. I don't recognize the land he describes. The loyal Americans I know are not fearful of infection. Those who suffered agonies from the loyalty check are all doing useful and constructive work. The young men who have come to me from the FBI have never asked me to denounce a friend as a "secret carrier" of Communism for what he said twenty years ago. And if I knew of any "secret carriers" in sensitive positions, I wouldn't suppose that keeping it to myself was an act of affirmation in the liberal faith. I'm short of breath from shouting about the loyalty program. But I know of no citizen branded traitor today because yesterday he practiced Americanism. As one of "the opinion formers who supported the New Deal, Republican Spain and the Russian alliance" I rub the neck that Mr. Crossman weeps for: I find no scar.

All conviction of course is intuitive in the end. My own intuition, like Mr. Crossman's, was pessimistic until now. The experiences that brought me into politics were the sight of the hunger marchers trudging toward London in the winter to plead for more than a dole, and the loss of close friends in Spain. All of us are bound by such early training, and the death of the Spanish Republic led me to expect the worst. Mr. Crossman and his friends have gone a little further down that road until they need disaster, like a drug to keep them on the march. So do those who blame society as a means of concealing the bitter truth—that the cause of their failure and unhappiness lies within themselves.

I don't trust these people any more, or feel them as my own. I have no compulsion to quarrel with a society that has permitted me to work for what I believe. On most of the occasions on which I differed with the majority of Americans I can see now that the majority was right and I was wrong. Of course, tensions divide us and fears distract us. Because tension reflects conviction, and fear is well grounded, I find them both far preferable to the calm borne of cynicism and apathy.

On the broad front of progress the political regulars are advancing in America. The scouts are out in front, where they should be. Of course, they stumble into pitfalls, lose their way, retrace their steps and pause for rest. Those who cry in alarm that all is lost because days pass without good news remind me of the story told by Adlai Stevenson in the 1952 campaign. A scout was found by troopers in our early days, with three Indian arrows in his back. They revived him with whiskey and when he could whisper they said, "It must hurt awfully."

"It sure does," he answered, "especially when I laugh."

IV
Trial by Television

Introduction

"He's a son-of-a-bitch, but he's our son-of-a-bitch." So said Charles Wilson, Secretary of Defense in the administration of President Eisenhower. His view was widely shared. Joseph McCarthy had played a large part in prying the Democrats out of power in 1952. It did not occur to McCarthy, or to those who made use of him, that when Eisenhower moved into the White House, his role would have to change. He continued to maul the government; his colleagues in the Senate let him do as he pleased. Lacking any restraints, he squandered his power on behalf of a narcissistic boy, beloved by his assistant. The confrontation with the Army followed and led to the Hearings.

I covered the Hearings for the *New Republic.* (I remember well the playful squeeze that McCarthy gave me on the opening day). Before long, I felt the need to record what was happening in a book. It demanded different perceptions, and it opened new doors. I needed, for example, to learn more about Senator McClellan. So I called at his office. His assistant went in to see if he would talk to me. "The *New Republic!*" I heard him cry, "Throw him out of here!" At that, I poked my head around his door. "Senator, " I said, "I'm here because I'm working on a book." "A book," he repeated, and he sighed: "Come on in."

The book was published by the Beacon Press in 1954. It is

reprinted here in abridged form. It was illustrated by Robert Osborn, who watched the Hearings on television. His ability to capture each participant is still astonishing to me.

The Collapse of Chairman Mundt

In the late spring of 1954, there occurred in Washington one of the most extraordinary dramas in recent American history. Its scenes were disorderly. Its actors seemed to comprehend only dimly the roles they were called upon to play. At first sight the plot concerned nothing more than the status of an Army private; yet twenty million Americans witnessed it, day and night. They sensed that the stakes were very high and included the control of the Republican Party, the integrity of the Army and of the Senate, the constitutional separation of powers, and the future careers of the men involved. Of all these, the last seemed the most important. For one among the participants was a man of great force and greater ambition.

Many Americans had no fixed opinions about the participants, when the hearings started. Others such as this reporter found that opinions and prejudices formed from prior knowledge were modified or transformed under the impact of events. As the drama developed it brought into sharper focus faces that were blurred, stories that were half hidden, issues that were only dimly seen, on the morning of April 22, 1954.

The millions of Americans who were watching their television sets at ten-thirty on that Monday morning participated passively. At a twist of the knobs, grey figures moved on the

flickering screen—sorting papers, pushing their way past reporters, bending over to whisper to each other, snuffing out
cigarette butts.

For those in the Senate Caucus Room it was not so simple.
At seven that morning the first group of spectators had gathered
in the rotunda of the Senate Office Building. Three hours later,
eight hundred were herded through oaken doors into the 74-
foot-long room, built in 1909 to hold three hundred people.

On three sides of the great room were pilasters of white
marble, brought from the South Dover quarries of northern New
York, and twelve marble columns whose florid Corinthian tops
sprouted against the high ceiling. On the fourth side between
brocaded curtains the color of dried blood three windows admitted the soft light from the courtyard and the sky.

But those in front could barely see the changing sky even
when spring thunderstorms approached and struck and passed.
In front of the windows had been raised four powerful floodlamps. Those who glanced up could hardly see anything else.
Those who looked, squinting and blinking across the room,
soon found that the sockets of their eyes were aching from the
glare.

So the subordination of the participants in the room to the
audience beyond it was at once established. On the scaffolding
raised between the floodlamps, crews of cameramen squatted
while two other men in shirtsleeves directed the television
cameras. These were the men in command.

Beneath them was the scene. Had there been any free space
for a stage it might have resembled most a theater-in-the-round
with the audience on all sides of the actors. But there was no free
space. Relatives surrounded the Senators. Spectators crowded
the witnesses. Reporters fought grimly to defend the little plots
of table on which they scribbled. Legal advisers hunted vainly
for places to perch. Cursing, snapping plates, and flinging out
flash bulbs in all directions, a pack of photographers rushed
from one incident to another like dogs fighting for scraps. And in
the confusion two Congressmen, protesting that they had as
much right to be present as anyone else, were led from the room
by Capitol policemen.

Only at the end of the long table where the Senators sat did the rush slow down to a measured pace. There, with folded arms, well-polished shoes, unsmiling faces, and constantly moving eyes, two bodyguards sat—assigned by the FBI to intercept any would-be assassin of Senator Joseph McCarthy of Wisconsin. Pressed by the crush of the crowd against the more fearsome of the two, this reporter inquired anxiously where the man kept his gun. He reached under one armpit, paused, and whispered, "I'd better not say."

In front of the bodyguards, surrounded by members of his staff, sat the individual more feared than any other man in the free world, the central figure in this dispute. Throughout government, and beyond government, men considered his attitude before they voiced opinions on great controversies. One after another, agencies of government had yielded to him a share in their control. Not many weeks earlier the Army of the United States had confronted him—and then caved in. By the force of his personality, the Senator had almost made himself into a second President, operating on Capitol Hill. Nor had the President of the United States been able to protect his pre-eminent place. On February 28, a Washington correspondent of the *New York Times* had reported: "There are quite a few politicians who believe that the administration is rapidly running out of opportunities on which it can grasp the initiative and fight it out once and for all with the Junior Senator from Wisconsin."

Now, two months later, Senator McCarthy was here beneath the floodlights. In the center of the stage were Army representatives now ranged against him. To his right were four Republican and three Democratic Senators.

Typical in its form among dramatic novels is *The Viper of Milan.* As it ends, the central figure, Gian Galeazzo Maria Visconti, stands at the peak of his power. And yet, in the magnificence of his surroundings are barely discernible the elements of his future decline.

Where other dramas ended, was this one about to begin?

Senator Mundt of South Dakota, the chairman of the subcommittee for this investigation, had been glancing up at the

television cameras. Their long noses were pointed toward him.
Their red bulbs, now lit up, told him that across the nation eyes
without number were watching him. He rapped his gavel. The
hearings were under way.

Leaning forward until his chin almost met its reflection on
the polished table, the chairman delivered a lucid statement of
the subcommittee's purpose. The Army, he said, had claimed
that Senator McCarthy, chairman of the Permanent Subcommittee on Investigations, its counsel, Roy Cohn, and its executive director, Francis Carr, "had sought by improper means to
obtain preferential treatment for one Pvt. G. David Schine." In
turn, continued Senator Mundt, giving a somewhat bowdlerized
version of their forty-six counter-claims, the three men had
presented charges that the Army's action was brought "to force a
discontinuance of further attempts by that committee to expose
Communist infiltration in the Army." Senator Mundt affirmed
the gravity of these charges and counter-charges. He promised:
"It is the purpose of this investigation to make a full and impartial effort to reveal that which is true and to expose that which is
false. . . ." He promised further:

> It is our joint determination to conduct these hearings with a
> maximum degree of dignity, firmness and thoroughness. We
> enter our duties with no prejudgment as to the verities in this
> controversy. We propose to follow the evidence wherever it
> leads and to give every party to this dispute the equitable treat-
> ment and consideration to which he is entitled.

Then the chairman called on John McClellan of Arkansas,
ranking Democrat on the subcommittee. The Southerner
commended the Republican on his "very frank, full and
thorough statement." Senator McClellan added that he and his
colleagues exceedingly regretted the circumstances of the inquiry, that they regarded the charges and counter-charges as
grave and beyond reconciliation, and that they were determined
to get at the truth "without regard to any personalities that may
be involved."

"Thank you, Senator McClellan," said the chairman, in the
manner of a moderator on a radio program. "Our counsel, Mr.
Jenkins, will now call the first witness."

Mr. Jenkins opened his cavernous mouth—but the voice heard in the room was that of the Wisconsin Senator.

> McCarthy. A point of order, Mr. Chairman; may I raise a point of order?

He had noted that the Army brief was labeled "Filed by the Department of the Army" and he protested.

> McCarthy. I have heard from people in the military all the way from generals with the most upstanding combat records down to privates recently inducted and they indicate they are very resentful of the fact that a few Pentagon politicians attempting to disrupt our investigations are naming themselves the Department of the Army. . . . The Department of the Army is not doing this. It is three civilians in the Army and they should be so named.

The intervention was forceful and characteristic. It was also improper as a point of order, and untenable as an approach to government. The "few Pentagon politicians" were the highest officials, appointed by the President of the United States to head the Army. They had at all times acted for the Department of the Army and in its name.

So, within the first hour of the hearings, the chairman's claim that he would be dignified and firm was challenged. Everyone in the room looked to see how Senator Mundt would respond.

Karl Mundt was a jovial little man with a large and simple face. The only son of a South Dakota hardware merchant, he had begun his adult life as a teacher. He later drifted into farming, real estate, and writing on outdoor life, before running for Congress. He was elected in 1938. He belonged to many of the fraternal organizations whose symbols politicians wear as generals wear battle ribbons.

There were seeming contradictions in Senator Mundt's career that fellow-politicians felt at a loss to explain. His life as a teacher, for example, had led him to become the joint sponsor of the Smith-Mundt act, a far-sighted program of international exchange which brought scholars and leaders around the world to a better understanding of the United States. Senator Mundt

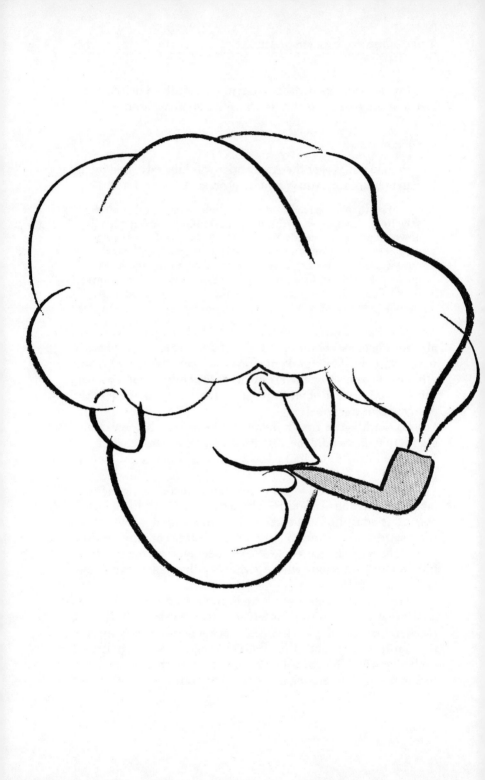

also sponsored the Congressional legislation authorizing United States participation in the United Nations Educational, Scientific, and Cultural Organization, a favorite target for Republican orators in the Midwest.

Senator Mundt was also one of the very few men who volunteered for service on the House Un-American Activities Committee. There he labored with Richard Nixon to gather evidence on Alger Hiss. In defense of McCarthy's acceptance of stolen secrets from government files, Senator Mundt was fond of declaring that if a State Department official had not awakened him at four A.M. to give him a secret personnel file stolen from the State Department, Alger Hiss might still be a ranking official of that department.

In 1946 Karl Mundt challenged Senator Chan Gurney in South Dakota's Republican primary and beat him after a bitter fight. Once in the Senate, he volunteered to serve on the McCarthy subcommittee. There, seated beside the Wisconsin Senator, he watched without protest as Roy Cohn and G. David Schine tore into the Voice of America and the overseas information service—two programs he had helped to found. He explained to this reporter that it was good for these agencies to be investigated—a view few of the officials concerned could share as they surveyed the wreckage McCarthy left behind.

Mundt alone had argued in an executive session of the subcommittee that the controversy should be investigated by some other group. When this view was defeated, he alone had added that he was not the man to preside over the hearings. Again he was defeated—but his reasoning proved sound. For on the first day he abandoned his role as chairman, a role which he never recovered until the day the hearings closed. Whenever rules were broken and a firm hand was demanded, Karl Mundt seemed lost in the cloud of smoke that rose from his pipe.

It was over the issue of McCarthy's crack about the "Pentagon politicians" the Karl Mundt was first tested. His response was simply to postpone the issue of whether Stevens was an irresponsible politician or the Army's appointed head until the Secretary of the Army might be called. At once Senator McCarthy saw that he was master. At once, therefore, he pressed his advantage. His tight voice made an explosive charge out of "Mr. Chairman." Then it rolled along the flat of his sentences until it glided up and over the key words "disgrace," "civilians," and "Communists":

> McCarthy. I maintain it is a disgrace and a reflection upon every one of the million outstanding men in the Army to let a few civilians who are trying, trying to hold up an investigation of Communists label themselves as the Department of the Army.

It was Senator McClellan who noted softly that the counter-charges had been signed for the subcommittee by "Joe McCarthy, Chairman." It was a sound point. But, before the day was over, Chairman Mundt had ruled in favor of McCarthy.

Now Senator McCarthy made his speech twice more to the television audience—and at last the first witness could be called.

A tall and well-groomed soldier made his way to the witness stand. He was Major General Miles Reber, Commanding General, Western Area Command, of the United States Army in Europe. His previous position had been at the Pentagon as the Army's chief of legislative liaison. There, in July and August 1953, he had tried to secure a commission for the former chief consultant of the McCarthy subcommittee, G. David Schine. General Reber recounted now the persistent efforts he had made on Schine's behalf. Yet he was careful not to charge any improper action against Roy Cohn or his employer. And neither friends nor critics of Senator McCarthy in the audience could detect any bias in General Reber's calm voice.

At last it was the turn of Joseph Welch, the Army counsel, whose birdlike manner belied a large, portly frame. He had just three questions for General Reber.

> Welch. Were you actually aware of Mr. Cohn's position as counsel for this committee . . . ?
> Reber. I was, Mr. Welch.
> Welch. Did that position . . . increase or diminish the interest with which your pursued the problem?
> Reber. . . . I feel that it increased the interest.

WELCH. Disregarding the word "improper" influence or pressure, do you recall any instance comparable to this in which you were put under greater pressure?

REBER. . . . I recall no instance in which I was put under greater pressure.

No fair-minded observer could conclude that General Reber was a hostile witness, to be cut down. But at this moment Roy Cohn leaned over to Senator McCarthy, his lips barely moving, while the photographers exploded flashes in their faces and the Senator covered the sensitive ears of the microphones with his hairy but well-manicured hands.

It was now McCarthy's turn to question the general. His questions were pointed but restrained, while General Reber's answers were conciliatory and polite. Then, under the rules set for the inquiry, the questioning passed to Senator McClellan. Quietly and peacefully his skillful questions came, and when he finished, the sand castle that Senator McCarthy had built in Schine's defense had dissolved on the beach.

Then Roy Cohn leaned over, his mouth working swiftly, and Senator McCarthy evidently determined that the vast television audience would respond to stronger tactics. Suddenly his tone altered.

McCARTHY. Now, General, Mr. Welch asked you whether or not you were acutely aware of the fact that Mr. Cohn was the chief counsel for our committee. Your answer was "yes." Will you tell us why you were acutely aware of that?

REBER. I knew in general the functions of your committee. And I knew that Mr. Cohn that spring had been appointed as chief counsel of the committee and I knew that as such he would have a great deal . . . to do with the Army. . . .

McCARTHY. Is Sam Reber your brother?

REBER. Yes, sir.

Suddenly all the reporters were bent over, scribbling hard. They knew Samuel Reber as a pleasant and distinguished foreign-service officer who, but for his added weight, might have been the twin of the witness.

McCARTHY. Now did anything about Sam Reber's ac-

tivities make you acutely aware of the fact that Mr. Cohn was
chief counsel?

REBER. No, sir.

McCARTHY. Do you know that Mr. Sam Reber was the
superior to Mr. [Theodore] Kaghan who Mr. Cohn and Mr.
Schine were sent to Europe by me to inspect . . . that your
brother, Mr. Sam Reber, repeatedly made attacks upon them and
that your brother, Mr. Sam Reber, appointed a man to shadow
them throughout Europe . . . were you aware of that at the time
you were making this great effort to get consideration as you say
for Mr. Schine?

Those allegations, as Chairman Mundt must have known,
were utterly untrue. With his sanction, and at the direction of
Joseph McCarthy, Roy Cohn and David Schine had made a
seventeen-day tour through Europe in the spring of 1953—an
episode that made the United States the laughingstock of the
world. The two young men spent seventeen hours in Bonn,
twenty hours in Berlin, and nineteen hours in Frankfurt, flinging out charges against United States policies and officials. So
they came up against Samuel Reber, who as Deputy High
Commissioner in Germany was second in command for his
country in that vital nation, in charge of political affairs. The
man whom Reber appointed "to shadow them throughout
Europe" was in fact an official from the Visitor's Bureau, sent
along to make arrangements for Cohn and Schine *at their request.* The repeated "attacks upon them" were nothing more
than Reber's refusal to comply with the demand of the 27-year-
olds that he publicly denounce a subordinate employee, Theodore Kaghan, who after a radical past had become one of the
most effective organizers of anti-Communist propaganda in
Germany.

All this Chairman Mundt surely knew. But he now sucked
on a pipe that David Schine had given him—and said nothing.

Counsel Jenkins intervened to instruct General Reber not
to answer, but Senator McCarthy, brushing him aside, claimed
the right to establish bias and prejudice on General Reber's
part. He went on to brand General Reber's testimony "completely false" and added that the general had once told him that

David Schine was entitled to a commission.

Mr. Jenkins sputtered. Senator Mundt continued to puff on his pipe. It was Senator McClellan who intervened—to protest that McCarthy was making charges even though he had not been sworn to tell the truth.

> McClellan. That is testimony.
> McCarthy. May I finish my statement?
> McClellan. You are giving testimony. I have a right to object at any time.
> McCarthy. Don't object in the middle of my question. Let me state my position.
> McClellan. I do not want you testifying unless you want to take the witness stand. Then I do not mind your saying it under oath.

Senator McCarthy paid no attention. Mr. Jenkins advised him to ask questions rather than make speeches, and Senator McCarthy agreed. So throughout the rest of the morning a question mark hung on the last sentence of his many speeches casting doubt on the integrity and truthfulness of General Reber. Puffing and sucking, Chairman Mundt stared at the ceiling.

In the afternoon Senator McCarthy's first question to General Reber was certainly a question.

> McCarthy. General, . . . are you aware of the fact that your brother was allowed to resign when charges that he was a bad security risk were made against him as a result of the investigation of this committee?

Mr. Jenkins held that the question was irrelevant. Senator McCarthy restated it in a much more damaging way. His voice was now abrasive and harsh:

> McCarthy. . . . this question is of the utmost importance . . . if his brother was forced to resign . . . because he was a bad security risk . . . I do think that it is important to have that in the record. . . .

Once again Mr. Jenkins requested Senator McCarthy to offer his comments in the form of questions. The chairman

said nothing. Only John McClellan showed an intense concern
for the law.

> McCLELLAN. ... there has been no testimony that the
> statements that the Senator makes as facts are true and until
> they are established in this record as facts then the question is
> incompetent.

Now the chairman rebuked McClellan for intervening:

> MUNDT. Senator, we will proceed in order.

McClellan felt too deeply on matters of propriety to give
up.

> McCLELLAN. Let us have a ruling on this because we may
> be trying members of everybody's family involved before we get
> through.

Mr. Jenkins ruled that Senator McCarthy's question was "a
perfectly legitimate question," and Chairman Mundt agreed.
The questioning passed to Mr. Welch, and the Army counsel
blandly inquired whether General Reber knew why his brother
had retired. At once Senator McCarthy protested: "That is a
completely unfair question!" His own question he held to be
"of the utmost importance," Mr. Welch's "a highly unimpor-
tant question." This ruling by Senator McCarthy was accepted
by Chairman Mundt and Mr. Jenkins, who agreed that Mr.
Welch's question was burdensome and not germane.

The well-disciplined soldier was trying to speak. Plainly
he was greatly upset.

> REBER. A very serious charge has been made against my
> brother in this room. I would like to answer publicly that charge
> right now.

Before he could do so, however, Senator McCarthy interrupted.

> McCARTHY. If General Reber is going to go into the
> grounds upon which his brother was separated then ... I have a
> right to cross-examine him on that subject.

Mr. Jenkins whispered to Chairman Mundt, and the chairman intervened: Senator McCarthy was right. The counsel added that there was no need for any such testimony.

> JENKINS. . . . General Reber I think is in error in stating that a serious attack has been made on his brother. Suggestions were asked . . . but no proof or statement has been introduced. . . .

This was too much for Senator Henry Jackson, a young journalist and lawyer from Washington.

> JACKSON. The statement, Mr. Chairman, has been made in this room and it is apparent to millions of Americans that General Reber's brother was dismissed as a security risk!

Then, said Mr. Jenkins, it was highly improper and should be ruled out of order. That he supposed was the end of it, but Jackson persisted.

> JACKSON. The statement cannot be stricken from all the newspapers tonight or from the television audience and radio audience and I think in fairness he should be given the opportunity to answer the statement . . . that his brother was dismissed as a security risk.

Once more Senator McCarthy's voice was breaking in over and over until he gained the microphones:

> MCCARTHY. . . . I am not concerned with General Reber's brother. . . . But if the general now denies that the brother was allowed or forced to resign because of security reasons . . . then I must demand the right to cross-examine the general on that subject and also produce witnesses from the State Department.

Speaking in his customary role as chairman—one that Senator Mundt had evidently abdicated—McCarthy continued:

> MCCARTHY. . . . If Senator Jackson, who obviously does not know the facts, is going to accuse me of making an improper accusation, then we will let the Senator hear the testimony.

For forty minutes more the debate continued, as John McClellan pleaded once more—and in vain—for proper procedure. At last Chairman Mundt instructed General Reber to testify on the one issue of his brother's resignation. But he was given no opportunity:

> MCCARTHY. Mr. Chairman, . . . I would suggest that you tell General Reber that as of now there is no question pending, that whatever he volunteers now is being volunteered gratuitously.

A good legal point—provided by Roy Cohn. Finally, two hours after the question had been raised, General Reber was allowed to speak.

> REBER. I merely wanted to say that as I understand my brother's case he retired, as he is entitled to do by law, upon reaching the age of fifty. That is all I wanted to say.

The general of course was right. No security-risk charges had been made against Samuel Reber. He had not been forced to resign. He had served for twenty-eight years in the foreign service. He had risen to its highest classification. But that classification offers no personal security commensurate with the responsibility it bears. The average foreign-service officer cannot save a dollar during the course of his career; nor can he provide adequately for his family on the pension offered; nor is he trained in the course of his public service for any alternative profession. So foreign-service officers often resign when they become entitled to their pensions, to seek new work while they are still active. Three years after he was entitled to retire, Samuel Reber did just this.

Now at the end of twenty-eight years of distinguished service for his country, false charges were broadcast against Samuel Reber, who was not even a participant of any kind in the dispute. Could either the one-sentence defense by his brother, or the cold release that the State Department would issue, erase those charges as Reber sought to establish himself in a new career?

The first day of the hearings was approaching its end. Only that morning Karl Mundt had pledged that he would conduct the hearings with "a maximum degree of dignity, firmness, and thoroughness," and that every party would be treated with equity and consideration. Where now was the "firmness" of the chairman? Where now was "equity" for Samuel Reber? The reporters who crowded around Chairman Mundt as the hearings broke up felt that his most accurate statement of the day had been his self-appraisal—that he was not the man to head the investigation.

In contrast to the unhappy chairman, Senator McCarthy seemed well pleased by the events of the first day. He gathered up his papers and marched behind his bodyguards to the doors. There a large and friendly crowd awaited him. He signed autographs for children and said, "Sure, I know him well," to men who spoke shyly of relatives in Manitowoc.

He was especially pleasant to the women who gathered around him.

"What a nice hat you're wearing!" he said to one admirer.

"I designed it myself!" she exclaimed in delight.

"Don't all women!" he replied with a grin.

The Power of Private Schine

For three years Joseph McCarthy had led forays against the federal government. Department after department had taken a beating and sued for peace. Of all departments, the Army was perhaps most sympathetic to McCarthy. Why, therefore, was it the Army that now confronted Senator McCarthy in an open fight?

Senator McCarthy's investigation of the Army between October 1953 and March 1954 had developed a new pattern of bitterness.

During these same months David Schine, the subcommittee's chief consultant, had passed into military service. And the reason why the conflict with the Army had passed out of control seemed to lie obscurely in the power of Senator McCarthy's commitment to Roy Cohn, and in Roy Cohn's commitment to his close friend.

David Schine was a tall and languid youth of twenty-seven with a fine physique, a pleasant manner, a strikingly handsome head. In the tiny kingdom of his father's hotels he was the adored prince. In the sprawling republic of the outside world he was one among the crowd. He chose the prince's part and sought to wrap himself in its myth when he ventured into the crowd. His doting parents conspired in his flight from reality by giving him money and power. The money set him apart from his contemporaries; and his experience hardly entitled him to the power conferred upon him as president and general manager of the Schine Hotels. Thus David Schine was deprived of perspective about himself and his place in society.

Schine went to Harvard as one among the crowd of freshmen in 1945. There, with his parents' support, he set out to re-create his kingdom. A study in the *Harvard Crimson* of May 7, 1954, records:

> Wealth of course is not out of place here, but Schine, certainly one of the richest men in his class, made it so. He lived in a style which went out here with the era of the Gold Coast: an exquisitely furnished room, a valet, a big black convertible equipped with a two way phone-radio and a fabulous electric phonograph.

Painstakingly, Schine attempted to make others see him in the mythical role in which he chose to see himself. The *Crimson* recalls his method of preparing his arrival at parties:

> This consisted of phoning from his car and saying, "This is G. David Schine. I'm now driving through Copley Square. Could you direct me a little further," and then later, "This is G. David Schine, I'm now at Kenmore Square. Could you give me more directions please."

If Harvard was not susceptible to fantasy, the world beyond it was still less so. The son of the Secretary of the Army was serving like any other private. The son of the President of the United States was facing enemy fire in Korea. Within the walls of the Waldorf-Astoria, the Boca Raton Club, the Ambassador, Schine might have preserved his myth. But he was ambitious and had half-formed notions about the world crisis. He described himself as an expert in psychological warfare—with emphasis on counteracting the Communist threat. So, late in 1952, he wrote his pamphlet, *Definition of Communism*. Senator McCarthy praised this document as "a fairly important pamphlet which shows a lot of study." Roy Cohn also cited it as proof that David Schine was well equipped to investigate the attitudes of America's leading diplomats and the overseas policies of the United States government.

The *Definition* runs to six pages and reads like a well-intentioned mixture of rhetoric and catalog prepared by a high school valedictorian. Three of its six pages recite the measures taken under the previous administration to combat Communism. In the other three pages Mr. Schine is on his own. His style is deplorable ("The theory of Communism . . . is repelled by the masses . . ."). The analysis is so inaccurate that it seems unthinkable that the author had read any work of Karl Marx or any serious study of Marxism or the Soviet state. Mr. Schine maintains that Marx sought a utopia in which there would be "no materialism, no classes, and no unhappiness"—views that Marx would have condemned as utopianism in its most infantile form. Then, in the following and somewhat contradictory passage, Mr. Schine affirms that under Marx's plan this non-materialist society would be inhabited only by a purely materialist man—one "with no aim in life other than the fulfillment of his material needs."

Mr. Schine goes on to consider the practice of Communism, dating the foundation of the Communist Party incorrectly by thirteen years and attributing to Lenin the first name "Nikolai"—one that Vladimir Ilyich did not use.

Nonetheless, the *Definition* impressed Cohn and McCarthy. And so David Schine found his way to the one enclave in this Republic where his myth of the prince could be fostered. For in Room 101 of the Senate Office Building, a boy of his own age had gained great power as counsel to the McCarthy subcommittee; and Senator McCarthy had been able to establish a real kingdom in the country of fear.

For four months David Schine led a charmed life as an unpaid consultant to the McCarthy subcommittee. McCarthy turned the boys loose on the world's third largest broadcasting service, the Voice of America, which handled more programs than the National Broadcasting Company or the Columbia Broadcasting System. Before long, Cohn and Schine were ushering into the Schine suite in the Waldorf Towers dozens of minor Voice officials ready to complain about their superiors. They were recruits to the "loyal American underground" organized by a dissatisfied Rumanian in a subordinate position.

Next Schine found a discontented engineer, who swore to the Senators of the subcommittee that two new transmitters on Cape Hatteras and in the Northwest were a waste of funds. The transmitters had been recommended by consultants from the Radio Corporation of America and the Massachusetts Institute of Technology. But these experts were not allowed to testify before the Senators. Even more fantastic stories developed as a girl accused her superiors of advocating free love; and the curtailment of the broadcasts to Israel was linked to the rise of anti-Semitism in the Soviet Union, despite the fact that the Israeli government had supported the curtailment.

As a result the agency was crippled, its organization broken, its staff demoralized, its audience dispersed. The damage to the United States was considerable.

But the two 27-year-olds had lots of fun.

Then, in July 1953, the magic spell was broken by Schine's draft board. Soon he was to become a serial number in the United States Army. Schine tried to maintain his role. His first proposal, according to General Reber, was that he drive over to the Pentagon "to hold up his hand"—that is, to be sworn in as an officer with no preliminaries of any kind. That course the Pentagon found irregular. Roy Cohn then blasted a road into the Pentagon for him. Much later, in a re-enactment of the calls from Copley Square and Kenmore Square, Schine arrived, expecting to receive his direct commission.

General Reber, who was waiting, politely presented him with a few forms. The first day's testimony records:

> REBER. . . . he apparently felt that the business of filling out forms and going through with the processing was an unnecessary routine step. . . .

Schine was persuaded to submit to the routine. He filled in the questionnaire until he arrived at the portion dealing with his career in the Army Transport Service. He paused there and left the remaining questions blank.

Once before, when he was at Harvard, David Schine had faced military service. On that occasion the Army rejected him for reasons that properly are not given out. Schine, whose

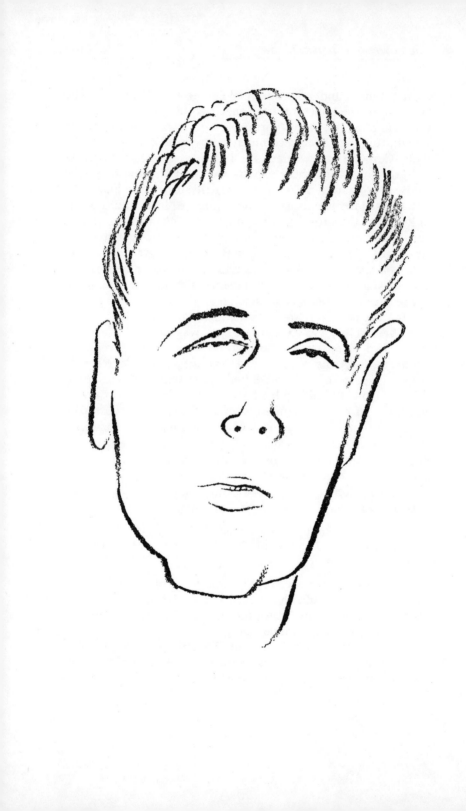

grades were failing, left Harvard in 1946 and returned in 1947. On his re-application to Adams House, according to the *Crimson,* he stated that he had served as a "lieutenant in the Army." In fact he had held a civilian job as assistant purser on an Army transport. The *Crimson* quotes a fellow student as saying: "We were all veterans, and his pretending to be one went over like a lead balloon."

The pretense apparently was maintained until it confronted the fact. Then a new pretense took its place. In a well-staged meeting, Secretary of the Army Stevens was ushered into the Schine rooms in the Waldorf Towers; on that occasion David Schine arranged to meet the Secretary the next morning and take him to watch Senator McCarthy probe into the Army in the courthouse at Foley Square. They rode down together in the Schine family Cadillac. Their conversation was later reconstructed, as Mr. Jenkins questioned Secretary Stevens:

> JENKINS. Was anything said to you . . . with reference to preferential treatment to be accorded Schine?
> STEVENS. Well, Mr. Schine and I had quite an interesting talk in the car riding downtown.
> JENKINS. Will you relate what the conversation was, Mr. Secretary?
> STEVENS. Well, the conversation was along the line that I was doing a good job in ferreting out Communists.
> JENKINS. Was that your statement or his?
> STEVENS. That was Mr. Schine's statement. . . . He thought I could go a long way in this field. And he would like to help me. He thought that it would be a much more logical plan for him to become a special assistant of mine.
> JENKINS. Than to do what?
> STEVENS. Than . . . to be inducted into the Army.

However, Stevens lectured his companion on serving as a private like everyone else.

So David Schine entered the Army as a private. Assigned to Company K at Fort Dix, he stopped the company commander, Captain Joseph Miller, in the barracks on their first encounter. The testimony records:

> MILLER. Private Schine asked me—or rather told me—that

if I ever wanted to make a little trip to Florida that he knew a Colonel Bradley and—but here I cut him off in the middle of a sentence.

Captain Miller warned Schine that special favors ran counter to the facts of military life. But to a determined man a myth can be more stubborn than facts. Three weeks later Captain Miller found Private Schine sitting in the cab of a truck one rainy day when he was supposed to be at the firing range. He was, he said, studying logistics. Captain Miller sent Schine out to the range. There he later found him in deep discussion with the field first sergeant.

> MILLER. I told Private Schine that he should not have approached the field first sergeant for any favors because I'd instructed both him and the "field first" that nothing was to be done without my authority. And I was admonishing him for this when he asked me if it might not be possible to lower my voice.
> . . .
> I continued to admonish Private Schine. He put his hand on my shoulder and attempted to draw me aside. I pushed his hand away. However . . . I stepped aside with Private Schine.
> He thereupon told me that it was his purpose to remake the military establishment along modern lines.

Once again the facts of military life were impressed upon the private. But the myth prevailed. David Schine, according to the Army's case, telephoned his friends on Capitol Hill to get excused from kitchen-police duty. In violation of Captain Miller's orders, he asked many favors of non-commissioned officers. He told Captain Miller that he would mention the company commander two or three times in reports he was filing. And Schine maintained that it was a little "obvious" for him to be required to put his name in the sign-out book when he left the post. Finally and without authorization, at 10:45 one morning he signed out as of 11:30 and departed for the kingdom of the Waldorf Towers—absent without leave.

Nor was this all the story. The rest was not told. "No one would believe it," said an Army officer laughing.

The Army's complaint was not that Private Schine received privileges or that his friends intervened persistently on his behalf. It was that Joseph McCarthy and Roy Cohn were acting, not as Senator and citizen, but as chairman and counsel of the Senate subcommittee when they pressed their demands—and that they used the subcommittee to harass the Army when their demands were not fully satisfied.

The hearings in the Senate Caucus Room had been called in order to determine the accuracy of the Army's complaint, and the heart of that complaint, backed up by sworn testimony, lay in nine of the Army's specific charges:

The Sixth Charge

During the period on or about October 18, 1953, to on or about November 3, 1953, Mr. Cohn ... sought to persuade or induce John Adams, Counselor of the Department of the Army, to procure an assignment for Mr. Schine in the New York City area. ... Mr. Cohn coupled these requests with threats that if they were not granted he would cause the Army to be exposed in its worst light and demonstate to the country how shabbily it was being run.

The Eighth Charge

On or about November 6, 1953, Senator McCarthy, Mr. Cohn and Mr. Carr sought to induce and persuade Secretary Stevens and Mr. Adams to arrange for the assignment of Private Schine to New York City. ... These requests were coupled with promises reasonably to limit or to terminate subcommittee hearings on Fort Monmouth.

The Fourteenth Charge

On or about November 18, 1953, and on numerous occasions thereafter, members of the staff of this subcommittee sought to and did obtain special passes for Private Schine and on each such occasion represented to the responsible officers at Fort Dix that the same were essential to subcommittee business. Private Schine was absent from Fort Dix on such special passes on occasions when in fact he did not work on behalf of this subcommittee.

The Sixteenth Charge

On or about December 8, 1953, Mr. Cohn, upon learning that special week day passes for Private Schine had been discontinued, called Mr. Adams and by abusive language and threats sought to have this decision reversed.

The Nineteenth Charge

On or about December 11, 1953, Mr. Cohn, upon learning that Private Schine had been assigned to duty the following Saturday morning, sought by threats and abusive language to get Private Schine relieved from his duty.

The Twentieth Charge

On or about December 17, 1953, Mr. Cohn, in the presence of Mr. Carr and Senator McCarthy . . . used extremely abusive and threatening language to Mr. Adams in an effort to obtain special privileges for Private Schine and in particular . . . to obtain his assignment to the New York City area. Senator McCarthy acceded in these demands. . . .

The Twenty-third Charge

On or about January 11, 1954, and on numerous occasions before and after that date Mr. Cohn sought to obtain special privileges for Private Schine upon his assignment to Camp Gordon, Georgia. . . . Mr. Cohn by innuendo and inference suggested that if his demands were not met the Army would be subjected to further investigations.

The Twenty-eighth Charge

On or about January 22, 1954, Senator McCarthy requested Mr. Adams to obtain a special assignment for Private Schine in New York and suggested that Mr. Cohn would continue to harass the Army unless this demand was acceded to.

The Twenty-ninth Charge

On or about February 16, 1954, and on several other occasions, Mr. Carr and a person purporting to act as a representative of Senator McCarthy indicated that the investigations of the Army then contemplated would be either terminated or be conducted along reasonable lines if the Army would accede to Senator McCarthy's request for a special assignment for Private Schine.

In response to these charges Senator McCarthy and his staff at different times took three different positions.

In the first place, Senator McCarthy argued that David Schine had been punished by the Army for his connection with the subcommittee. Thus, on December 22, 1953, Senator McCarthy wrote to Secretary Stevens: "Mr. Schine would never have been drafted except because of the fact that he worked for my committee." This was also the position taken by Senator McCarthy on March 11, 1954. On that occasion the Senator published memoranda which he announced had been written months before. Among them was one dated December 9 from Francis Carr. It stated:

> ... I am getting fed up with the way the Army is trying to use Schine as a hostage to pressure us to stop our hearings on the Army. John Adams ... refers to Schine as our hostage whenever his name comes up. . . . I am convinced that they will keep right on trying to blackmail us as long as Schine is in the Army. . . .

No evidence was introduced to show that David Schine had suffered discrimination. On the contrary the Army seemed guilty of granting him too much. More interesting was the question: What value did Private Schine possess that could make him a "hostage"—as Frank Carr claimed? The most that the McCarthy staff was seeking, according to the Army, was to keep Private Schine available in the New York City area. The worst that the Army was trying to do, according to Carr, was to refuse to assign Private Schine to New York. To whom and why was this a sword that the Army could hold poised over a Senate committee?

Senator McCarthy apparently was well aware of the dangers of this position. His second argument was that he cared not a whit what happened to Private Schine. This was the main burden of the letter of December 22, written, so McCarthy said, because Drew Pearson had published the first revelation about Schine's record at Fort Dix. Roy Cohn echoed that his only concern for Schine was his insistence on finishing up subcommittee work.

In the case of the Senator, the argument was partially convincing, for Secretary Stevens testified that Senator McCarthy had told him that Schine was a pest that he wanted to be rid of. In the case of Roy Cohn, however, indifference was a claim difficult to accept. Too many witnesses were ready to testify to the intensity of his concern for his friend.

The third explanation offered for the pressures brought to bear upon the Army by Senator McCarthy and Counsel Cohn was that Private Schine was indispensable to the subcommittee. But this seemed difficult to credit. Schine had come to the subcommittee without any background in investigation. At the time he learned he was due for induction, he had worked for the subcommittee for just five months—on a part-time basis. Thereupon he still had four months in which to clean up his five months' work. And yet, three months after his induction, Roy Cohn maintained that Schine was still needed for subcommittee work.

But if these arguments seemed weak, the brief filed by Joseph McCarthy, Roy Cohn, and Frank Carr was not. The vigor of the attack, with its allegations of bribery and blackmail, concealed the weakest and most curious aspect of the McCarthy brief; of its forty-six separate counts, just two mentioned G. David Schine.

The Credulity of Mr. Jenkins

In his book *Trial Judge,* Mr. Justice Botein writes, "I know of no child prodigies among trial lawyers." By the end of the fourth day of the Army-McCarthy hearings Ray Jenkins might have argued the point.

It was a dramatic day, and a humiliating one for the special counsel. On the previous afternoon he had flourished a photograph at the Secretary of the Army. It was a damaging photograph—but not quite in the way that the special counsel had foreseen.

Now he announced a surprise witness to testify on its origin:

JENKINS. The next witness is myself.

The giant of the Tennessee bar was sworn to tell the whole truth—and he told how he had been made to look a fool by the 27-year-old Roy Cohn.

It was not all the fault of Mr. Jenkins. In the weeks before the hearings began, the subcommittee had first picked for the crucial role of counsel a Boston attorney, Samuel Sears. But Sears's claims to impartiality were blemished by the disclosure of his arduous efforts on behalf of Senator McCarthy.

During the public outcry that followed, the subcommittee

canvassed the nation until, at the suggestion of Senator Dirksen, it fell on Ray Jenkins of Knoxville. He had the leading criminal practice in the state, an unblemished political career as a Taft Republican, and a record of unbroken silence on the sharpest domestic issue of the day. So he was rushed to Washington, ten days before the beginning of the hearings.

Jenkins went first to the peach-colored labyrinth of the Pentagon, where messengers roll by on tricycles and travelers stop hurrying men in uniform to ask their way. Jenkins spent six days there, reviewing the Army charges. Granting for the sake of argument all that the Army said about Private Schine, Jenkins thought as he crossed back over the Potomac that two questions remained: How many of Private Schine's privileges were volunteered by the Army? Why, unless the Army was hiding something, did it give way so far?

Jenkins and his two assistants went to Capitol Hill. There, when the hearings ended each day, they closeted themselves for briefings with Roy Cohn, spreading out on a table the counter-charges filed by Joseph McCarthy, Roy Cohn, and Frank Carr.

The fourth charge opened the case:

> At the threshold the core of the matter stands in bold relief: There are and were Communists and other security risks in the Army. . . .

The sixteenth charge established the origins of the dispute:

> On or about September 7 . . . Chairman McCarthy publicly announced his determination to pursue [his Army] investigations to the point of calling those . . . responsible for the clearing of Communists. Secretary Robert Stevens then commenced a series of efforts to interfere . . . with the investigations, to stop hearings. . . .

The twenty-third charge accused the Army of misconduct:

> As part of the attempt to halt the subcommittee's investigation of Communist infiltration in the Army, Mr. Adams frequently and Mr. Stevens on two occasions offered up the Navy, the Air

Force, and the Defense Department as "substitute targets." . . .

The thirty-seventh charge offered a reason for the earlier Army action in releasing its files on Cohn and Schine:

On or about January 22, 1954, Mr. Adams made to the Chairman and Mrs. McCarthy the threat that unless the investigation of the loyalty set-up was halted he would cause to be issued a report on Mr. Cohn casting events in such a light as to attempt to embarrass the committee and its staff. The Chairman told Mr. Adams that the investigation would continue despite any threat.

The forty-sixth charge was a summary:

The pattern followed by Secretary Stevens and Mr. Adams is clear. As long as only individual Communists were the object of the subcommittee's investigation they made continuing offers of cooperation with the investigation. But as soon as the probe turned to the infinitely more important question of who was responsible for protecting Communist infiltration and protecting Communists who had infiltrated, every conceivable obstacle was placed in the path of the subcommittee's search for the truth.

Where, asked Mr. Jenkins, did the charges regarding Private Schine conflict? The counter-charges filed by Joseph McCarthy declared that David Schine was "a prime mover in the successful exposure of Communist infiltration," a man whose knowledge was important for the nation's security. All arrangements for his leaves were "open and proper." The thirteenth charge affirmed:

To call participation in arrangements to have Private Schine devote many hours over and above Army training which could otherwise have been spent in recreation to the completion of vital subcommittee work a request for preferential treatment defies reason. All such arrangements were made with the full concurrence of Secretary Stevens.

Yet Secretary Stevens maintained that the pressures were improper and extremely embarrassing. To this McCarthy, Cohn, and Carr had a simple reply: "Bad faith." Their fifteenth charge affirmed:

Five days after the Secretary claimed that attempts were made to induce and persuade him by improper means to give preferential treatment to Private Schine, Mr. Stevens posed for smiling photographs with Private Schine at Fort Dix.

This was a telling argument, if it could be proved. Now, Mr. Cohn—asked Ray Jenkins in the conference that followed the third day of hearings—what proof do you have? Plenty, replied Roy Cohn, Their conversation was re-enacted five days later when Cohn was called to the witness stand to explain the little discrepancies in the "proof" of "bad faith" that he had provided, and that Jenkins had, without pause for reflection, employed.

Jenkins was plainly upset; Cohn was rather vague.

JENKINS. You stated to me on that occasion that Mr. Stevens as Secretary of the Army on that date [November 12, 1953] requested David Schine to be photographed with him.

COHN. I stated that, and that is the fact, sir. . . .

JENKINS. Did you or did you not tell me who was present on that occasion?

COHN. . . . I believe I told you some of the people who were present. I might have told you all the people who were present.

JENKINS. Did you or did you not tell me you had documentary evidence . . . ?

COHN. . . . I told you, sir, I believe, that I thought very substantial proof of the bad faith of Mr. Stevens in making these charges now was the fact that long after the threats had supposedly been made . . . Mr. Stevens was not only solicitous of Private Schine but . . . asked that he be photographed with Private Schine. . . .

JENKINS. I will ask you whether or not you told me that you had documentary evidence in the form of a photograph of Mr. Stevens and Mr. Schine corroborating your statement to me that Mr. Stevens requested his photograph be taken with Schine. Is that correct?

COHN. I told you, sir, that as far as I knew there was a picture of Mr. Stevens and Private Schine taken on November 17. . . .

JENKINS. Did I ask you to produce that photograph for me prior to any cross-examination of the Secretary of the Army?

COHN. I believe you did that. . . .

JENKINS. Did or did you not tell me it was taken on that
occasion at the request of the Secretary of the Army?
COHN. I said that then, sir, and I say that now.

It was a dramatic photograph of the Secretary and the private standing and facing each other in front of an Air Force
plane. And, well-armed, Jenkins had sprung the question on
Secretary Stevens on the afternoon of April 26. The Secretary
had been baffled.

JENKINS. Mr. Stevens, did you ever have your photograph
taken with G. David Schine?
STEVENS. Well, there were a lot of photographers down
there at the hearing and it could be.
JENKINS. Did you ever at your suggestion at a meeting any-
where, any time, say that "I want my picture taken with David"
and have it done?
STEVENS. I am sure I never made a statement just like you
make it there.

Jenkins rose from his chair behind the long table. His left
hand quivering in the excitement of his first big moment, he
brandished the large reproduction before the startled Secretary,
with the prosecutor's cliché:

JENKINS. Let me show you a picture, Mr. Stevens, for the
purpose of refreshing your recollection. I ask you whether or not
that is a photograph of you, the Secretary of the Army, and
David Schine, a private in the Army?

The Secretary floundered in confusion. Then Jenkins
struck:

JENKINS. Mr. Stevens, isn't it a fact that you were being
especially nice and considerate and tender of this boy Schine—

The Secretary protested indignantly, but the prosecutor
overrode him:

JENKINS. —Wait! Wait! Wait! Wait!—in order to dissuade
the Senator from continuing his investigation of one of your
departments?

The ex-manufacturer sputtered in anger.

STEVENS. Positively and completely not!

The victory of the hour was McCarthy's. But the next morning, as the subcommittee reconvened, the special counsel for Secretary Stevens had an announcement:

WELCH. Mr. Chairman, Mr. Jenkins yesterday was imposed upon and so was the Secretary of the Army by having a doctored or altered photograph produced in this courtroom as if it were honest.

He brought out a picture, well hidden until that moment.

WELCH. I show you now a photograph in respect of which I charge that what was offered in evidence yesterday was an altered, shamefully cut down picture so that somebody could say to Stevens, "Were you not photographed alone with David Schine," when the truth is he was photographed in a group.

Mr. Jenkins had said "alone" in one exchange. Now here was the real photograph from which Cohn's "proof" of "bad faith" had been taken. It showed a figure which proved to be that of Frank Carr, in addition to a colonel standing beside Private Schine. This was Colonel Jack Bradley (whom Private Schine had cited as the friend who presumably would arrange to transport Captain Miller to Florida for a vacation if the captain treated the private in the manner to which he was accustomed).

Senator McCarthy and Roy Cohn bent together in urgent whispers. The Senator intervened with a soft-spoken and proper request that Welch be put under oath. Then the fury that was rising within him at this exposure of his techniques boiled up and ran over the room—labeled a "point of order."

McCARTHY. The point of order is this: that Mr. Welch under the guise of making a point of order has testified that a picture is doctored . . . and he makes the completely false statement that this is a group picture and it is not.

McCarthy also was testifying—although he also was not under oath. And leaning across the discomfited Senator Jackson, Stuart Symington pounded on the table and shouted

in McCarthy's face that he was out of order. "Oh, be quiet!"
said the Senator, filled with hatred, while between them—
unmoved by the bloodletting—sat Frank Carr, as round and
impassive as a buddha chipped from stone.

By now Senator McCarthy was out of control. Up with the
anger was coming a good deal more that had lain in his
stomach over four days of these hearings, in which he was no
longer the chairman:

> McCARTHY. I am getting awfully sick of sitting down here
> at the end of the table and having whomever wants to interrupt
> in the middle of a sentence. . . . I suggest that the chair make the
> record clear that Mr. Welch was not speaking the truth. . . .

Jenkins broke in at last, and finally the reluctant chairman. Agreeing as usual with the last person who spoke, Karl
Mundt said that both Mr. Welch and Senator McCarthy were a
bit out of order. It made little difference to McCarthy, who by
now often showed open contempt for Mundt.

> McCARTHY. Mr. Chairman.
> MUNDT. Do you have a point of order . . . ?
> McCARTHY. Call it a point of order or call it what you may,
> when counsel for Mr. Stevens and Mr. Hensel and Mr. Adams
> makes a statement . . . do I have a right to correct it or do we find
> halfway through my statement that Mr. Welch should not have
> made his statement and therefore I cannot point out that he was
> lying?

Already, according to the Senator, Welch was "lying."

The subject changed. The tension hung on in the room and
then mounted again as Roy Cohn was called to the witness
chair. He sat with head tilted like one of those saints of Giulio
Romano on whose lower cheek rests one perpetual tear.

The subcommittee counsel began the cross-examination.

> JENKINS. Was anything ever said to me up to this time
> about any person being cut out of that photograph?
> COHN. No, sir, I do not think anything was said. . . .

By this time Cohn wasn't even sure that on April 23 he had
known there was a photograph.

COHN. I believe you asked me, sir, whether or not such a picture was in existence. I believe I told you that I thought it was. . . .

That was April 23. This was a curious assertion in the light of the fifteenth charge that McCarthy and Cohn had released on April 20, in which the picture was described in detail. Cohn, moreover, had been standing beside the plane when the photograph was taken.

It was a petty issue, made significant because McCarthy, Cohn, and Carr had enlarged it to huge proportions even as they cropped it, and because the gullible Jenkins had taken Cohn at his word. But even as it became clear that Jenkins was the victim of a little hoax, he was again demonstrating his credulity on a much larger scale. As he cross-examined Secretary Stevens, the Tennessean made it plain that he was accepting without question Senator McCarthy's concept of himself as the nation's guardian-in-chief; hence he pictured Secretary Stevens as a man blind to the great problems of subversion that McCarthy understood so well.

The Education of Secretary Stevens

In the 1954 Armed Forces Day Manual the portraits of the Commander in Chief and of the Secretary of Defense were closely followed by the round and confident face of the Secretary of the Army. His solemn message to the nation stated: "The Army is well aware that we live in an age of peril and not of military peril alone." But, said Robert Stevens, the equipment, the training, and above all the fighting morale of the service he led would guard this country against all perils that threatened.

The military photographs that bristled through the pages of the Manual seemed to justify the Secretary's proud boast. And yet there were perils against which he could not direct those fearsome cannons, those splendid troops. On the day the Manual appeared, the Secretary himself was held prisoner in a red leather chair within two miles of the Pentagon, and none could rescue him.

There is a line in Ford Madox Ford's novel, *Parade's End*, about schoolboys of the Sixth Form—"sinister, hobbledehoy, waiting in the corners of playgrounds to torture someone weak and unfortunate." Now the Senate Caucus Room seemed to be the playground, Joseph McCarthy and Roy Cohn the schoolboys of the Sixth Form, and Robert Stevens, pink-faced and chubby, the weak and unfortunate one, cornered, frightened, forced at last to fight—to fight alone before the cameras and in the glare of the floodlamps.

The Secretary of the Army was surrounded by generals, but they could not move to aid him. The three Democratic Senators tried vainly to prompt him; the Senators of his own party seemed hostile. The jaws and hands of Ray Jenkins protruded toward him from the committee table. He could not tell which seemed worse—the deadly insinuations of the Senator he had called his friend, or the brutal disbelief of the stranger from Tennessee.

One by one the Secretary's past efforts to win Senator McCarthy's good will were laid out on the long table, as embarrassing as the love letters of a man now married to someone else. As each was read aloud the Secretary squirmed in his seat. And Counsel Jenkins could not believe what he saw. He pursued the Secretary of the Army with the determination of a sheriff hot on the trail of a moonshiner in the Smokies.

In November, Secretary Stevens had learned with horror that Senator McCarthy was offended at him. At once he had sought McCarthy out to patch things up.

> JENKINS. Now why did you, the Secretary of the Army, having released a statement . . . take it on yourself in your high position . . . to go traipsing off to New York City hunting up this man to change your statement and make peace with him . . . if you weren't afraid of him. . . ?

Roy Cohn had made wild threats against the Army when, in the course of a tour of Fort Monmouth, he and other staff members and Senatorial assistants were kept out of a top-secret laboratory. Secretary Stevens had publicly apologized.

> JENKINS. Why did you in your exalted position as head of the Army . . . humble yourself so to speak or kowtow to this young man . . . if it wasn't a part of a pattern on your part to . . . keep the good will of the McCarthy committee so that they would lay off of you? . . .

According to the brief filed by McCarthy, Cohn, and Carr,

the Secretary of the Army had invited David Schine to a Pentagon luncheon after his induction as a private and had expressed disappointment when Schine did not come.

> JENKINS. What possibly could have been your purpose in inviting David Schine there . . . to lunch with you, the Secretary of the Army, if it were not for the purpose of offering tidbits, so to speak, sweet morsels of tidbits, to lull to sleep this three-headed monster that you say was about to devour you?

To all such questions Secretary Stevens had the same answer—these were "acts of cooperation."
Why had the Secretary of the Army gone so far?

Robert Ten Broeck Stevens was a New Jersey businessman. He had manufactured uniforms for the Army and had served in a wartime federal agency. He had generously supported the candidacy of General Eisenhower for President. In February 1953, his good friend brought him back to the Pentagon. He worked happily and earned a Labor Day weekend rest at Harlowtown, Montana. There, on September 2, 1953, he read in a local newspaper that Senator McCarthy claimed to have found "a disturbing situation" in the Department of the Army.

Robert Stevens had watched as Senator McCarthy continued his course of invading one executive department after another. He had seen Secretary of State Dulles remake the nation's overseas libraries at Senator McCarthy's demand. He had seen the Voice of America weakened. He had seen the Mutual Security Administration undermined when Senator McCarthy signed an agreement with 118 Greek shipowners—in plain violation of the Constitutional separation of powers.

Now, in September, the Senator had placed his foot in the door of the Pentagon, where the bronze bust of the tight-lipped James Forrestal stands grimly on guard. A very different sort of man, Robert Stevens, rushed to welcome Senator McCarthy. From Montana he sent Senator McCarthy a wire that represented his "whole philosophy." It read: ". . . will call your office to offer my services in trying to assist you to correct anything that may be wrong. . . ."

On October 2, Frank Carr and Roy Cohn told Secretary Stevens that the McCarthy subcommittee had been investigating Fort Monmouth. They told him that every other agency of government had given them free access to personnel—an assertion he accepted without question. However, they added, the commanding officer of Monmouth, General Kirke Lawton, had limited their questioning of his men. The Secretary's response was immediate.

> STEVENS. I said, "Well, I want to cooperate with the committee to the very limit of my ability," and in their presence then and there I called General Lawton on the telephone. . . . I told General Lawton that I wanted full cooperation by him and the members of his staff.

In the same spirit the Secretary of the Army went to New York on October 13 to listen to the McCarthy subcommittee hearings. Again acting without dignity or wisdom, he took the Senator and his staff to lunch at the Merchants Club. The same day he went to dinner at the Waldorf Towers as a guest of the Schine family. The next morning he rode back to the hearings, discussing privileges for a private, in the Schine Cadillac.

One week later, on October 20, Secretary Stevens arranged a joint trip to Fort Monmouth with the McCarthy subcommittee. Its purpose was not to educate the staff in the secrets of radar but to review problems of personnel and security. The first group, consisting of elected officials, was taken into a secret laboratory. The second group, consisting of staff assistants who lacked passes, was kept outside. At this point, according to an Army colonel, Roy Cohn declared: "This is war! We will now really investigate the Army!"

The Secretary of the Army apologized.

By then David Schine's induction was near at hand. So, Stevens testified, he called on Allen Dulles, director of the Central Intelligence Agency, to ask if a commission could not be arranged there. The Secretary did tell Schine on October 21 that it looked as if he was stuck with sixteen weeks of basic training. But, he added, he had given in to Roy Cohn's request that Private Schine's career in the Army start with a furlough in New York.

On November 6, Secretary Stevens once more invited Senator McCarthy and his staff to luncheon at the Pentagon. Both sides later agreed that the discussion had passed from Fort Monmouth to Private Schine.

Normally soldiers during their first four weeks of basic training are not permitted to leave their posts. But Secretary Stevens himself suspended this rule for Private Schine. He argued, in justification of his action, that Private Schine was needed by the subcommittee. Yet on the following day Senator McCarthy exploded this convenient theory. Once out of earshot of Roy Cohn, the Senator had called Secretary Stevens to tell him that Schine was not needed for subcommittee work.

> STEVENS. Senator McCarthy said that one of the few things he had trouble with Roy Cohn about was David Schine. He said: "Roy Cohn thinks that Dave ought to be a general and operate from a penthouse in the Waldorf-Astoria." Senator McCarthy then said that he thought a few weekends for David Schine might be arranged . . . for the purpose of taking care of Dave's girl friends.

Thus on November 7 Secretary Stevens must have realized that Senator McCarthy and his staff were exploiting the Army and applying improper pressure upon it. A man conscious of the dignity of his office would have canceled all special privileges—or at least would have demanded written assurance that each leave was in fact for subcommittee work. Instead, the Secretary ordered General Ryan at Fort Dix to grant special leaves. So Private Schine took sixteen passes, returning so late that General Ryan, the commanding officer at Fort Dix, called a halt, lest the bleary-eyed soldier kill himself or someone else on the firing range.

One storm had blown up and then passed over during the first trip to Monmouth. Now in November a second storm was approaching. Sensational newspaper charges inspired by Senator McCarthy in the course of his Monmouth hearings were causing alarm across the nation and demoralization at the base. The Secretary reviewed the whole story—and told the press on November 13 that there was no evidence of current espionage at Monmouth. Three days later he was visited by Roy Cohn and Francis Carr.

STEVENS. Mr. Cohn indicated that Senator McCarthy was very mad and felt that I had double-crossed him.

Cohn threatened to hold public hearings to prove McCarthy right. So Secretary Stevens flew up to New York and again invited Senator McCarthy to luncheon at the Merchants Club. After a long meeting, a new statement was made to the press by the Secretary, who now held that he had meant to emphasize only that the Army had no *proof* of espionage.

JENKINS. It was designed for the purpose of, shall we say, pacifying the Senator?
STEVENS. I had been cooperating right along with the Senator and his committee, and I wanted to continue.

The Secretary of the Army then made the services of the Merchants Club available to the Senate subcommittee investigating the Army. When Senator McCarthy remarked that he had to be in Boston that evening, but wanted to see Private Schine at Fort Dix on the same afternoon, Secretary Stevens flew them to New Jersey and then to Boston in his Army plane.

Thus the second storm blew over.

Then for six weeks the Secretary was left in peace, as the subcommittee wrote its reports and John Adams worked with Roy Cohn. In January, after a long and friendly conference with Senator McCarthy, Robert Stevens left for the Far East. When he returned in February his department was in an uproar. Members of the Army's Loyalty and Security Screening Board had been threatened with subpoenas to appear before the subcommittee—and then spared, thanks to the intervention of Senator Dirksen. But this crisis was followed at once by a new crisis over one Major Peress.

Irving Peress was a dentist, commissioned in October 1952 under the Doctor Draft Law. When he filled out a question-

naire, he declined to answer questions concerning his political affiliations. There was no regulation requiring him to do so. He was automatically advanced under the Doctor Draft Law, until in November 1953 the Army caught up with the case of this dentist, who was by now suspected of Communist sympathies.

It was a difficult case for the Army. It could court-martial Major Peress. Yet he had committed no overt crime, and precedent indicated that the case would be lost.

It could discharge him under conditions other than honorable. This course, the Army concluded, might take nine months.

It could release him without prejudice as part of a reduction-in-force. This course the Army chose to follow.

But the Army did not count on Senator McCarthy. Although he had promised to drive out in carloads the Communists whom the Democrats had kept in Washington, in twelve months of hunting among two million civil servants he had found just two suspects. Now, hearing of a Communist suspect in the Army, he rushed in with a roar.

On December 30, 1953, the Adjutant General ordered the First Army to discharge Major Peress within ninety days.

On January 30, Senator McCarthy questioned Major Peress who cited the Constitutional privilege against self-incrimination.

On February 1 Senator McCarthy wrote Secretary Stevens demanding that Peress be court-martialed.

On February 2 Major Peress requested and was granted an honorable discharge.

On February 16 Secretary Stevens sent a reply to Senator McCarthy. He conceded that the Army had been in error. He promised that "there will be no repetition of the circumstances" of the Peress case. He added:

> I have directed the Inspector General of the Army to initiate an exhaustive investigation for the purpose of determining whether there are any additional areas where correction should be made and secondly whether there is any evidence of collusion or conspiracy which might have been inspired by subversive interests in the assignment, transfer or other personnel handling of the officer in question.

This time Senator McCarthy was not to be appeased. He denounced the Secretary's letter as "double talk" and "evasion" and added that it contained "Communist jargon". He demanded the receipt within twenty-four hours of the names of all Army personnel concerned with the discharge of Major Peress, and he threatened contempt citations for those responsible if the names were withheld. The Pentagon, he declared, was "coddling Communists."

Major Peress was discharged at Camp Kilmer. There the commanding officer was Brigadier General Ralph Zwicker, an old comrade-in-arms of President Eisenhower and former chief of staff of the Second Infantry Division; but for his action in the Battle of the Bulge, the President had stated, the war might have turned against the allies. Zwicker had apparently talked freely to a subcommittee staff member, James Juliana. But, after a briefing by John Adams on the law, he refused to name the men responsible for the Peress discharge. He was acting under specific provisions of Public Law 84 of the Eighty-third Congress.

But Senator McCarthy expelled John Adams from his hearing, rewrote the subcommittee rules on the spot to justify his act, drew the baffled general into a discussion of crime, and then berated him. He said that General Zwicker did not have the brains of a five-year-old child, and he ended: ". . . any man promoted to general who says, 'I will protect another general who protected Communists,' is not fit to wear that uniform."

General Zwicker was a heavy, slow-moving man who had previously thought well of Senator McCarthy. Afterward he said: "I took the stand—and boom! I never anticipated anything like it!"

General Zwicker protested to General Matthew Ridgway, the Army Chief of Staff. Ridgway knew well what was involved. He had seen the foreign service demoralized when the State Department failed to resist encroachment. He believed that morale in the officer corps was already unsatisfactory. He knew what would happen to the Army if every malcontent could get back at his commanding officer merely by forwarding charges and complaints to Senator McCarthy. So General

Ridgway went to Secretary Stevens—and at last the Secretary responded. "This," said Secretary Stevens, "is the end of the line." Without waiting for the transcript of the testimony he wrote to Senator McCarthy:

> I have directed Brigadier General Ralph Zwicker not to appear before Senator McCarthy on Tuesday in New York. . . .
>   I cannot permit the loyal officers of our Armed Forces to be subjected to such unwarranted treatment. The prestige and morale of our Armed Forces are too important for the security of the nation to have them weakened by unfair attacks on our officer corps.

To this Senator McCarthy answered:

> The favorable action in the case of this Fifth Amendment Communist was stupidity at best and treason at worst. Those who committed it are now being officially shielded by order of the Secretary of the Army. . . .

From a legal point of view the Stevens letter went too far in seeming to deny to Congress the right of subpoena. Politically, as a move to withdraw recognition from a particular Congressional subcommittee that had abused its powers, it was a position that the President of the United States could have backed with substantial Congressional support. But the President was in Palm Springs, California, and for him the notable event of February 18 was a mashie shot from fifty yards out that rolled close to the pin.

In the absence of the President, others became very active. James Reston of the *New York Times* later reported:

> Bernard M. Shanley, the White House legal counselor, thought the Peress case was a "bad case" and told Stevens so. . . . Vice President Nixon was worried about the political effects of a public fight over television. The President, who knew Zwicker well, . . . was very silent, and when Stevens inquired about this he was told that "everybody thinks we should keep the President out of this."

Secretary Stevens had declared that he would testify before Senator McCarthy on February 25. He had called the three Democratic members of the subcommittee to inform them of his intention to stand fast against Senator McCarthy and to seek their support. At noon on the previous day he had met with H. Struve Hensel, counsel for the Department of Defense. They read over a powerful declaration of resistance that Stevens proposed to make and rehearsed his supporting testimony. Then the Secretary left, saying he would return soon.

Instead he went to a chicken luncheon in the Senate office of the Republican Campaign Committee. There he met in secret with Republican Senators McCarthy, Dirksen, Potter, and Mundt. And at the end of the luncheon, Senator Mundt typed up a "memorandum of understanding" that was read to the press. It endorsed every one of Senator McCarthy's demands. It made no mention of a single concession gained by Secretary Stevens. The memorandum stated:

> There is complete agreement that the Secretary . . . will give the committee the names of everyone involved in the promotion and honorable discharge of Peress and that such individuals will be available to appear before the committee. If the committee decides to call General Zwicker . . . General Zwicker will be available.

Back at the Pentagon a large group had gathered to await the Secretary's return. He told them he had gained what he wanted. They congratulated him and went their ways.

Later in the day Secretary Stevens was called by a newspaperman who reported Senator McCarthy's version of the luncheon: "Stevens could not have given in more abjectly if he had got down on his knees." (The Senator denied under oath in the hearings that he had made this remark.) That night, Senators reported, Secretary Stevens sobbed over the telephone and threatened to resign his post because of reports that he had sacrificed the Army. In the Pentagon, high-ranking officers greeted each other by waving white handkerchiefs. "Private Schine," said one, "is the only man left in the Army with any morale."

On the following day the President—now back from his vacation—intervened. He called Senator Dirksen to the White House and asked him to secure a statement from the subcommittee that, in the future, Army witnesses would not be abused. McCarthy—and Dirksen himself—declined to sign any such statement. And so, while the President practiced approach shots on the lawn outside, a face-saving statement was prepared in the White House for Secretary Stevens.

In the *New York Times* of February 28, Hanson Baldwin wrote:

> The Army today is a far call indeed from the tough units that sailed from the ports of Europe to the assault on Fortress Europe a decade ago. Its morale is depressed, discipline and efficiency leave much to be desired. . . .
> Whether President Eisenhower realizes it or not, Senator McCarthy is now sharing with him command of the Army.

That was the inevitable end of a futile endeavor. Ten days later the Army released a "chronology of events," giving the story of the case of Private Schine.

Now, six weeks later, Secretary Stevens sat in the red leather chair in the Senate Caucus Room. In front of him as judges sat the three Republicans who had brought about his surrender of February 25; three Democrats whom he had ignored on that day; and a seventh Senator named temporarily to Senator McCarthy's subcommittee seat. At the end of the table was the man the Secretary had trusted—so repugnant to him now that he could hardly bear to look at that swarthy face. Yet if he turned to stare ahead he saw Ray Jenkins, snorting at his petty efforts to gain the Senator's favor and demanding "Why! Why! Why!"

During the hearings the Secretary was at all times at a disadvantage. The solid testimony on his side was to be given, if given at all, by John Adams. The weighty evidence, if there was to be weighty evidence, would come in the transcripts of telephone conversations between John Adams and Roy Cohn. Those were the moments that were frozen hard in the Army brief.

In contrast, the events that Secretary Stevens sought to recreate lay hidden in the shadows. The Secretary had put his name to the allegation that McCarthy and his staff had linked their treatment of the Army to the Army's treatment of Private

Schine. On each occasion, as the Army's brief conceded, the link was established by "inference and innuendo."

Where in the charges and counter-charges might the truth be found? The dilemma of Secretary Stevens—which for Senator McCarthy was no dilemma but an opportunity to create further confusion—was put in allegorical terms by a leading figure in the case:

> You are driving in a restricted zone and a policeman draws up beside you and cries, "Pull over!" Then he takes out his book and licks his pencil and says, "You were speeding!" You deny it, and then the policeman looks in the window. "I just thought," he remarks. "You weren't by any chance speeding on your way to the policemen's ball were you?"
>
> You gulp and stammer, "Well, maybe I was." So he sells you a ticket for $10—and then arrests you anyway.
>
> The case goes to court, and you protest. You say the policeman brought improper pressure to bear on you. He retorts that you were trying to blackmail him.
>
> Just what is the court to do?

In the course of three days the direct Ray Jenkins completed his direct examination, and the cross Ray Jenkins completed his cross-examination—a process which one leading jurist described as "professionally very funny."

Then the special rules that had been established in order to win Senator McCarthy's participation in the hearings went into effect. By these rules each member of the subcommittee had ten minutes in turn to question the witness; when all but one had finished, that one man could continue his cross-examination as long as he wished.

With an unerring instinct for a victim's sensitive spot, Senator McCarthy and Roy Cohn began at once to tear at the honor of the New Jersey businessman. Stevens had signed his name to the charge that Frank Carr had "sought to induce and persuade the Secretary of the Army to give Schine some kind of special treatment." Cohn asked what Frank Carr had said or done in the conference of October 2 that the Army complained about:

COHN. Would you tell the committee what he said, please?

STEVENS. I cannot tell you. You did most of the talking and Carr backed you up . . . in a minor . . . way.

COHN. Can you remember one word that Mr. Carr said on the subject of Schine?

STEVENS. I say in a very minor way.

McCARTHY. May I interrupt, Mr. Cohn. . . . Do I understand that you mean he backed him up by silence or backed him up by conversation? And if he backed him up by conversation then let us have the conversation.

STEVENS. Well, first of all, he did nothing to stop the conversation.

McCARTHY. . . . you make the charge one day that Frank Carr did something improper, and then you appear under oath and you say he did nothing. And then three days later you say, yes, maybe he said something, and maybe he didn't, and you don't know, and you think he did, and maybe it was his silence.

McCarthy's manner was brutal; but his point was perfectly fair.

From then on, the questions that held Secretary Stevens in the witness chair for eleven more days arose largely from events at Fort Monmouth.

Fort Monmouth was the principal research development and training center for the Signal Corps, with four main laboratories scattered over New Jersey. In this area, the Army raised its employment during World War II from 150 employees to 14,000. It employed 4,000 civilians, of whom 200 were engaged in radar work.

Among the highly skilled technicians in one laboratory were scientists drawn from a generation for whom the great formative experiences in politics had been the misery of the depression and the persecution of the Jews by Hitler. Many of them had turned, in reaction, to anti-Fascist organizations. And among them, without doubt, were some who had given their loyalty to the Soviet Union ahead of the United States. If the Soviet Union had chosen to cooperate fully with the allies in their combined war effort, it would have participated in the benefits of our science. Instead, in innate hostility and blind ambition, it stole what it might have been given and turned its well-placed followers in America into spies.

In the post-war years, as the story came to light and the public demanded action, the Truman administration began to move against this threat. The President's loyalty order of March 1947 treated present membership in the Communist Party as proof of disloyalty and grounds for expulsion from government service. Past membership in the Communist Party or its front groups was to be judged in terms of the time and the awareness of the individual involved.

The Army did not adopt these procedures. It had its own more powerful statute of 1942, by which Congress had granted to the Army the right to summarily remove any employee. Fort Monmouth of course was subject to this pattern. Its special weakness lay in its reliance on private industrial installations, where security was somewhat harder to enforce, and its subjection to an organized espionage drive led by Julius Rosenberg during World War II.

The cleaning out of the espionage ring had left at Monmouth a group of men suspected of some radical association in the past, but cleared under the terms of the existing security orders. In May 1953, however, the standards of security were revised by President Eisenhower. Under the tougher standards that he established, employees at Monmouth were due for review and some for release.

Cohn and Carr knew this. They had the names from an FBI document that had been slipped to McCarthy. Here, as in other agencies, they prepared to move in and take credit for what the department was itself about to do. Their task was made easier because Monmouth had been the subject both of a House committee inquiry and of a series of articles in the *Chicago Tribune.*

This was the material that led Roy Cohn and Frank Carr to Fort Monmouth in September, while Senator McCarthy was on his wedding trip. Soon they wired him that they had uncovered sensational evidence of espionage. McCarthy returned to conduct the inquiry in person. From secret sessions, stories were "leaked" of spy rings bigger than those involving Rosenberg and

Hiss. Willard Edwards, who had written the 1951 articles for the Chicago *Tribune,* reported on October 1 that McCarthy had discovered definite ties with the Rosenberg spy ring. Edwards added:

> The military world was shaken to the core by the realization that its latest experiments in defense against atomic attack may be known to the Russians.

In the uproar that followed, thirty-five highly placed employees were suspended. In the explosive atmosphere of Monmouth County, car pools were broken up as other men refused to be seen with the suspects. The suspects' children were persecuted in schools; milk bottles were left on porches; neighbors refused to be seen near the homes of scientists called away to prepare their defenses against charges still unknown.

Slowly the charges came partly to light. One man was charged with belonging to the Young Pioneers of America in 1933. Accusations against another apparently grew out of his attendance at a men's club meeting at which Max Lerner spoke on Israel. A third was charged with membership in a veteran's organization to which the President himself belonged. A subcommittee of the Federation of American Scientists, appointed to review the charges, concluded:

> Of over 120 charges against 19 employees which were analyzed in detail, only six involved Communist membership or affiliations, five of which were denied under oath; the sixth was an admission of attending Communist meetings with the employee's mother at the age of 12 or 13.

As the facts were developed the subcommittee staff lost interest in Fort Monmouth and made it clear to newsmen—as they did to Secretary Stevens—that they wanted to turn the investigation back to the Army itself. Stevens was content. He held a press conference to announce his course. But he did not at first reveal the actual situation at Monmouth. Some of the facts were known to two responsible reporters, Philip Potter of the *Baltimore Sun* and Murray Marder of the *Washington Post.* These two reporters, shocked by the Secretary's cover-up, led

him, in the course of 260 questions during the press conference, to concede that there was no evidence of espionage at
Monmouth.

It was this frankness that brought McCarthy back into the
picture. He claimed that Stevens was trying to conceal the
facts. So Stevens and McCarthy divided. And between the two
men was General Lawton, now looking primarily to McCarthy
for support.

With some reason Stevens considered relieving Lawton of
his command. But the Secretary moved hesitantly and asked
the Senator how he would feel—about the transfer of an officer
responsible to the Secretary alone.

Now, five months later, the case was before the subcommittee and the cameras. *Did you want the hearings suspended?* demanded Senator McCarthy. As this question was
asked sixteen times, the Secretary seemed to answer in sixteen
ways. On the fourth day McCarthy pressed an exhausted man.

> McCarthy. Now, can you tell us today whether or not you
> wanted the hearings at Fort Monmouth suspended?
> Stevens. I wanted them suspended in order that the Army
> could carry out the hearings themselves and stop the panic that
> was being created in the minds of the public on a basis that was
> not justified by the facts.
> McCarthy. How did you finally succeed in getting the
> hearings suspended?
> Stevens. How did I succeed?
> McCarthy. Yes; they are suspended as of today. How did
> you succeed?
> Stevens. They aren't suspended as far as I know.
> McCarthy. Bob, don't give me that. You know that the
> hearings were suspended the day you or someone filed your
> charges against Mr. Cohn, Mr. Carr, and myself . . . let's not be
> coy!

Secretary Stevens could only stammer that McCarthy's
charge was unfair and untrue. Very well, Senator McCarthy
had further evidence to present: Robert Stevens had punished
Kirke Lawton because the general had refused to be soft on
Communists and because he had cooperated with the sub-

committee. Choking with indignation and embarrassment, the Secretary gave an incoherent reply.

This was his worst hour. On the one issue on which he had been right, not only McCarthy but the majority of the sub-committee seemed to be against him. As for Ray Jenkins, the Tennessean accepted the McCarthy approach. He referred to all the men suspended at Monmouth as "subversives." He insisted—and got Stevens to agree—that time was of the essence in driving them out. He did not examine the question as to whether the enforcement of security at an Army post was the responsibility of the Army. He affirmed that McCarthy was the man who went in with a hose to extinguish the flames of treason while the Army was puttering around with a watering can.

For fourteen days the Secretary was held in the witness chair. At last the questions of Senator McCarthy became so repetitious and peripheral that it seemed clear that he was striving to make a farce of the hearings—and then to call them off on the grounds that they were a farce. But in retrospect the sixth day seems of particular significance. By noon on that day, it was clear that the Secretary was all in. His voice broke, tears welled up in his eyes. He could no longer stand up to the onslaught of Ray Jenkins. And when the special counsel bore down on him once more, Joseph Welch gently intervened.

> WELCH. I am informed, Mr. Jenkins, that you have tried many murder trials, and with great success. But may I remind you, my friend, that this is not a murder trial, and that you are examining the Secretary of the Army.

On the Democratic side of the table, Senators Symington, McClellan, and Jackson moved to end the Secretary's long ordeal, and Jenkins agreed. But Senator McCarthy objected.

> MCCARTHY. In view of the fact that the Secretary of the Army had made charges and asked for the discharge of two of the most competent Communist fighters I have ever been in contact with . . . I don't think that the Secretary should object to answering my questions.

But that day the Secretary had difficulty in answering even friendly questions.

When the subcommittee reconvened that afternoon, Chairman Mundt announced that the Secretary would be excused, at his own request, on grounds of exhaustion. At this Welch demurred. He whispered to his client and then replied:

> WELCH. . . . I do not make any such request. . . . Mr. Stevens wanted me to make it entirely clear that he is a member of the Army and that he would go forward if the committee required him to. . . . He would not permit me to ask for quarter. He would prefer to go on rather than see any signal flag go up of any lack of courage on his part.

The Secretary sat there, blinking and staring in front of him. Senator McCarthy complained at length, protesting, "I have no personal sympathy for this particular witness." But eventually he left it to Jenkins to decide. Jenkins waved the Secretary from the witness chair.

The Art of Mr. Welch

The spirit in the Senate Caucus Room was bright and cheery as the subcommittee reconvened on the morning of May 5. The generals who sat behind Secretary Stevens had put on their summer tans. The guards joked as they herded the crowd of spectators into the room. And through the crowd, with police in front and aides behind, came Senator McCarthy, happy and natty in a dark-blue suit and light-blue tie. Moving down the long committee table, he gripped each Senator in turn with the politician's arm-and-hand clasp. So he came to Stuart Symington of Missouri and Henry Jackson of Washington—two Democrats he had worked hard to defeat in 1952. Leaning over them with his arms around their shoulders and glancing up to see that the photographers were recording the scene, he drew discomfited smiles from them in response to his loud chuckles. Settling into his chair at the end of the table, he looked around him as a cocky batter surveys the field.

Nor was the prevalent mood broken as the hearings started. Senator McCarthy began by proposing to give Secretary Stevens a long weekend so that he could "come back Monday and start fresh." Later General Reber was excused, only to be halted by the resonant voice of Senator McCarthy as he reached the door. Only one week earlier the Senator had as-

serted that Reber's brief testimony was motivated by a desire
for revenge because McCarthy had helped drive his brother
from the government as a security risk. Now, in the name of
the entire committee, McCarthy loudly and beneficently bade
him Godspeed.

In the midst of all this good humor, only Joseph Welch
seemed to stand apart. To Senator McCarthy, Senator
Symington was "Stu," Senator Jackson "Scoop," Secretary Stevens "Bob"; and they all suffered it in silence. But Senator
McCarthy would not address the formal Bostonian as "Joe."
Two days earlier McCarthy had insinuated bad faith in claiming that Welch had "welshed" on an agreement; therefore,
when an executive session was proposed, the Army counsel
absented himself, explaining that "the Senator has said such
ungracious things about me that I prefer not to attend."

On the surface all was calm. But beneath the camaraderie
there was discernible a thread of tense and purposeful activity
on Senator McCarthy's part. As the hearings opened, he accused Senator Jackson of possessing transcripts of the telephone calls monitored by the Army. Evidently McCarthy was
attempting to determine by this device what use had been
made of these records, and if possible to control their publication. He failed—and thereupon attempted to read into the record a telegram he had sent that morning to Secretary Stevens.
Again his demand was turned down.

Then, as the day's events unfolded, the reason for the
Senator's second request became clear, and the tension of the
hearings heightened until May 5 became, of all the days that
had passed, the most extraordinary in its dramatic force.

Until that day, by the force of his personality the defend-
ant had made himself prosecutor, judge, and jury. He had
succeeded because he understood that the investigation was
not a court proceeding, where order would reign and rules of
evidence would prevail, but a vast, disorderly drama whose
plot would be shaped and whose end would be written by the
actors possessing enough power to take command of the stage.

To the extent that the subcommittee was a court, McCarthy made a poor showing as a lawyer. Of all the arts of advocacy, the highest is cross-examination; its purpose is to elicit information. In this McCarthy was wholly inept. His questions, save when Roy Cohn was using him as a transmitter, were a jumbled outpouring of verbiage. When he finished breathless, not only Stevens but Mundt and frequently McCarthy himself could not remember what question lay concealed in the snarl of his oratory.

But if Senator McCarthy tripped on occasion, he did not fall. For McCarthy, a master of trial by television, did not formulate his questions with a view to obtaining information. He formulated them to convey deadly insinuations to untrained minds transfixed before ten million television sets.

> McCARTHY. May I say, Mr. Stevens, I think that much of what has gone on here has not been your fault. I would like to know who has been shoving you into this deal . . . ?

Outwardly the other actors in the drama conveyed a sense of consciousness that they were on a stage. Everett Dirksen of Illinois held high the noble ruins of his face. Charles Potter of Michigan made admirable efforts to clarify points that were easily grasped in the Senate Caucus Room but that were difficult to comprehend in Detroit. Stuart Symington took every opportunity to rebuild in the public mind a proud image of an Army now humbled. And Karl Mundt tried harder than anyone else. He introduced new characters like a master of ceremonies at a giveaway show. He restated issues so often that reporters leaned to whisper at the start of each review: "For the benefit of those who tuned in late."

But all of these men were indicating respect for the outward aspects of theater rather than a grasp of its inner essence and central demands. Among these indecisive debaters, Joseph McCarthy worked purposefully toward his own ends.

McCarthy, ill-tempered from the first, seemed to know that he should never have permitted himself to be caught defending the privileges of the overly-indulged son of a millionaire. Yet he was also a great showman who loved a fight. And when the hearings began the showman rose in him, and he cast aside his prior assertion that this was nothing but a private feud between Roy Cohn and John Adams.

Each afternoon Joseph McCarthy appeared freshly shaved, his face caked with a cream-colored make-up which from nearby gave a startling aspect to his jowls. In the same way, Roy Cohn succeeded in projecting a public image that reporters knew to be at variance with his private self. Resting pensively as the cameras turned upon him and his master, Roy Cohn might have been molded of terra cotta, holding a bird bath on his head in some forgotten garden. No need for him to shave twice a day. He seemed rather like a cherub gone to seed: his cheeks puffed, his sensual mouth turned down at the corners, his complexion sallow, his black hair matted down, and the purses swelling under his eyes. Those who knew him knew well his rudeness and his haughty scorn. Yet the vast audience must judge far-fetched any allegation that this boy—who now spoke respectfully, with his mouth far open and his tongue laid out on his lower lip—could be the same one whom the Army charged with foul language and wild threats.

But to appeal to a vast audience this drama must be more than a show. It demanded the selection of problems, the simplification of the plot, the concentration of attention and emotion on one or two focal points. And it demanded that all issues, however obscure, be presented in language familiar in every sitting room. The other Senators spoke of anonymous security risks; McCarthy spoke of "Communists" who but for him might have destroyed the nation. The others voiced compliments or criticism; McCarthy proffered wreaths or curses. He had brought to the debate on subversion neither new information nor new ideas. He had simply taken facts gathered by Democrats, ideas formulated by Republicans, and given them terrifying force. Like Caliban in Shakespeare's *Tempest* he could cry to Republicans and Democrats:

> *You taught me language, and my profit on't*
> *Is, I know how to curse!*

In the hands of Dirksen, Potter, and McClellan, the dispute between the Army and a Senate subcommittee might

have brought a dozen bored reporters, a handful of harassed
officials, and a clump of nervous relatives to some small Senate
chamber. It was McCarthy who, giving the dispute a melo-
dramatic form, had filled the Senate Caucus Room.

On the face of it, McCarthy's case was absurd. It was that,
in the highest reaches of the Pentagon, Communist sym-
pathizers were protecting Soviet spies, and that to prevent exposure of these traitors the Republican Secretary of the Army
had attempted to blackmail, coerce, and smear McCarthy and
his staff. From such fantasies comic strips are fashioned—
and it was to the readers of comic strips that McCarthy was
talking. His voice, tense and vibrant, had the underplayed,
charged-with-emotion authority of Sky King, Captain Midnight, and all the heroes of the bedtime hour who war
ceaselessly against the forces of evil while citizens sleep, secure. Every issue McCarthy took up flamed with melodrama. If
Stevens stumbled, he was "lying"; if Welch bent over, he was
"eavesdropping"; if the Army, obedient to orders, had removed
security information from personnel files given to McCarthy,
then in McCarthy's translation this routine procedure became
a nefarious act. "We caught them stripping the files!" McCarthy said, looking at the television camera whose long nose
pointed at him. A moment later he cried to John Adams, "We
caught you redhanded!"

In all this, McCarthy and Cohn worked together as cleverly as a team of all-in wrestlers—the big one gouging and
heaving until the opponent was staggering, then climbing back
through the ropes as his little partner hopped into the ring to
pin the helpless man with a series of nimble twists. Master
though he was, McCarthy without Cohn was only half a man.
Or rather McCarthy was Caliban to Cohn's Stephano. McCarthy used words charged with explosive force. "Thief!" "Liar!"
"Traitor!" "Spy!" he cried, over and over. Cohn by contrast
seemed mild and considerate. "Now, sir, my next question is
this," he would begin. He was quick to take the blame if the
question was not understood. Cohn gave the television audience the impression that he was reasonable—while McCarthy
clawed at raw emotion. Cohn separated the audience into indi-

viduals and appealed to each. McCarthy molded them into a
mass again and exploited the barbarous instincts of the crowd.

Compared to these two masterful actors the rest who filled
the stage were like extras in a chorus. The chairman was
good-natured and ineffective. Jenkins failed early in the hearings. The Republicans asked tentative questions and winced
under McCarthy's lash. Nor was the Pentagon much better.
The reason why the audience found the drama frustrating soon
became plain. In all great dramas there must be a protagonist,
someone with whom the audience can identify itself. In this
drama the antagonist was always present, oppressive and
threatening; the audience searched desperately for some
counter-force, a hero on whom it could focus its faith and
hopes. There was none. The Secretary of the Army of the
United States lacked not only the ability to assert himself, but
a sense of the dramatic as well. *Come on! Hit me!* McCarthy
taunted the Secretary of the Army and Stevens gazed plain-
tively into McCarthy's leering face. Thus McCarthy invited
him to describe how he and the Pentagon had been manhan-
dled. Stevens declined. "Just try to tell us what you objected
to!" McCarthy insisted. Surely at that moment the whole story
could have been told to the nation in unforgettable terms. Instead, this exchange took place:

> STEVENS. I objected to the hammering over the head of the
> Army, and the unfair publicity.
> McCARTHY. You talk about "hammering over the head." It
> sounds rather rough.
> STEVENS. I think that.
> McCARTHY. Who up to that point had been hammered over
> the head?
> STEVENS. I think the *New York Times* editorial this morn-
> ing gives a pretty good picture of what I am trying to talk about
> here.

To one in a hundred thousand listeners that allusion conveyed some meaning. To the rest, it was lost. So this opportunity passed. Contemptuously McCarthy closed out the exchange: "You mean a few Communists in the Army were
hammered over the head, don't you, Bob!"

At these moments it was the job of counsel to place his client in a favorable position. This Welch failed to do. Evidently he hoped that his client's honesty would satisfy the nation, and that his disabilities were his best defense.

Beyond that, Welch himself was new to the world of security orders and loyalty checks, and still newer to the world of plots and spies. He was the son of English parents; his mother had been a domestic servant and his father had run away to join the Royal Navy at fourteen. Leaving his parents' new home in Iowa, the young man worked his way through Harvard Law School waiting on tables, selling maps and flagpoles, doing odd jobs. Now he was a senior partner of the Boston firm of Hale and Dorr. He was known to H. Struve Hensel and other Pentagon lawyers as one brilliant in jury trials and, as a lifelong Republican, he took the assignment for no fee.

"I carefully explained that I had no political experience whatever," Welch said, "and I told them I would not know how to comport myself in the presence of television and radio. It didn't seem to make much impression—they said they still wanted me to represent them."

So Welch was thrown into the Senate Caucus Room. He confessed later that he had been terrified. "So many cameras, so much television, those movies, that bank of lights, all those reporters . . . for once in our lives we felt great fear and paused at the threshold."

The truth was that in this floodlit spectacle the 27-year-old Cohn was the veteran and the 63-year-old Welch the novice. Welch knew only how to conceal his handicap. He nodded to the Senators and walked through the marble halls of the Senate Office Building in the recesses, his hands in his pockets and his toes pointed outwards. He listened courteously, head tilted, as friendly people fed him scraps of praise or advice, and he grew in understanding as the audience grew. McCarthy never forgot the vast audience; Welch seemed not to remember it. McCarthy spoke with contempt for the mob. Welch seemed to be conversing respectfully with one individual, and so he gained the audience's devotion in the end.

In the beginning, however, Welch was not of much use to

his embattled client. Only when Roy Cohn took the Secretary's
place in the witness chair did the elderly Bostonian bestir himself. It was plain that he would either poke fun at the young
man's pomposity or else treat him as a stern father would a
wayward child. Seating himself comfortably beside Cohn, the
Army counsel chose the first course.

> WELCH. Mr. Cohn, I assume you would like it understood
> that although I sit at the same table, I am not your counsel.
> COHN. There is not a statement that has been made at this
> hearing with which I am in more complete agreement. . . . Roy
> Cohn is here speaking for Roy Cohn, to give the facts. I have no
> counsel and I feel the need of none.
> WELCH. In all modesty, sir, I am content that it should
> appear from my end that I am not your counsel.

Cohn joined a little late in the laughter; and the cross-
examination continued. Welch asked for the photograph. Cohn
had argued that it was a picture of Private Schine and Secretary
Stevens smiling at each other. Now Welch suggested that Secretary Stevens was not smiling and might well be looking at
the third man, Colonel Bradley.

> WELCH. I think I observe on Colonel Bradley's face a faint
> look of pleasure. Do you, sir?
> COHN. I would say I know that Colonel Bradley had a good
> steak dinner shortly afterwards. Maybe he was anticipating it.
> . . .
> WELCH. If Bradley is feeling good about a steak dinner,
> Schine must be considering a whole haunch of beef!

There was a burst of laughter, indicating that Welch had
scored. But this was the manner of the courtroom, not the
mastery of the theater. And as the drama wound on with Secretary Stevens as its unhappy principal, Welch sat and listened,
his elbow on the table and his chin in the palm of his hand, as
distant and bemused as a senior professor listening to the
prattling of his freshman class. The veteran of the court, the
perfect Ephraim Tutt, Welch seemed ill equipped for this tele-
vised spectacle with its lawlessness and vulgarity, its mass
techniques and mob appeal. He uttered none of the brand

names of emotion on the rare occasions when he spoke.

And yet at times a rapier flashed in his hand and McCarthy found himself wounded. In these moments Welch demonstrated that he understood, if he did not admire, the popular images.

The first moment, of course, was the exchange over the cropped photograph. Welch was asking McCarthy's assistant, James Juliana, where the cropped photograph of Stevens and Schine came from. "Did you think it came from a pixie?" he asked innocently, and then McCarthy broke in:

> MCCARTHY. Will the counsel for my benefit define—I think he might be an expert on that—what a pixie is?
>
> WELCH. Yes, I should say, Mr. Senator, that a pixie is a close relative of a fairy.

McCarthy and Cohn were hurt by Welch's wicked thrust, and from then on they reserved for him a special venom. For the moment, however, McCarthy responded like any hurt fighter by flailing out with both fists. Thus he attempted to regain the initiative that he had lost. Yet he was at a disadvantage. In previous hearings of the subcommittee when he was acting as chairman, it was McCarthy who held the evidence, who alerted the press, who softened up the witness—and then exploded the charge, deftly timed for the afternoon news break. Now it was Ray Jenkins who held the Army records and who dictated the pace of the hearings. Over and over McCarthy and Cohn struggled through a morning to command the sensation of the day, only to have Jenkins cap their efforts with a fresh charge, a surprise witness, a new letter from the Attorney General or the FBI.

So it happened that McCarthy gambled a second time, seeking to regain the initiative by releasing a secret document that was both peripheral to the inquiry and dangerous to himself.

Late in the afternoon of May 4 McCarthy thrust a document marked "Copy" toward Secretary Stevens. It was, he said, "part of a series of letters from the FBI, warning of the tremendous danger of Aaron Coleman and his associates," at Fort

Monmouth. And he added, "those repeated warnings were disregarded, ignored, until this committee opened its investigation."

Welch was skeptical.

> WELCH. I would like to have Mr. J. Edgar Hoover state that he wrote the letter and mailed it. Then we'd know what we were dealing with.

But the Senator broke in:

> McCARTHY. Mr. Chairman, if Mr. Welch is going to say there's not a copy of this in the Army files, he should be sworn in because that statement is untrue as far as I know.

Curiously, Welch had not mentioned the Army files.

McCarthy hastened on to deride Secretary Stevens for refusing to read the document which bore the highest security classification of the FBI, and to criticize him because he was unaware of its existence in the Pentagon. So the day ended, with Secretary Stevens promising to track down the original of the letter and Robert Collier, an assistant to Jenkins and a former FBI man, heading down Pennsylvania Avenue to determine whether the document was real.

So the hearings of May 5 began with Secretary Stevens swearing that he had failed to find the original, and Robert Collier reporting on his journey to the FBI office. J. Edgar Hoover, he affirmed, had sent a fifteen-page memorandum to the Pentagon—but he had not sent a letter of two and a quarter pages. The paragraphs of the letter, with some deletions and changes, were taken from the memorandum. But the date was different, and the letter was "materially different in form." There were, Collier testified, seven minor differences in form, and then the major difference: the original memorandum carried the "To"-"From" form; the McCarthy document began "Sir" and ended "Sincerely yours, J. Edgar Hoover, Director," There was no identification of the typist on the copy, and no indication that other carbon copies existed. Hoover, said Collier quietly, had stated that he had neither written nor seen the letter held by McCarthy and ending with Hoover's typed name.

At that McCarthy broke in on a "point of order." All this he claimed was known to him. (He had been tipped off, he later conceded, at 11:30 the night before.) His telegram to Secretary Stevens had been to demand the "additional pages" that made up the true document. Over and over, McCarthy repeated to the television audience that the letter was a "verbatim copy," an "abbreviated form," "an accurate summary" of the real report.

Collier held before him the letter that Cohn had certified as the one an informant had given McCarthy. At the end of the table McCarthy held a copy of the same letter. The two men checked the copies to make sure they were the same; and it was apparent from differences in spacing that McCarthy's copy had, in fact, been retyped. This apparently insignificant point was a fact of potentially great significance, for the retyping of a classified document amounts legally to its "publication." Thus the episode involved a possible crime.

The tension fell, and Senator Mundt prepared to call back Secretary Stevens. Then Ray Jenkins leaned forward to announce that he would first call a surprise witness. The remark hung over the hearings until, as Collier stepped down, Jenkins called the next witness—Senator McCarthy.

Was the Senator surprised? At that moment McCarthy was studying a memorandum. With feigned indifference? No muscle moved in his face. Slowly he stirred himself to the soft-spoken demand that Senator McClellan also reveal his sources. McClellan answered angrily that he held no secrets. McCarthy shrugged his shoulders, lifted his heavy frame, and picked his way through the reporters to the witness chair where he had held Secretary Stevens a prisoner over nine days.

He took the oath that some had sworn he would not take; and the first question was asked. The witness mumbled; the microphone was pushed closer to his lips. Then he was talking, and it was evident that he was addressing not ten million Americans but his little private army of informers in the federal government.

McCARTHY. I want to notify the people who give me information that there is no way on earth that any committee, any force, can get me to violate the confidence of these people.

McCarthy continued by equating an executive department which gathered information as part of its enforcement of the laws, and himself, a legislator, holding a document that he had no right to possess.

> McCARTHY. May I say that this is the rule which every investigative agency follows. Mr. J. Edgar Hoover insists that no informants be disclosed and brought up in public. They will not be brought out today.

A young patriot had given him the letter, McCarthy added, one whose "duty to his country was above any duty to any Truman directive." His voice rose in pitch until in his excitement and confusion he addressed the startled Ray Jenkins as "Mr. Welch."

From then on McCarthy's testimony was uncertain and confused. The Republicans handled him gingerly. Jenkins in his malaprop manner revealed that McCarthy had given the secret document to him, and that he, McCarthy, and Cohn had all used it in further harassing the bewildered Secretary of the Army. At last it was Welch's turn. Seated in the chair recently vacated by McCarthy, he leaned on his elbow, dapper in a brown suit and green bow tie, his face crossed with purplish veins, his finger crooked on his cheek, his brows furrowed as he looked with an air of unbelief at the witness.

Through the smoky brilliance of the floodlights, McCarthy glared back. He too crouched over the table, waiting, and looked sideways at the Army counsel. A roll of flesh beneath his black eyebrows came down over his upper eyelids, making slits of his eyes, and giving to his face an almost Satanic look.

Slowly the two men circled and closed.

> WELCH. Senator McCarthy, when you took the stand you knew of course that you were going to be asked about this letter, did you not?
>
> McCARTHY. I assumed that would be the subject.
>
> WELCH. And you, of course, understood that you were going to be asked the source from which you got it. . . .

McCARTHY. . . . I won't answer that. . . .

WELCH. Could I have the oath that you took read to us wholly by the reporter?

MUNDT. Mr. Welch, that doesn't seem to be an appropriate question. . . . it's the same oath you took.

WELCH. The oath included a promise, a solemn promise by you to tell the truth and nothing but the truth. Is that correct, sir?

McCARTHY. Mr. Welch, you are not the first individual that tried to get me to betray the confidence and give out the names of my informants. You will be no more successful than those who have tried it in the past.

WELCH. I am only asking you, sir, did you realize when you took the oath that you were making a solemn promise to tell the truth to this committee?

McCARTHY. I understand the oath, Mr. Welch.

WELCH. And when you took it did you have some mental reservation, some Fifth or Sixth Amendment notion that you could measure what you would tell?

McCARTHY. I don't take the Fifth or Sixth Amendment.

WELCH. Have you some private reservation when you take the oath that you will tell the whole truth that lets you be the judge of what you will testify to?

McCARTHY. The answer is that there is no reservation about telling the whole truth.

WELCH. Thank you, sir. Then tell us who delivered the document to you!

McCARTHY. The answer is no. You will not get the information.

WELCH. You wish then to put your own interpretation on your oath and tell us less than the whole truth?

McCARTHY. . . . you can go right ahead and try until doomsday. You will not get the names of any informants who rely upon me to protect them.

WELCH. . . . will you tell us where you were when you got it?

McCARTHY. No.

WELCH. Were you in Washington?

McCARTHY. The answer was I would not tell you.

WELCH. How soon after you got it did you show it to anyone.

McCARTHY. I don't remember.

WELCH. To whom did you first show it?

McCARTHY. I don't recall.

WELCH. Can you think of the name of anyone to whom you showed it?

McCARTHY. Oh, I assume that it was passed down to my staff most likely.

WELCH. Name the ones on your staff who had it!

McCARTHY. I wouldn't know.

WELCH. . . . You wouldn't know?

McCARTHY. No.

WELCH. Would it include Mr. Cohn?

McCARTHY. It might.

WELCH. It would, wouldn't it?

McCARTHY. I said it might.

WELCH. Would it include Mr. Carr?

McCARTHY. It might.

Next Welch established that the document belonged to the subcommittee. So, if the subcommittee voted to obtain the name of the informant, Senator McCarthy would be bound by its decision. At that Everett Dirksen intervened to pull McCarthy out of his own trap. Still better for McCarthy, Ray Jenkins saved him from a possible citation for contempt of Congress by ruling that he could protect his sources of information because he was a "law enforcing officer . . . ferreting out crime." This incredible ruling granted McCarthy's whole claim to a share of the law enforcement powers of the executive branch. Yet, if McCarthy's peril was passed, the damage was done. Once again the Army counsel had shown a matchless dramatic sense. Before twenty million Americans he had led McCarthy to behave in the same manner as surly witnesses before his own committee. McCarthy had taught the nation to despise those witnesses, branding them "Fifth Amendment Communists" for their refusal to tell what they knew. What was the nation now to infer? Whether or not he understood fully the profundity of his action, Joseph Welch had penetrated to the heart of the matter. In the deepest and most classical sense McCarthy was a revolutionary. And now the likeness was exposed to millions to whom it could never have been explained.

As if to confirm Welch's point, Senator McCarthy from then on acted in a reckless manner. He began the next morning by asserting that General Zwicker had lied under oath. He next

accused Secretary Stevens of trying to block his investigations
of Communism by prolonging the hearings. Slowly he regained
control of himself, and then at noon Robert Collier read out a
new letter, from Attorney General Brownell. It held that
McCarthy's "FBI" letter "constituted an unauthorized use of
information which it classified as confidential," and forbade its
publication.

Caught in one possible law violation, the acceptance of
stolen documents, McCarthy now promised to commit
another—the unauthorized release of the information he possessed. He denounced the letter "allegedly from Mr. Brownell."
He cried that no "Truman directive" or any other directive
would prevent him from publishing secrets. He claimed that
no Congressional committee was bound by any ruling of a
member of the executive branch; now, he insisted, was the
time to test it, because he had promised the voters in the 1952
campaign that, once elected, a Republican Congress "would no
longer be honoring blackout orders." So he incited his colleagues to rebellion, demanding that they determine "once for
all . . . whether or not we are the lackeys to obey—afraid to
overrule—a decision made by someone in the executive department."

But the "someone" was the nation's highest legal officer.
And to justify his defiance of constitutional authority it was
necessary for McCarthy to carry the whole controversy beyond
the outer boundaries of reason. He cried that Brownell released
files about dead spies while he himself was concerned with live
ones, who were "poised with a razor over the jugular vein of
this nation." He added, "We have no secrets from the Communists as far as the A- and H-bombs are concerned." He cried,
"I am getting very, very weary of sitting here and acting as
though we're playing some little game! This committee, this
committee's activities may well determine whether this nation will live or die!" So he claimed for the committee all of the
executive's functions. His voice rose like a siren, winding and
grinding upwards until it became a shrill monotonous whine.
Then, close to hysteria, the happy and natty man of the previous morning seemed truly like the wild Caliban, crying:

For every trifle are they set upon me:
Sometimes like apes, that mow and chatter at me
And after bite me; . . . sometimes am I
All wound with adders, who with cloven tongues
Do hiss me into madness.

In contrast, for a man who had seemed a little disconsolate on the morning of May 5, Welch was now all smiles.

"Sir," said one of a group of reporters as the hearing ended, "how will all this affect your work in Boston?"

"Perhaps," he answered, "I shall become so famous in the course of these hearings that I won't have to work ever again!"

The Employment of Mr. Adams

On the fourteenth day of the hearings Secretary Stevens developed a fever. He sat in the Caucus Room after his counsel announced that he was under a doctor's care, protesting feebly that he could go on. But Welch asked that he be excused, and there was no objection. The issue of adjournment was before the committee, and in his desire to call an end to the hearings not even McCarthy demanded the loyalty file of the doctor who had prescribed penicillin. So the little manufacturer took his fever home and watched the hearings on his television set.

John Adams, Counselor to the Department of the Army, was now called to the witness chair. He was so well groomed that one observer compared him to a floor walker. Many times the television cameras had caught him smiling and shaking his head as Senator McCarthy and Roy Cohn recounted their stories in the form of questions to Secretary Stevens. But now he looked drawn and pale. "If Stevens needed penicillin when they finished with him," said one reporter, "Adams will need a blood transfusion!"

Prompted by Ray Jenkins, Adams told his story. At the end of the first morning he concluded:

ADAMS. If you would pile together all of the abuse that I

had from all of the other members of Congress and all of the other Congressional employees over a period of five years it would not compare to the abuse that I took over this situation.
    JENKINS. The abuse from whom?
    ADAMS. From Mr. Cohn.

What was John Adams's part in this drama, and why did he have to take such abuse? Perhaps the best answer was given three centuries before, when in the end of another tragedy, Hamlet described to his friend Horatio the fate of Rosencrantz and Guildenstern.

They were two courtiers—faithful to whatever king they served. Their deaths served no purpose of Hamlet's. But to the protesting Horatio, Hamlet answered:

> *Why, man, they did make love to this employment!*
> *They are not near my conscience; their defeat*
> *Does by their own insinuation grow.*

John Adams was a good and faithful courtier, playing the same role.

There were many Democrats skilled in this profession after twenty years in office, and very few Republicans. Among the few was a young lawyer who had supported his family from adolescence, when his father died. Adams had been brought to Washington as the secretary of a South Dakota Republican, Senator Chan Gurney. He had returned from three years of combat to become chief clerk of the Senate Armed Services Committee through the Republican Eightieth Congress, an attorney-advisor to the Secretary of Defense, and finally Deputy General Counsel of the Army. In September 1953 Secretary Stevens picked Adams as the man to handle the McCarthy subcommittee. He knew the chairman by reputation. He knew that the Democrats had left the committee with justifiable complaints. He knew that a powerful member of the committee was Karl Mundt, who had no affection for Chan Gurney's protégés.

He knew also that the Republican National Committee looked on the job of liaison with McCarthy as one of great

importance. So Adams took the job on October 1. By then, as
was later proved, Secretary Stevens had made vague promises
to G. David Schine which the Army could not keep. It was John
Adams who had to break these promises—promises of some
ill-defined post for Schine following his basic training—and
Cohn, as Secretary Stevens noted, was "tremendously interested in David Schine."

The qualities that are demanded of the liaison man—the
courtier of 1954 in the kingdom of Washington—are several.
He must be anonymous by instinct, self-effacing in nature,
long trained in conciliation, and well disciplined in subordinat-
ing his own prejudices and opinions in order to get along with
all types of men. These were the qualities that equipped John
Adams for his assignment, and they are caricatured, but not
disputed in essence, by the McCarthy-Cohn-Carr brief. Adams
was accused by the three men of "using every effort to in-
gratiate himself personally with the subcommittee personnel,"
of trying to "handle the committee," of being a "close personal
and social" friend of Cohn, and of endeavoring to maintain this
friendship long after he allegedly complained of the intolerable
abuse heaped on him by his young companion. Of course! That
was Adams' job! Over and over, in his own words, John Adams
conceded in his testimony that he made the overtures, tried "a
little placating or conciliation," attempted to "get back in good
with Mr. Cohn."

Ray Jenkins apparently was staggered by the courtier's be-
havior. "Wasn't it for the purpose of appeasing Mr. Cohn?" he
demanded harshly. And Adams murmured, "It was living with
people."

If John Adams had possessed the qualities of the courtier
and nothing more, he might have survived unscathed. Unfortunately, in the manner of Shakespeare's courtiers, he was inclined to talk too much, to be flippant, to do a little intriguing
on his own. Far more important than these minor faults was
the major truth—that living with Cohn and McCarthy required
more than the courtier's art.

At first, Adams recalled, relations were very friendly. He
handled the privileges won for Schine in late October, when

Roy Cohn was calling two or three times a day on his friend's
behalf. He followed Cohn and McCarthy into the men's room
at Fort Monmouth, and prevented Cohn's anger from causing
an early break. He arranged the luncheon of November 6 in the
Pentagon to talk about Fort Monmouth, and he kept the Monmouth hearings on a friendly basis. Thanks to his work, the
subcommittee turned over the transcripts of its executive hearings to the Army, and let Army representatives attend.

John Adams had strong feelings about wrecking the lives
of innocent men at Monmouth, as he later testified. To express
them at the time was not his role. His role was to be friendly;
and it was only the status of David Schine, Adams recounted,
that "caused the degeneration of an otherwise very friendly
relationship" between Roy Cohn and himself. For as Schine
was pressed into the military mold by his field commanders,
Roy Cohn interpreted each change as "a double cross."

At last Adams told Senator McCarthy that he could stand
no more abuse. Soon after that conversation, Roy Cohn
phoned.

> ADAMS. He said he would teach me what it meant to go
> over his head. I said to him, "Roy, is that a threat?" He said, "No,
> that's a promise." . . . he made quite a point of the fact that . . . I
> could only talk to him.

Early in December, Schine's schedule of basic training was
changed by his officers at Fort Dix. Roy Cohn, said Adams,
called to denounce this "Stevens double cross."

> ADAMS. This was as difficult as any of the telephone con-
> versations I had. I would state that the extreme pressure, abu-
> sive pressure and very, very abusive criticism of Mr. Stevens was
> generated in this telephone call.
> JENKINS. Mr. Adams, was there any abusive language used
> toward you at that time?
> ADAMS. . . . these telephone calls . . . were extremely abu-
> sive and they were very obscene.

Later Roy Cohn denied this. But another witness, Colonel
BeLieu, testified that Cohn's language was "a little lower than a
mule skinner's," and those few who saw the unexpurgated ver-

sion of the Army's first Chronology of Events will agree.

On the steps of the courthouse at Foley Square, on December 17, Senator McCarthy stood waiting for John Adams. He was disturbed by the actions of his staff—as he himself testified—and now:

> ADAMS. Senator McCarthy stated to me that . . . he wished to tell me that as of then and now it was through, it was to cease, he was not going to permit it any more.

That day, when the hearings recessed, Adams, McCarthy, Cohn, and Carr went to lunch. All of them later agreed that a bitter quarrel broke out.

> ADAMS. . . . Because I wanted Senator McCarthy to restate before Mr. Cohn what he had told me on the courthouse steps, I said, "Let's talk about Schine."
> That started a turn of events similar to none which I have had in my life. Mr. Cohn was extremely agitated and became extremely abusive first to me, and then to Senator McCarthy. . . . it went in waves. He would be very abusive . . . and then it would abate and everybody would eat a little bit more and then it would start in again.
> JENKINS. . . . Was there not any obscene language used?
> ADAMS. Yes.
> JENKINS. Well, do you remember the subject?
> ADAMS. The subject was Schine. . . . the thing that Cohn was so violent about was the fact that the Army was not agreeing to an assignment for Schine and that Senator McCarthy was not supporting his stand. . . . His abuse was directed partly to me and partly to Senator McCarthy. . . . At first Senator McCarthy seemed to be trying to conciliate Cohn and not to state anything contrary to what he'd stated to me in the morning. But then he more or less lapsed into silence.

On the claim of improper pressure, Adams' testimony was convincing. But the Army claimed more, and Adams had yet to prove that the subcommittee's investigations of the Army were shaped by the Army's treatment of Schine.

First Adams described the less convincing story of January 13 when once again Secretary Stevens took the undignified step of lobbying at the Capitol, and Adams went to warn Cohn that 80 percent of draftees were sent overseas.

> ADAMS. I asked [Cohn] what would happen if Schine got
> overseas duty, and he responded with vigor and force, "Stevens
> is through as Secretary of the Army."
> I said . . . , "Come on, really, what is going to happen?"
> And he responded with even more force, "We'll wreck the
> Army!"
> Then he said, "The first thing we are going to do is get
> General Ryan for the way he has treated Dave at Fort Dix. . . .
> We're not going to do it ourselves. We've got another committee
> interested. And then he said, "I wouldn't put it past you to do
> this. . . . we'll start investigations. We've got enough stuff on the
> Army to keep investigations going indefinitely and if anything
> like such a double-cross occurs that's what we'll do."

"I wouldn't put it past you. . . ." The single phrase implies
that Cohn took the hint as a threat. Cohn claimed that he did,
and that Adams angered him by seeming to use Schine as a
lever. In his own defense, Adams was able to show that he had
honestly erred in supposing that Schine was due for early transfer overseas—a view Cohn knew to be mistaken.

John Adams was far more persuasive in describing the final
break with Cohn on January 18, 1954. On that day Roy Cohn
was enjoying life in Florida at the Boca Raton Hotel and Club,
of which G. David Schine was president and general manager.
Adams told Carr of the Army's schedule for Private Schine at
Camp Gordon, Georgia. Soon after, Cohn telephoned Adams
for the full story. It was not new to him.

> ADAMS. He asked me to repeat to him what I'd told Mr.
> Carr with reference to the future of Schine, and when I did so it
> was obvious to me he was very upset.
> I asked him if he intended to continue his vacation in
> Florida . . . he said . . . , "How can I when this has happened
> . . . ?"
> On the following morning, the 19th, I received a telephone
> call from Mr. Carr requesting the appearance of certain mem-
> bers of the Army Loyalty and Security Appeal Board for ques-
> tioning by the Committee. I objected very strenuously. . . .
> I asked him why it happened and he said that there was
> nothing he could do about it, that Mr. Cohn had returned the

night before at 8:50 P.M. from Florida which was just six-and-
one-half hours after he talked to me on the telephone from Boca
Raton. . . .

To the Army, Cohn's decision amounted to a declaration
of war.

> ADAMS. This was a matter of vital importance to the Army.
> The boards are quasi-judicial in nature and they have somewhat
> the function of an appellate court. The Army always felt that to
> subject their actions to review by other bodies would be similar
> to requiring a judge to appear before a legislature to explain the
> reasons for his decision.
> We knew that the performance of these difficult tasks
> would be jeopardized and objectivity would be lost if there was
> even a remote possibility of a board member having to appear
> and explain the reasons behind his decision.

The Secretary of the Army was in the Pacific; so Adams
went to H. Struve Hensel, general counsel of the Defense Department. Hensel sent him on to see William Rogers, Deputy
Attorney General. Adams insisted that the Army could not act
alone, and so on January 21 Rogers called together a conference
of decisive importance.

The meeting was held in the Attorney General's office, and
there were present Herbert Brownell, William Rogers, Sherman
Adams, Gerald Morgan, and Henry Cabot Lodge, then attached
to the White House. The group was concerned with legal
precedent—and much more. Brownell was the leader who had
directed Mr. Eisenhower's nomination and election; Lodge had
been the first spokesman of the Eisenhower movement and
was still a Senate power. Sherman Adams, the "Deputy President," was the man who executed the domestic tasks of the
Presidency day by day; William Rogers was the administration's spokesman in resisting or appeasing McCarthy. Until
that time administration policy had been to deal with McCarthy behind closed doors. That policy was reaffirmed at the
meeting on January 21; but Sherman Adams advised John
Adams, as a precaution, to prepare a written documentation of
his long ordeal.

The January 21 meeting shifted the whole basis of the

conflict between Stevens and McCarthy. The revelation of this meeting fifteen weeks later came so quietly upon the Senate Caucus Room that it passed unnoticed. Soon it would send the hearings off in a new direction, but for the moment the Senators listened without stirring. McCarthy showed no sign of interest, and John Adams continued his story; thus he came to the Army charge that the McCarthy side had made offers of a trade.

The first offer, if Adams was to be believed, came not from Cohn directly but from Cohn's close friend, George Sokolsky. He was the Hearst philosopher, and his intervention was not unusual, since he and the Hearst apparatus had proved helpful to McCarthy in providing investigators, receiving leaks, and publishing stories which—as in the case of the Voice of America—formed the basis for subsequent investigations by McCarthy. It was George Sokolsky who had brought Cohn and McCarthy together.

Cohn, a good lawyer, would certainly have made no offers of a trade. But, Adams testified, Frank Carr urged him many times during January and February to call Sokolsky. So five days after Private Schine arrived at Camp Gordon, Adams took Carr's advice.

> ADAMS. On the fifth of February I called Mr. Sokolsky . . . we talked forty-nine minutes. . . . Mr. Sokolsky pointed out to me that . . . there was a Course 95 which was ready to start very shortly and that Schine wanted to get into it. . . .

Course 95 was the Criminal Investigation Department School which Private Schine was not entitled to apply for until he had completed another eight weeks of basic training. But Adams continued:

> ADAMS. He suggested that I get Schine assigned to Course 95 and he said . . . , "I'll see if I can't . . . soften this pressure on the Army that's coming from Senator McCarthy."

A week passed, during which, Adams testified, Frank Carr urged him many times to call Sokolsky again.

> ADAMS. He [Carr] pointed out to me that if . . . he

[Sokolsky] isn't consulted he gets mad, and he said, "He's got a great deal of influence with the Senator," and he said, "You ought to talk to him. You ought to talk to him."

. . . So I called Sokolsky again on the twelfth of February.

. . . We talked for a long time again. . . . Mr. Sokolsky said to me that if we would assign Schine to Course 95 he would move in and stop this investigation of the Army.

According to John Adams, the task of trading fell to Frank Carr when Sokolsky failed. The staff director called Adams many times in March in an effort to halt the drift toward an open break. They met at a quiet place for lunch.

ADAMS. A great part of the luncheon was given over to conversation with reference to Schine. Mr. Carr stated to me as he had on numerous other occasions that he felt that I should understand that as long as the assignment for Schine was not satisfactory to Mr. Cohn the Army was in for continued trouble. . . . He had no personal interest in Schine. He made that clear. But if he could give me advice in a friendly way his advice would be: You take care of this matter and we will get these investigations off your neck.

But no trade was agreed upon, either for Course 95 or for a more permanent assignment to New York. Why not, Senator McClellan demanded of the courtier; Adams gently pointed out that he was bound by very large considerations.

ADAMS. Well, I guess as good a reason as any was that we had—25,000 men killed in Korea who didn't have the money or the influence to get themselves a New York assignment.

Why, man, they did make love to this employment!
They are not near my conscience . . .

The point was still true. John Adams, in the witness chair, seemed the archetype of subordinate officials, overburdened, underpaid, obedient to directives—and now stretched out on the rack for the errors of those he served. "I was hounded and hounded and pounded and pounded," he said. Few could doubt it. Yet the same people whose hearts had gone out to Secretary Stevens lacked sympathy for the man who suffered most for the Secretary's mistakes. Stevens was the amateur who never saw the pits into which he fell; Adams was the professional who knew the pits and yet made love to this employment. Stevens was the child lost in the dark forest of Washington, Adams the denizen of the forest who knew its secret places where, at the approach of the marauder, the hunted hide.

The time for cross-examination came, and first the counsel for the inquiry repeated the clumsy ceremony of "Putting on his other hat." John Adams remained good-natured and calm while the Tennessean shuffled round him with all the grace of a bear attempting to grasp a bee.

First Jenkins spent a half-hour attempting to make Adams admit that he had been "indifferent" to what happened at Monmouth. When Adams agreed, in order to speed the inquiry, that he had been "indifferent," the Tennessean spent the next half-hour upbraiding him for admitting that he was "utterly indifferent" when obviously he could not have been. Next Jenkins attempted to break down the Army counselor by intimidation as a mountain farmer might be broken in a city trial. He accused Adams of trying to buy off Senator McCarthy. "You know that's the truth!" he cried. "It is not," said Adams quietly but firmly.

At last, late in the third day of the counselor's testimony, McCarthy's turn arrived.

"Just a few questions," McCarthy said—"or maybe a few hundred," he muttered in a good-natured aside to Frank Carr. Still in good humor he took full responsibility for summoning the members of the Army's loyalty board. Next he pressed Adams to say, not what Cohn had threatened, but what he had *done.* It was a powerful shaft aimed at Adams, at the end of a tiring day. Adams thought for a moment and mentioned the single incident of the subpoenas. McCarthy brushed this aside and ordered Adams to name another. There was a long moment of silence. "I don't at the moment recall specific incidents," said Adams weakly. McCarthy leaned back grinning, and said, "Roy Cohn!"

Never was the young prosecutor better than when he looked, smiling and demure, at his detractor. He did not review

the acts with which he was charged—and wisely. He left it to
the vast audience to ask: How could one so deferential have
threatened to wreck the Army? How could one so polite have
shouted obscene curses? For those who might miss the point,
Cohn gently rubbed it in, and in doing so subtly attacked the
credibility of his enemy. "Didn't I call your aunts in Brooklyn
when you asked me?" he inquired. "Didn't I get the theater
tickets for you that no one else could get? Didn't I arrange the
little theater party at Sardi's at your request?" "You were always very gracious about that, you always were," murmured
Adams, whose face by now seemed drained of blood. And all
this after I cursed you and abused you? inquired Cohn. The
witness sighed.

> ADAMS. When we had difficulties ... it would ebb and
> flow....
> COHN. I see. ... During the ebb do you think you might
> have asked me to get those theater tickets for you?
> ADAMS. It is conceivable.
> COHN. I see. Did you cancel the order during the flow?

It was exquisite, a brilliant legal tour de force. Adams
stared in silence at the table before him. He must have suffered
something of the fate of Rosencrantz and Guildenstern while
at the side of his young tormentor the heavy shoulders of
Joseph McCarthy and Frank Carr shook in silent laughter.

The Sanctimony of Senator Dirksen

A path was opened in the crowd, the cameras turned toward the doors, and into the Senate Caucus Room on the morning of May 11 marched the man for whom ten million Americans were waiting—Everett Dirksen. His hair as usual was carefully mussed. A herd of scarlet and white elephants tramped up and down his shirt-front on a black tie. In his breast pocket he wore a handkerchief folded with precision and bearing in blue embroidery the initial 'D'. In the side pocket of his grey suit he carried a motion. "The reason for the motion," Senator Dirksen explained later, "was to ring down the curtain" on the hearings, now in their fourteenth day.

The first concerted drive to close down the hearings had developed a week before under the leadership of the same Senator. On that occasion the Republican majority had sat down comfortably in the assurance that an agreement to close had been reached the night before. But Welch upset the plan by announcing that the agreement was not acceptable to the Army side. "We must," he said, "plow the long hard furrow." "To the bitter end," added Chairman Mundt, who conducted himself on that morning with wisdom and dignity. So all the Senators had settled down in resignation—all save Senator McCarthy, who, furious, charged that Welch had "welshed," and, in near-hysteria, employed for the first time his colorful simile about spies, razor blades, and jugular veins.

For two days now a new plan had been in the making. Discussion of the first draft had taken half of the previous day—and no decision had been reached. Its terms in closing out debate were too extreme, and after Senator Dirksen tried unsuccessfully to transfer its consideration to a secret session it was rejected publicly by Mr. Welch. By mid-morning of May 11 the new draft had been prepared; the cue was given, the Senator began. His voice, a masterpiece of the elocutionist's art, rose up from his diaphragm through thick neck muscles and a loose mouth. First he explained why he was an hour late.

> DIRKSEN. Mr. Chairman . . . , there is so much work to be accomplished that I just find it almost impossible in the space of an eighteen-hour day to get around to everything. Then sometimes my feeble talents are not too facile in seeking to interpret viewpoints and human reactions when it comes to language.

But it came to language at last, and the language was to cut off all public testimony and to limit secret testimony to rebuttal—to such rebuttal as Senator McCarthy cared to invite by pressing new charges in the course of his closing remarks.

The Republicans seemed drawn to the suggestion like flies to molasses. The three Democrats were less enthralled. When the chairman asked them to reflect that they had better things to do than hold the Secretary of the Army a prisoner in the Senate Caucus Room, McClellan aptly remarked that if McCarthy's charges were true, Stevens could do a lot less harm to the nation there than in the Pentagon.

The unhappy majority attempted to defend itself. Dworshak spoke of "the circus," Potter of "this public brawl." In three long speeches Mundt predicted that if they were not cut short now the hearings would go on "many long melancholy weeks," "two months," "until the fourth of July," "ad nauseam," and "indefinitely." Very quietly, McClellan suggested that the principals be consulted. Mundt was reluctant, but the Secretary of the Army broke in. The people, he said, were entitled to watch the other side testify as they had watched him. Mundt was appalled. He had made it plain that he would oppose the resolution if one of the principals felt it did violence to justice and equity; he now added that any such principal would bear the responsibility on his own shoulders. He begged every man to commune with his soul during the lunch hour.

The lunch hour passed and the hearings reconvened. Almost at once the vote was taken. Senator Dworshak was in favor of the resolution, of course—the forthright Czech had never concealed his impatience to call off the hearings and get back to his work. Senator Dirksen and Senator Potter were for the motion. The three Democrats voted "No."

Next the principals were polled. The first was the lawyer for H. Struve Hensel, who seemed agreeable to the proposal. The next was Joseph McCarthy. He had earlier expressed the hope that the Senators were smarting from these hearings, and now he added that he would be happy to cut the hearings short.

At last all but Secretary Stevens were accounted for. The Secretary had gone home ill, and so the chairman looked imploringly at Welch. But Welch murmured that his client had not changed his mind.

All through the morning the chairman had held the feet of the feverish man to the fire. Through the lunch hour and long before, Secretary of Defense Wilson, Deputy Secretary Fred Seaton, and other top leaders of Stevens' party had argued with him to give in. Senator Dirksen had brought in his motion in the belief that the President would see to it that Stevens went along. But Stevens had refused to retreat. Now Chairman Mundt sent Welch out to telephone the Secretary, and the Bostonian walked through the crowd and down the marble halls, fishing in his pocket for a dime. He returned at once, and was sent a second time by the unhappy chairman. Both times he returned to report meekly but firmly that the Secretary's answer was still the same. The chairman kept his word, and the Dirksen resolution was defeated by his vote.

So the hearings continued, with John Adams in the witness chair. As Adams approached the events of late January, Senator Dirksen again became restive. The three Republican Senators of the subcommittee had evidence to give on the events of that time.

But what embarrassing evidence to give in mid-May! The three had been part of the McCarthy apparatus in January, and the apparatus had been regarded as an asset by the Republican high command. Now the break was evident, and they were caught in the most painful of positions—in between.

For Dirksen it was no new position. For he had been on more sides of more issues than any man in Washington since he had come to Congress from the county seat of Pekin, Illinois.

In the thirties Dirksen had survived the Roosevelt election landslides by becoming an advocate of the New Deal. He backed the Wagner Act and other basic measures demanded by President Roosevelt, and when Roosevelt's reforms were halted by the Supreme Court, Dirksen was for Roosevelt and the NIRA, proclaiming "constitutionality is no match for compassion." His sympathies were such that the leading Democrats rose to acclaim him when he left the House. Ten years later, however, he saw nothing but socialism in the measures he had fought to enact.

In the same manner, Dirksen was an isolationist in foreign policy in 1935, strongly opposing Roosevelt's first moves for adequate defense. In 1936 he reversed himself and advocated a "large and adequate defense establishment." In 1939 he was back in opposition to new defense measures such as the strengthening of fortifications on Guam. In 1940 he cried, "Thank God there is a national defense program under way!" He opposed compulsory military training, but backed the rest of Roosevelt's policies in 1941. Then, when the outraged Colonel McCormick berated Dirksen in the *Chicago Tribune*, he again reversed himself. To the horror of the *Tribune*, he supported the Marshall Plan in 1948. Then in 1949 (when Thomas E. Dewey had lost) he reversed himself again and denounced the Marshall Plan for "throwing money down into a bottomless pit." Of General Marshall himself Dirksen once said, "Thank

God we have leadership like that." Not long after, he was allied with Joseph McCarthy, who denounced Marshall as one of the greatest villains in American history.

On the morning of May 12, Dirksen testified first.

"Do you solemnly swear?" inquired Chairman Mundt. And nothing certainly could have been more solemn than the Honorable Everett McKinley Dirksen holding his right hand up in silhouette against the floodlights. He then began:

> DIRKSEN. Mr. Chairman, let me just say . . . for the benefit . . . of those who may be watching this proceeding that there arrived at my office about 2,500 letters and telegrams today. Some of them are so intemperate and so abusive and so unrestrained that my office force is afraid they might affect my finer sensibilities and they don't even show them to me. It would occur . . . that I have been charged with being belligerently partial to one side or the other.

Heaven forbid! With the injured and innocent air of a schoolboy falsely accused of stealing jam, Senator Dirksen told his story.

Three times he swore that when Mr. Adams and Gerald Morgan of the White House visited him on January 22, that was the first he knew of any trouble. By that time the controversy between the subcommittee staff and the Army had raged for four months. It had been raised during public hearings and in private meetings. It had preoccupied the Secretary of the Army and shaped the subcommittee's course if the Army was right. But Dirksen knew nothing of all this and felt no responsibility for the actions carried on in his name. His responsibility, he explained, was to take "judicial notice" when the charges were breaking into the public view. At that point, as he admitted, he became concerned.

> DIRKSEN. The thing that stuck in my mind mainly was not pressure but . . . an alleged effort to secure preferred treatment for a private which certainly would not look good on the front page and might enmesh every member of this subcommittee if it could be established and that we might find ourselves charged with . . . neglect of duty.

So, he testified, he called the subcommittee together and told its members—Senators McCarthy, Potter, and Mundt—that if the charges were true Cohn should be fired to keep the dispute from becoming a public scandal; and for good measure John Adams should be fired as well.

Now came the cross-examination. Senator McCarthy pressed the unhappy Dirksen as far as he could in undermining John Adams. Soon it was Welch's turn. Senator Dirksen was no man to say "could be" if "peradventure" would do as well, and Welch's vocabulary was at least as good. Armed with prose forgotten since the time of Carlyle, the two portly gentlemen circled in a solemn waltz, smiling sweetly as they tramped deliberately on each other's toes.

Next it was the time for Chairman Mundt to testify. He too was sworn, so that he might describe the visit of John Adams on January 22. Senator Mundt did not claim that the story of the dispute came to him as a shocking surprise. The privileges granted to Private Schine had been discussed for a month in the press, and the story was well known to the South Dakotan in January. The Senator added that he had supported on principle the action of Joseph McCarthy in issuing the subpoenas for the members of the Army's loyalty board and that he had told Adams just what the Army should do.

> MUNDT. I do recall . . . saying this: that if I were running the United States Army there would be no problem with me at all after the second time a committee staff member called me up. I would tell him from that time, "I am running the Army, you run your committee" and I wouldn't talk with him on the subject one additional time.
>
> I pointed out further that, speaking for myself, as a member of this committee, Dave Schine was just another John American. . . . they could put him—and I think I used this phrase—on KP duty for the rest of his natural life as far as I was concerned.

What brave advice to give the Army on January 22! How much better it might have been three months before!

The third to testify was Senator Potter of Michigan. He was a young man of thirty-seven, who had taken up social work when he left his state's Normal College and entered the

Army as a private in 1942. In the forests of Colmar, shrapnel fired by the retreating Germans tore off both his legs. Now each morning he worked his painful way through the crowded chairs, always with a pleasant smile. Of the Republicans on the subcommittee, Potter was the most independent of McCarthy, and it was he who, at Vice President Nixon's request, had touched off the public dispute by sending his written request for the John Adams file.

Charles Potter was the most persuasive of the three Republicans. He testified that he had known of the "considerable effort . . . on the part of Mr. Cohn to secure preferential treatment for Mr. Schine." He conceded by his silence that he had made no move to review the subcommittee's course.

There was, the three Republicans knew, a Presidential directive in force, forbidding executive officials to answer questions on loyalty and security matters. Senator McCarthy had ordered that the Pentagon board members appear to answer questions on matters including personal graft and corruption. Dirksen, Mundt, and Potter might well have inquired what evidence their subcommittee possessed to justify the grave and damaging step of singling out these few men from among two million civil servants. But they knew, of course, that McCarthy's real intent was to question the board on forbidden matters of loyalty; he had long made it plain that this was his purpose. And any other purpose would have served to prove the Army's contention that his action was motivated by Roy Cohn's desire for revenge. All three men held that the loyalty board officials should come but then refuse to answer questions about their work. Yet they must have known that at Fort Monmouth, McCarthy had summoned loyalty officials on extraneous issues and then cross-examined them about loyalty files. Knowing their chairman, they must have anticipated that any member of the Army's board might suddenly be told: "State whether or not it was the Communist Party that ordered you to reinstate Aaron Hyman Coleman at the secret radar base!" The refusal of the board member to answer this one question would have provided the headlines of the following day, as evidence of treason high in the Pentagon.

Fearing publicity, Senator Dirksen managed to delay the subpoenas. But neither he nor his colleagues, before or after that crisis, faced the responsibility of restraining the chairman and directing the subcommittee that was also theirs. Their solidarity with Senator McCarthy, as much as the weakness of Secretary Stevens, brought on the public fight.

Once they had affirmed their impartiality and lack of prejudice. Chairman Mundt had declared in his opening address, "We enter our duties with no prejudgment as to the verities in this controversy." But now three of the four Republicans who were sitting as judges affirmed that they had indeed prejudged the verities on the climactic issue of the Army's Loyalty and Security Screening Board.

This was the first bitter fruit of the defeat of the Dirksen resolution. And the unhappy Republicans supposed that there would be many more weeks of increasing unpleasantness for their party and themselves. Then on the morning after the defeat of the Dirksen resolution, a new reason for cutting short the hearings loomed up in the form of a letter from the White House. Leaning on the stern figure of Andrew Jackson, President Eisenhower forbade further testimony on the meeting of January 21 or any other conference within the executive branch.

The impact of the letter on Joseph McCarthy was devastating. He was cornered for the first time. He looked in desperation for a door of escape—and Everett Dirksen opened it for him. Playing instinctively for time, McCarthy demanded an executive session of the subcommittee. His demand was granted and, behind the closed doors where he functioned best, it was once again Dirksen's turn.

Three hours later, as on the morning of the previous day, the path was again opened in the crowd, the cameras turned, the Senators filed in. The reporters noted that Symington was flushed and angry, Jackson wan, and McClellan sorrowful, while Potter, Mundt, and Dworshak were beaming. Joe McCarthy came in happily, squeezing the shoulders of his friends. And Everett Dirksen was the happiest of all.

Once again he had a motion.

This time Senator Dirksen was dressed in a dark-blue suit and a dark-blue tie. The reason, he confided to the television cameras, was that he was going to the funeral of a friend. He presented a motion for a recess, but he argued once more for a final adjournment.

And it was adjournment that was plainly desired and feared. McClellan and Jackson tried to shorten the period of recess. Symington in his impulsive and dramatic manner denounced the whole move as "a flagrant denial of fairness and justice" and a "transparent device to let the other side avoid the necessity of testifying under oath." "I predict, he ended, "that if these hearing are recessed they may never start again." The Republican Senators smiled and the chairman read once again his opening address.

Then the four Republicans voted "Aye" and the three Democrats voted "No"—and so the curtain that had remained up while Everett Dirksen tugged at it came crashing down at last.

As if to confirm that Dirksen had won his fight, Welch was discovered on the following day gossiping idly with Ray Jenkins in a Senate office. The Bostonian explained that he was now unemployed, that he had come to seek his friend out in his loneliness, and that he expected to return to his home soon.

He was wrong. The protests mounted across the continent and the President himself voiced the demand of the majority of the nation that the hearings continue to the end. A chastened Senator Mundt emerged from the Attorney General's office to announce that the following Monday would find himself and his colleagues back in the Senate Caucus Room. So millions of hands were laid on to raise the curtain that the Junior Senator from Illinois had managed to lower. It seemed that Everett Dirksen was doomed to be forever successful in all but his central aim.

The Pacifism
of President Eisenhower

The pretext for the Army-McCarthy hearings was the treatment of Private Schine. The real issue was Joseph McCarthy's bid for power. He was not, like Alexander Stephens a century before, striving to gain supremacy on behalf of the entire Congress. He was in fact refusing to share with his colleagues the power that he wrested from the executive branch. In his own name he raised the flag of personal power. With the encouragement of Dirksen and Mundt he kept that flag flying.

It was the Attorney General's order forbidding the release of his FBI "letter" that led McCarthy to rebel on the ninth day of the hearings. He called then on his fellow-Senators to ignore the ruling of the nation's chief legal officer. But not even Dirksen could follow his friend here. John McClellan, carefully avoiding all mention of McCarthy's name, suggested that a crime might have been committed by the man who received secret material without authorization as well as by the man who gave it out. At that the relevant Army regulations were re-examined. It seemed clear that McCarthy and his informant had violated these regulations, as well as the executive order which he had openly defied.

The firing died down for a time and then flared up again on the eighteenth day of the hearings. On that morning the chairman read another letter from the Attorney General in response to his second request that the information in the FBI document be released. The Attorney General stated:

> The Department has under consideration at the present time possible violations of the Criminal Law as the result of the referral of the transcript of the hearings to the Department by your Sub-Committee. The two-and-one-quarter page document is involved, and its declassification at this time might adversely affect or even defeat the proper prosecution of the offenses involved.

The letter from President Eisenhower was read, forbidding any testimony on the January 21 meeting, or on any other conferences within the administration, as an encroachment upon the rights of the executive branch.

At last the President had marched out to confront the challenger who had advanced to the gates of the White House and had held it in a kind of siege throughout the President's first year in office.

Would the President follow the pattern established by his administration—make a brief stand, only to retreat once more? In the course of the White House press conference held on the fifth day of the hearings the following exchange between the President and a reporter took place:

> ARTHUR SYLVESTER. At the McCarthy hearing yesterday, Secretary Stevens was rather chided for letting the Army go so long under pressure by Mr. McCarthy in behalf of Private Schine, and he subsequently testified that his two bosses were Mr. Wilson and the President of the United States and said that he had taken it up with Mr. Wilson. I wonder if Mr. Wilson had taken this problem up with you during the seven months?

The President asked if Sylvester meant the talk about a private. "Yes," said Sylvester, "and pressure being put on for him." The President then stated that he had never heard of the private.

At this, the reporters of this nation's friendly press laughed openly at the President of the United States. He flushed, and balled up his fists until the knuckles turned white. A second reporter continued the exchange.

RICHARD WILSON. As a former commanding general of the United States Army what do you think of all the excitement at the Capitol over the privileges granted this private?

The *New York Herald Tribune* correspondent noted: "There was a silence. The President drew up his shoulders and clenched his hands together and when he answered it was in a deeply husky voice."

The President said he trusted that the ladies and gentlemen would excuse him for declining to talk at all about something he didn't think was something to talk about much. He just hoped it would all be concluded very quickly.

Then, the *Herald Tribune* reported, "The President, nearly speechless with emotion . . . strode from the room. . . ."

The reason for this scene was obvious. The hearings were dramatizing the tragic inability of President Eisenhower to cope with Senator McCarthy's usurpation of his authority. This inability stemmed from Eisenhower's rigid adherence to an anti-political concept of the President's role.

Any President, on moving into the White House, must choose between two concepts of the Presidency. The choice is not, as some have said, between a constitutional monarch on the one hand and a prime minister on the other. It is part of a President's task to be both a head of state and a man of action. In the field of action, he must choose to be guided by the precepts either of James Buchanan or of Abraham Lincoln.

In the Buchanan view the President can do nothing except what the Constitution expressly permits. Even within this limited area the Presidency has no way to guide itself. It moves only when the Congress turns on the switch. It stops when the switch is turned off. In the interval when it is in motion, it merely administers the objects and situations entrusted to it by Congress. It has no duty to show a political consciousness of its own, or to encourage that consciousness in others.

Where the Buchanan concept of the Presidency ends, the Lincoln concept begins. Lincoln believed that the President could do everything for the people except that which the Constitution prohibits. According to this concept, the least part of the Presidency is the mechanical work of administering under law what the Congress alone can approve. The greater part lies in the President's extralegal powers and duties as the party leader, the teacher of public opinion, the keeper of the national conscience, the prophet of warning and encouragement. It lies in the artful combination of all these extralegal powers and their use in the political work of winning legal approval from the Congress in the furtherance of great national projects.

In the light of some of his words, President Eisenhower seemed committed to the Lincoln concept of the Presidency. He often talked of a "dynamic" program. He stressed his own role as a party leader: "The responsibility of the President as party leader," he said, "is recognized as an inescapable duty, essential to democracy itself." He emphasized the importance of being "fearless and uncompromising in speaking the truth to the people," since "public opinion is the force that keeps the United States in being, and runs all its parts." He correctly observed that "our form of government is in peril unless each branch willingly accepts and discharges its clear responsibility."

Yet these phrases did not follow from the Lincolnian concept of the Presidency. They concealed a Buchanan image instead.

It was in June 1953 that President Eisenhower made his most explicit commitment to the Buchanan tradition. The place and the occasion could not have been more historically tactless. It was during the ceremony dedicating Theodore Roosevelt's house at Oyster Bay as a national shrine. There, in a justification of his own policies as President, Dwight Eisenhower scoffed at the notion that Theodore Roosevelt "galloped down Pennsylvania Avenue on a spirited charger with his sabre drawn, rushed into the Senate or the House, demanded what he wanted and rode out with everybody cowed." The true fact, said President Eisenhower, was that Theodore Roosevelt sought "to win his objectives by cajolery. He used every form of polite advance that was open to him including . . . many breakfasts."

Cajolery, then, was the way to avoid the fatal cross fire between the branches of the government, to guarantee that each branch of the government would discharge its clear responsibilities. But what this apologia, spoken at Oyster Bay, left out, was Theodore Roosevelt speaking in his own voice. "I have used every ounce of power there is in the office of President," Roosevelt said on one occasion. "And I have not cared a rap for the criticism of those who spoke of my usurpation of power; for I know that the talk has been all nonsense and that there has been no usurpation." And of his efforts to get along with Congressional leaders, Theodore Roosevelt said: "I was forced to abandon my efforts to persuade them to come my way, and then I achieved results only by appealing over the heads of the Senate and House leaders to the people, who are the masters of both of us."

Even had there been no Joe McCarthy in the Senate, the resort to the Buchanan tradition in the White House would have led to trouble in 1953. The first crumbling at the edges began overseas. Walter Lippmann, traveling through Europe, reported with alarm the collapse of confidence in the United States among conservative allies committed to Western unity. These men understood that Congress was dictating American foreign policy—and dictating it, not in terms of America's national interest, but as a reflection of the relative power of the domestic pressure groups that converged on Capitol Hill.

But it was Joseph McCarthy who dramatized and magnified the President's disability.

Nature abhors a vacuum in politics as well as in physics. Just as at a lower level Roy Cohn was drawn further than he meant to go as Stevens retreated, so Eisenhower's unwillingness to discharge the presidential role encouraged McCarthy to set himself up as a second president. By December 1953 Lippmann foresaw a constitutional crisis, brought about by the "abdication of the powers of the Executive and the usurpations of Congress."

McCarthy was the usurper by invitation as well as instinct. His execution of the presidential power was on a very broad front of foreign and domestic affairs. On the matter of China trade, for example, he came close to splitting Britain and

the United States at the end of 1953 in pursuit of his own
foreign policy of blockading Communist China, a policy which
Secretary Dulles declared "attacks the very heart of United
States foreign policy." Dulles defended his prerogative—but he
was saved essentially by the fact that McCarthy had no clear
objectives in mind.

On one issue, however, McCarthy knew just what he
wanted—he was the Protector of the Nation's Security and
neither President Eisenhower nor even J. Edgar Hoover himself
could deny him this primacy.

The President, however, made an early attempt. Perhaps
the most important statement in his first message to Congress
was that thenceforth the protection of the United States government against infiltration by subversives was the province of
the Executive. With marvelous clarity, the President stated:

> The primary responsibility for keeping out the disloyal and the
> dangerous rests squarely upon the Executive Branch. When this
> branch so conducts itself as to require policing by another
> branch of the Government it invites its own disorder and confu-
> sion.
>
> I am determined to meet this responsibility of the Execu-
> tive. . . .

This was a strong affirmation of executive power. Accordingly 1953 should have been an idle year for McCarthy and his
subcommittee. But McCarthy declared, in his annual report for
1953, that never had he been so busy in hunting Communists
in government as during President Eisenhower's first year of
office.

The Eisenhower administration prepared a new loyalty order. It reflected the Republican belief that the Democrats had
been soft in dealing with subversives. Reviewing the status of
two million federal workers under its new standards, the
Eisenhower administration fired the few suspects that it found.
Including them under the new security rules with drunks, per-
verts, the insane, and some dead men, it fired as security risks a
total of 1456 federal employees during the first year of
Eisenhower's administration.

To McCarthy, all this was "a breath of clean fresh air." But it made not a whit of difference in his own design. He proceeded to summon General Zwicker before his subcommittee and to berate him as a protector of Communist-coddlers in the Eisenhower administration.

Dwight Eisenhower had made it a habit not to know about events that, properly appraised, would force an abandonment of his concept of the Presidency. But when the humiliation of his friend, Ralph Zwicker, took place, he could not turn away. His response was to avoid a clash on the real issue by affirming in the most general terms that "fair play" was the American way. "We can be certain," he said, "that [Congress] will respond to America's convictions in this regard."

Congress, of course, did no such thing. A meeting of Senate Republicans was held to pay lip service to the Rule of Fair Play on Capitol Hill. It prohibited any "dictation"; it barred a uniform code of rules for Congressional committees. McCarthy's friend, Senator Jenner, appraised it correctly as "much ado about nothing." But the President was satisfied.

As the party leader, he could have engineered the political isolation of Senator McCarthy. He could have demanded of his party lieutenants in the Congress that they deny to Senator McCarthy the chairmanship of his committee. He could have demanded that they withhold funds for the operations of his committee. He could have issued orders to all employees of the government directing them to ignore the demands of Senator McCarthy. And he could have done this last on the legal grounds that the President has a duty to see that the laws are faithfully executed, while the McCarthy course constituted an open invitation to faithlessness. He could have done it on the further legal grounds that the President has a constitutional duty not alone to uphold and defend the Constitution, but to uphold and defend his office when it comes under attack. None of this would have meant a curb on the legislature's proper investigating powers. It would have meant a curb on McCarthy's flagrant abuse of those powers, an abuse leading to a direct usurpation of executive functions in the name of investigation.

If the will for battle was lacking, it was not because Eisenhower liked McCarthy. He loathed him with a sincere and dedicated loathing. And, though his language was indirect, the President on numerous occasions made plain the extent of that loathing. But there was in all of this a reversal of the Biblical injunction to hate evil and not the evildoer. In obedience to the Buchanan view, the hatred seemed to be for the evildoer, and not for the evil itself.

For months McCarthy abused his authority as committee chairman and for months the administration suffered the abuse. It suffered abuse also with respect to an issue it later embraced in the course of the hearings—the injunction that "the reports, records and files relative to the employee loyalty program be preserved in strict confidence." The quotation here is from the Truman directive of March 13, 1948, which was kept in force—on paper—by the Eisenhower administration. And that directive said further:

> In accordance with the long established policy that reports rendered by the Federal Bureau of Investigation and other investigative agencies of the executive branch are to be regarded as confidential, all reports, records and files relative to the loyalty of employees or prospective employees (including reports of such investigative agencies), shall be maintained in confidence, and shall not be transmitted or disclosed except as required in the efficient conduct of business.
> Any subpoena or demand or request for information, reports, or files of the nature described, received from sources other than those persons in the executive branch of the Government who are entitled thereto by reason of their official duties, shall be respectfully declined, on the basis of this directive, and the subpoena or demand or other request shall be referred to the Office of the President for such response as the President may determine to be in the public interest in the particular case. There shall be no relaxation of the provisions of the directive except with my express authority.

But in practice the secrets of loyalty-board reports were made available to Senator McCarthy—and not because this was required in the efficient conduct of business. In the case of the Fort Monmouth investigations, the efficient conduct of business would have called for a continuation of the Army investigations that were then in progress, and not the retreat in favor of a McCarthy investigation of the same subject. But the Buchanan view remained the dominant motif until the hour when Roy Cohn, learning that Private Schine was to be sent overseas, flew up from the Schine establishment at Boca Raton to issue subpoenas for the members of the Army's Loyalty and Security Screening Board.

The bid was to make the board responsible to Senator McCarthy for its decisions and to use the files of the board as an instrument with which to embarrass the Army still further. For the Army, this was the intolerable act. It was also in direct contravention of a Presidential order and, therefore, a declaration of war that the administration could ignore only at the risk of surrender.

There was, at that moment, a true crisis in the executive branch. James Reston, writing in the *New York Times*, noted that government officials were "identifying themselves with the people who protect them, and if they cannot count on protection from the heads of their own departments, they seek it through association with the McCarthys or through passing information to the McCarthys." Executive authority was crumbling; the imitation White House, Room 402 of the Senate Office Building, was becoming the real center of power. The FBI "letter" passed to McCarthy was simply one in a flow of government secrets so serious that government was becoming, as Symington said, "a bloody sieve." The President seemed powerless to halt this mounting crisis, as Buchanan had been powerless to halt the drift toward civil war a century before. But there were men around the President who were conscious of what was at stake. The Attorney General and Sherman Adams, the real dispenser of the Presidential power, understood the nature of the challenge perfectly. When John Adams took to the Justice Department McCarthy's challenge on the subpoenas, Brownell and Sherman Adams counseled resistance and the preparation of a written file on Cohn and Schine. Even then no decision was made to take a public stand against

McCarthy. Among the opponents of McCarthy in the administration (and he also had friends) the view was that McCarthy should be handled behind closed doors. But by now the story was leaking too fast to be contained. And so, in an inadvertent and almost ignoble manner, the administration was pushed into the public stance that the President called "a posture of defense."

Even when the television cameras brought to the nation the scene of Eisenhower's embattled subordinates, the President held back from public identification with his own side. John Adams was on his own when he let fall the remark about his January 21 meeting with the President's advisers. And it was the insistence of the Democrats on developing the facts about that meeting, together with Mundt's persistent pleas to release the FBI "letter," that finally brought forth the administration's affirmation of its powers on May 17. The affirmation came in the form of a letter from President Eisenhower to Secretary of Defense Wilson, and a memorandum from Attorney General Brownell to the President.

In his letter to Secretary Wilson, President Eisenhower gave due recognition to the investigatory function of the legislature. His administration, he said, would continue to provide Congressional committees with information relating to any matter within the jurisdiction of the committees. However:

> It is essential to the successful working of our system that the persons entrusted with power in any one of the three great branches of government shall not encroach upon the authority confided to the others. The ultimate responsibility for the conduct of the Executive Branch rests with the President.

As to the case in point:

> Because it is essential to efficient and effective administration that employees of the Executive Branch be in a position to be completely candid in advising with each other on official matters, and because it is not in the public interest that any of their conversations or communications, or any documents or reproductions, concerning such advice be disclosed, you will instruct

employees of your Department that in all of their appearances before the Subcommittee of the Senate Committee on Government Operations regarding the inquiry now before it they are not to testify to communications or to produce any such documents or reproductions. This principle must be maintained regardless of who would be benefited by such disclosures.

I direct this action so as to maintain the proper separation of powers between the Executive and Legislative Branches of the Government in accordance with my responsibilities and duties under the Constitution. This separation is vital to preclude the exercise of arbitrary power by any branch of the Government.

The Attorney General's memorandum to the President was in the same vein.

It is essential to the successful working of our system that the persons entrusted with power in any one of these branches shall not be permitted to encroach upon the powers confided to the others, but that each shall be limited to the exercise of the powers appropriate to its own department and no other. The doctrine of separation of powers was adopted to preclude the exercise of arbitrary power and to save the people from autocracy.

The Attorney General continued:

Nor are there instances lacking where the aid of a court was sought in vain to obtain information or papers from a President and the heads of departments. Courts have uniformly held that the Presidents and heads of departments have an uncontrolled discretion to withhold information and papers in the public interest; they will not interfere with the exercise of that discretion, and that Congress has not power, as one of the great branches of the Government to subject the executive branch to its will any more than the executive branch may impose its unrestrained will upon the Congress.

The letter and the memorandum belatedly acknowledged what the Buchanan concept did not acknowledge: that the President all along was not the helpless victim of fate, represented by McCarthy; that he had a free will, a constitutional duty to prevail against that fate.

In the Senate Caucus Room, when the substance of the executive communication was read, it was not without reason that McCarthy's hand trembled and his reply came in a halting voice. "I must admit," he said, "that I am somewhat at a loss as to know what to do. . . ." McCarthy had never before been at a loss over what to do. He floundered as Eisenhower spoke in Lincoln's voice. He stammered that the President could not be responsible for his own act, saying, "I don't think his judgment is that bad."

The administration was suddenly ranged against him, and in his bewilderment McCarthy became almost humble during a rare and admirable moment of self-doubt as he thought out loud about the January 21 meeting.

> McCARTHY. I fear that maybe in my mind I was doing an injustice possibly to Mr. Adams and Mr. Hensel.

That is, an injustice in attributing to them the dark desires to bring his investigation of alleged Communist-coddling to a halt. Then, drawing perhaps some resolution from the sound of his own voice, the Senator denounced the "Iron Curtain" that had fallen on the January 21 meeting because of the President's order. He said of the President:

> McCARTHY. I'm sure if he knew what this was all about, he would not sign an order that you cannot tell a Senate committee what went on when they cooked up those charges against Mr. Cohn, Mr. Carr, and myself.

Then the bitterness and anger and hysteria within him boiled over once more.

> McCARTHY. Who. . . . Who was responsible for the issuance of the smear that has held this committee up for weeks and weeks and weeks and has allowed Communists to continue . . . with a razor poised over the jugular vein of the nation?

The answer evidently was Sherman Adams of the White House, and Herbert Brownell.

For McCarthy, a crisis had come. He spoke in a series of unrelated assertions. After each one, he returned to the claim that Frank Carr had been completely cleared. This was a hope rather than an accomplished fact; it suggested that the Senator was thinking of walking out of the hearings, but only if he could take Frank Carr along. Suddenly, he demanded a ten-minute recess. He marched out, and many of the reporters believed that he was gone for good. Evidently it was a moment of great difficulty for him. Yet when he returned, he was look-ing for new openings even as he defended himself against the unexpected blows. He needed time to regroup his forces, to wear down the President's resolution, to permit the figure of Buchanan to find its way back to the White House again. He won his way with a week's recess. So a week with no hearings passed—but there was no sign of weakening on the President's part. McCarthy was at a loss to know where to turn. His fol-lowers, waiting anxiously by their television sets for his ap-pearance in the evening news programs, were treated to the spectacle of a baffled McCarthy muttering, "I'm frankly con-fused. I just don't know what to do." After a week of indecision he conceded that he would be on hand when the hearings started up again, but for how long he would not say.

The hearings reconvened in the Senate Caucus Room and at the close of the following week, the debate over the Con-stitution boiled up again. Roy Cohn was in the witness chair and he was endeavoring to prove that the subcommittee in-terest in the Army predated by four months its interest in the military career of Private Schine. As proof, Cohn introduced a memorandum of March 1953 by Paul Crouch, who—unknown to the Democrats—was a subcommittee employee. Crouch, a professional informer, was under investigation by the Depart-ment of Justice for perjury at the time the hearings reconvened. His memorandum seemed to consist of an unpublished chapter of his autobiography concerning the events of 1928, to which one paragraph was tacked on—alleging that there were a thousand Communists in the Army.

John McClellan, however, was more concerned with the fact that, despite his membership on the subcommittee, he had never heard of the existence of the Crouch memorandum until that morning. He protested, and McCarthy countered with the charge that McClellan wanted to jail his informants and himself for wrongdoing. McClellan denied this, but McCarthy plunged toward an uncompromising defiance of the President.

MCCARTHY. In view of Senator McClellan's statement, I would like to make it clear that I think that the oath which every person in government takes to protect and defend this country against all enemies—foreign and domestic—that oath towers far above any presidential secrecy directive.

And I will continue to receive information such as I received the other day. ... That will be my policy. There's no power on earth can change that. Again I want to compliment the individuals who have placed their oath to defend the country above and beyond any presidential directive. ... None of them, none of them will be brought before a grand jury because of any information which I give. If any administration wants to indict me for receiving and giving the American people the information about Communism, they can just go right ahead and do the indicting.

The ranking Democrat was never more penetrating or concise than in his answer.

MCCLELLAN. You may be right, but I do not know of any oath that any man ever took that required him to commit a crime.

Symington joined the dispute; Mundt attempted to shut it off with the extraordinary claim that it was wholly irrelevant to the controversy. McCarthy disagreed and continued his course of defying President Eisenhower.

MCCARTHY. I would like to notify two million federal employees that I feel that it is their duty to give us any information which they have about graft, corruption, Communists, and treason, and that there is no loyalty to a superior officer which can tower above and beyond their loyalty to their country.

Once again, McClellan showed his matchless ability to discern the central issue.

MCCLELLAN. If this principle is adopted, that every federal employee shall reveal everything he knows, then you have no security system in America. It will be destroyed totally and irrevocably if all who have information give it out indiscriminately.

Again Mundt intervened in an attempt to close out the debate. Although the chairman again maintained that it was "irrelevant," it was the most important exchange in the thirty-six days of the hearings. In recognition of its importance, the White House returned to the battle with its most powerful answer to McCarthy's challenge.

> The obligations and duties of the executive, judicial, and legislative branches of the government are defined by the Constitution. The executive branch of the government has the sole and fundamental responsibility under the Constitution for the enforcement of our laws and presidential orders.
>
> That responsibility cannot be usurped by any individual who may seek to set himself above the laws of our land or to override the orders of the President of the United States to federal employees of the executive branch of the government.

The three Democrats applauded this statement. Two Republicans, Mundt and McCarthy, attacked it. McCarthy spoke in scorn, saying that he would disregard it and adding, "I hope to remain in the Senate and see many Presidents come and go." Mundt spoke in cynicism, treating the separation of powers and the security of the United States as a game. "I don't mind if President Eisenhower calls it reprehensible," said Chairman Mundt. "If I were President Eisenhower I'd do everything I could to stop it [the leaking of secret information to Senators]. But I'm down here [in Congress] and so I would do all I could to get it. That's the way you play the game."

From then on, the debate continued with rising force and eloquence.

"Federal officials," said McCarthy, "are bound only by their oath."

"Then," answered McClellan, "you are advocating government by the individual conscience as against government by law."

"No phony stamp of secrecy should keep from the Congress any evidence of wrongdoing," McCarthy declared.

"Then," McClellan retorted, "no committee member is under any obligation to protect the wrongdoer."

"I have instructed a vast number of federal employees," McCarthy continued, "that they are duty-bound to give me information even though some little bureaucrat has stamped it 'secret' to defend himself."

"I am sorry," remarked McClellan, "to hear you refer to Mr. J. Edgar Hoover as 'some little bureaucrat.'"

"Senator," said McCarthy, "I will just not abide by any secrecy directive. You and I have seen and will see Presidents come and go."

"Senators, too," McClellan replied.

"The issue," said McCarthy, "is whether the people are entitled to the facts."

"No," said McClellan, who despised loose thinking above all else; "the issue is whether a Senate subcommittee is entitled to gain by theft what it cannot legally obtain by subpoena."

Cornered, McCarthy reverted at last to his maudlin complaint that the Southerner was trying to send him to jail. McClellan shook his head.

> McClellan. I'm asking no such thing. I don't care.
> McCarthy. You wouldn't worry about me.
> McClellan. You stay in or out. No one's afraid of you out any more than they would be in, as far as I know. The point I'm making, Joe, and you know it, is that you've reached the cross-roads. And we're entitled, in the course of these hearings to have this thing settled, if there's any way to settle it.

There was, of course, no way. But the issue was drawn at last between the Constitutionalists—the Democrats and the newly recruited President—and the anti-Constitutionalists, led by McCarthy with the support now of Chairman Mundt. And this debate alone, by arousing the President and the nation to the constitutional crisis that had slowly matured during years of indifference, outweighed the pain and sordidness of other hours, and promised that the Army-McCarthy hearings would gain a lasting place in the annals of America.

The Integrity of Senator McClellan

On the twenty-first day of the hearings, late in May, Jenkins made an announcement which he supposed would make everyone happy. With Welch's consent, he was about to close the Army's case. But Welch, sitting by the witness chair, was not at all happy. First he wanted some assurance that two witnesses would be heard from; they were Frank Carr and Private Schine. Jenkins invited the Army counsel to criticize any dereliction of duty on his part; and with that inconclusive answer he called the name of Senator McCarthy's first witness, Mr. Roy M. Cohn.

Cohn rose, fastening the button on his coat, and then there was heard the little-known voice of Senator Dworshak. He made a motion.

DWORSHAK. I now move that the charges involving Mr. Struve Hensel be dismissed for lack of any testimony whatsoever involving him or sustaining such charges and he no longer be considered a party in interest in this controversy. And he be dismissed as a witness.

And also that at this time the charges preferred against Mr. Frank Carr be dismissed because the proof and testimony concerning Mr. Carr are wholly insufficient to sustain such charges.

And I further move that he no longer be considered a party

in interest in this controversy. And that he be dismissed as a witness.

The resolution was seconded at once by Senator Dirksen.

On the face of it the resolution was indefensible. Of course there was lack of testimony on Hensel—the McCarthy witnesses had not yet been called. Frank Carr had neither been allowed to testify on his own behalf, nor required to affirm under oath the grave charges to which he had signed his name. And yet, it was learned, the four Republicans had discussed this resolution and agreed on it in advance.

Twenty-one days before, Senator Mundt had promised, "We propose to follow the evidence wherever it leads and to give every party to this dispute the equitable treatment and consideration to which he is entitled." Now the promise was broken on all counts for the sake of rushing the hearings through.

On that opening day John McClellan had also made a promise—that the three Democrats would seek to "develop the facts, and to seek the truth . . . without regard to any personalities that may be involved." Where would they stand now?

The three men were very different in their approaches. John McClellan, the son of a tenant farmer, was concerned with procedures. Stuart Symington, the son of a judge, was driven by an emotional involvement on the Army side. Henry Jackson, the son of a Norwegian mason, had a craftsman's approach: a keen sense of the law and an active political instinct; a long-standing awareness of the meaning of McCarthyism; and an ability, as his friends said, to walk down a cow lane without dirtying his feet.

Now the three stood together. McClellan, as the ranking Democrat, spoke first. He denounced the resolution as "manifestly unfair to Senator McCarthy." Jackson added that legally it made no sense at all.

Then Senator Dirksen spoke eloquently for his motion, holding that no charges had been made against Hensel and none sustained against Carr. But Jackson intervened in a series of brilliant questions, to reveal the absurdity of the Republican position. Next Chairman Mundt laid the responsibility for the motion concerning Hensel at the door of the White House, saying that the President's order made any discussion of Hensel's role impossible. Again Jackson pointed out that the charges against Hensel had nothing to do with the January 21 meeting and that if the charges against Hensel should be dismissed for lack of testimony, then all the charges brought by McCarthy, Cohn, and Carr should be dismissed since no testimony had been given by their side.

McCarthy, Cohn, and Carr had charged that Hensel was a liar and a war profiteer who had deliberately instigated false charges against the subcommittee and its staff in order to cover up his own "misconduct and possible law violations." Hensel in turn had branded McCarthy's action "scandalous malice and . . . cowardly irresponsibility," and had called McCarthy's charges "barefaced lies." It was unthinkable to McClellan that any man would not insist on the right to seek vindication. Another Democrat might have welcomed the Republican motion as proof that McCarthy's charges were fraudulent. McClellan condemned the motion for denying to McCarthy the opportunity of proving his charges real.

> McCLELLAN. I have witnessed some peculiar proceedings in my lifetime but never before have I witnessed charges brought and then somebody moving to dismiss them before the man who made the charges was given an opportunity to testify.
>
> This would be one of the grossest reflections upon those who made the charges for this committee at this stage in the proceedings to dismiss them because it would be tantamount to saying to Senator McCarthy and Mr. Cohn, "Your charges are baseless, they were an imposition upon this committee and upon the country and they are irresponsible!"
>
> If you want to place that stigma upon Senator McCarthy and Mr. Cohn you may do so. But so far as I am concerned we are going to get the proof or see the charges withdrawn by those who made them, and I shall vote against the motion.

Those who listened smiled at the political sophistication of the rural Democrat in opposing a Republican motion in the

name of another Republican. They were altogether wrong. For John McClellan, who had never finished his schooling, was the one truly judicial figure in the Senate Caucus Room. His dedication and self-restraint in adhering to absolute impartiality were ultimately the most memorable qualities shown by any man in the hearings.

Where did that integrity come from?

Arkansas is one of the poorest of the forty-eight states, and stands next to the bottom in its expenditures for each child in school. And Grant County, where McClellan was born, is one of the poorest counties in Arkansas. Facing a visitor in his Senate office, lined with the photographs of national leaders, John McClellan says first of himself, "I am an uneducated man."

John McClellan's grandfather was a Confederate veteran who never owned a foot of land in his life and could scarcely write his name. "When he was seventy-five and I was fifteen," McClellan recalls, "we ploughed the same field and he did more work than I was willing to do."

McClellan's mother died three weeks after he was born; his grandparents helped to raise him. His father left home at eighteen to enter the third grade in school. There were no high schools in Arkansas then, but his father worked his way through country school and gained a first-grade license to teach. From then on he taught school, worked as a tenant farmer, and studied law. He borrowed law books, since he could not buy them. McClellan as a boy of twelve looked on the books with fascination. McClellan himself went to school from twelve to seventeen, and worked his father's new farm with his grandfather and a hired hand. He spent his spare time reading and watching in his father's law office. When he was seventeen the Arkansas legislature passed a special bill removing his civil disabilities and authorizing him to practice law in the circuit and inferior courts, on the basis of an oral and not-too-rigid examination.

So John McClellan worked in the law office of his father in Sheridan, a town of six hundred people, until he went off to officer's training camp in the First World War. He was twenty-three when it ended. He and his father took a written law examination and were admitted to practice before the state supreme court on the same day.

McClellan was elected to Congress in 1934 and 1936. He ran for the Senate in 1938 against Mrs. Hattie Carraway. Her record was more liberal than his, and she won with New Deal support. For a time he was depressed. But in 1942 he was elected to the Senate in a four-way race. There he established a record as a Southern conservative, hostile to legislation backed by organized labor, bent on economy, on many issues a hostage to the past in a state that by now was swiftly changing.

The Committee on Government Operations grew out of an older standing committee of the Senate to which John McClellan belonged. As its chairman, he appointed himself in 1948 to the Subcommittee on Investigations which Joseph McCarthy took over after the Republican victory of 1952. In his bitterness over his lack of education and his suspicion of big government, McClellan was inclined to look with favor on Joseph McCarthy as the Wisconsin Senator tore into the city intellectuals of the Voice of America and the international information services. He was even persuaded that there was something of a Communist plot in the distorted picture that Cohn and Schine presented of the Voice's proposed transmitters.

It was on a matter of procedure rather than principle that McClellan led the Democrats off the subcommittee. He felt that it was proper that the Democrats should have a minority counsel of their own. When McCarthy insisted on treating the staff as his personal instrument, McClellan was outraged; he returned in February only when McCarthy agreed to give in to all of the procedural demands.

Now McClellan sat at the chairman's left, suspicious, sardonic, humorless, unafraid. More than any man present he had the right to feel bitter at the privileges gained for Private Schine. His own three sons had volunteered for combat and he had refused to even consider special assignments for them. One son had suffered from extreme exposure in the landings in

North Africa in 1942, developed spinal meningitis, and died. A second son was killed in a crash on the day before his first son was buried in Arlington. Nonetheless, he never wavered in his detachment and restraint. His examination of witnesses was far more impartial than that of Ray Jenkins. His points of procedure were frequently in support of Senator McCarthy. But when McCarthy transgressed, McClellan's intervention was as swift and as deadly as a moccasin's strike. Brilliant lawyers worked to help Jackson and Symington. A large staff labored at the Pentagon to back up Welch. John McClellan worked entirely alone, scorning advice, going home to work into the night on his mail. But it was McClellan, more than any other man, whom McCarthy feared.

Now McClellan watched McCarthy, waiting for him to act in honor. Everett Dirksen was also watching him, and it was Dirksen who spoke. "It occurs to me," he said, "that we have ventilated this matter long enough." And so he called for a vote on the Dworshak resolution.

But Stuart Symington had caught McClellan's closing point, and he leaned forward.

> SYMINGTON. . . . First I would like to ask . . . have the charges against Mr. Hensel been withdrawn? . . .
> McCARTHY. I think perhaps I should answer that. May I say that nothing has been withdrawn. . . . I have one objective now, now that we know we can never get all the facts, and that is to get the show off the road as soon as we can. . . .

So the Senator who had made the gravest of charges against a high government official, and been called a malicious and cowardly liar in return, washed his hands of the matter by saying that he had better ways to occupy his time. Those who watched or listened that afternoon did not know it, but ten days earlier, in an executive session of the subcommittee, Senator McCarthy had conceded that he had no evidence whatever to support his charges against Hensel—that, given the opportunity, he could not present a case. And yet, without exception, the Republicans who knew this failed to suggest that the charges be withdrawn.

For a very different reason, Stuart Symington joined McClellan. He had worked in the Pentagon, and been attacked because of his business connections. He knew what damage Hensel would suffer, and into the mounting tension of the scene he brought now the shattering force of a morally outraged man.

> SYMINGTON. I have known Mr. Hensel for a long time. He is in a position of great authority in the Department of Defense. . . . He was appointed by the President of the United States to this high office. I have no reason to think that he is guilty in any way of the charges that have been made against him but I join with my colleagues in holding that to dismiss these charges at this time and to leave this man as the number one legal official in the Defense Department where everybody is looking for corruption to me is just unbelievable! . . . from this day on he will operate on the basis of the charges that were made and were dismissed before he was even given the opportunity to answer them.

But the point was lost. H. Struve Hensel was a fighter who had forced his way to the top of a dozen prominent law firms or government agencies. More than anyone else in the dispute, he was capable of trading punches with McCarthy. But he had returned to the Pentagon, leaving his attorney, Mr. Bryan, who resembled a Colonel of the Guards in a Gilbert and Sullivan operetta. With a grand roar, Mr. Bryan supported the Dworshak motion. He claimed that it fully vindicated his client, and he ridiculed Symington's assertion that the charges would be left hanging over Hensel's head. To his claim that every citizen was innocent until proven guilty, Symington, the non-lawyer, retorted that every citizen also had the obligation of clearing himself of charges. Jackson, whose arguments throughout the day were most decisive, called Bryan's argument "the grossest violation of Anglo-Saxon law . . . and of plain common sense." They were right, and one week later, Hensel himself asked to be heard. By then it was too late. For now, ignoring the fact that the charges had not been withdrawn, the Chairman reasoned that if McCarthy were content "not to press them," why then "the committee would be in a most unhappy position to try to prod people to prolong the hearings and expand our witness list and extend the evidence ad infinitum, ad nauseam."

Upset and angry, Senator Symington shouted "Whitewash!" and threatened to take the issue to the Senate floor. At that everyone protested. At last they yielded to McClellan once more. It had occurred to his suspicious mind that the Pentagon was breaking up and joining the Republicans, leaving the Democrats without a defense or a case. The image of the January surrender rose in his mind. He lifted his haggard head.

> MCCLELLAN. I want to make one more brief statement and then I am through. I do not know whether there has been another Memorandum of Agreement that the Democrats didn't have an opportunity to know about or not.

This piercing thrust was greeted with more ardent protests. Then once again Senator Dirksen demanded a vote on the Dworshak motion. The vote was called.

At this point, the voice of the Army counsel was heard.

> WELCH. . . . Senator Dworshak, I would count it, sir, a great courtesy to me if you would split your motion into two parts because you have in the same motion a dismissal as to Mr. Hensel and a dismissal as to Mr. Carr. There is no lawyer . . . nor I think any human being in the court room who does not know that very different considerations apply to these two men. . . . I have no right to ask it, but I beg it as a favor.

Senator Dworshak refused to grant the favor and for a revealing reason.

> DWORSHAK. Mr. Welch, . . . you are practical enough to know that you must have some balance or compensating feature.

The motion was a trade, a wrong for a wrong, and it came as a shocking revelation to a lifelong Republican. But Welch still had some faith in the leaders of his party.

> WELCH. I am bitterly disappointed . . . I am sure there is some sympathy for me on that side of the table when I point out the different considerations that apply.

"I think," said Mr. Welch, "that certain Senators on the other side of the table have not been as appreciative of the seriousness of the case that has been made against Mr. Carr as I am, on reading the record." And so he reviewed the record of five months. He sensed that there was little sympathy for his indictment of the one he described as the strong silent man. He knew that a motion to strike Carr as a principal was inevitable at the conclusion of the Army's ineffective case. But he knew also that the Dworshak motion eliminated Carr not only as a principal but as a witness. Carr was McCarthy's witness, but Welch ended in an eloquent plea that he be heard. He said of Carr:

> WELCH. I do not want anyone in this room or anyone that hears my voice to think that I could bear a grudge against a man that I have never yet actually met.
>
> I have heard Senator McCarthy say that the Army wants his neck and wants his job. Mr. Chairman, I would not know what disposition to make of either the neck or the job if it were offered to me. I want to try this case and bring out the facts fully.

Welch looked appealingly at each of the Republican Senators. Only in Senator Potter's manner could he discern any sign of indecision. He turned to the Tennessean.

> WELCH. Mr. Jenkins, my friend, I think I am looking at you more than anyone else. I have not the power to keep Mr. Carr in the case as a principal if this vote goes as it seems somewhat indicated that it will. As long, Mr. Jenkins, as I have your promise that Mr. Carr will be called so that I can examine him . . . whether he helps me or hurts me, I want him as a witness.

The committee counsel seemed then to be genuinely distressed. He also was shaken and left outside by the political twist of the day's developments. He spoke now to his fellow lawyer, as a lawyer.

> JENKINS. I address my remarks directly to Mr. Welch. . . . I want you to understand as I am sure you do that I work for the committee as its special counsel. I am in no wise responsible for the policies of the committee. I have no vote . . . you are bound to know . . . that my hands are tied . . . please don't cast the

burden or the onus upon me because as you know and as everyone knows I am taking orders from those who employ me.

The crowd was hushed as the two men spoke to each other. The mood in the great room had passed from burning anger to deeply felt sadness. Then Senator Dirksen spoke, replying very effectively to Welch's summary of Carr's record. He ended with unusual sarcasm.

> DIRKSEN. This is amazing, isn't it! Where are the facts, Mr. Welch? Where is the affirmative testimony? We have been waiting for it! So, silence and profundity are now the basis of the proof. There has been no proof and . . . it becomes our duty now to relieve Frank Carr of this cloud.

Mr. Welch was very, very sad. He knew there was little use, but he tried once more.

> WELCH. I wish to say to my friend Senator Dirksen, whose voice I always so much envy: you don't strike me, Senator, as being open to conversion. I am afraid I may not gain your vote. But I do wish to point out to you. . . .

As he spoke, his forearm on the table, his head low, his fingers drawn together against his forehead, he strained to see Senator Dirksen in the half-darkness on the other side of the shaft of blinding light from the floodlamps. Only Senator Dirksen's eyelashes fluttered. As Welch's head turned to look down the table past the four Republicans, he saw the head of John McClellan nodding in agreement. The Army counsel remarked lamely:

> WELCH. I observe a nod from a lawyer I respect, although I differ with his politics.

Summoning a little more vigor he turned back to Senator Dirksen.

> WELCH. Let me say this, Senator. If at the close of the case Mr. Carr is found free of all fault by you, you will see me advance towards him smiling. I have, sir, a genius for losing cases. I wish, however, not to lose them until the evidence is in.

This was an allusion to the monitored telephone calls, and evidently it roused anger in Senator McCarthy.

> McCarthy. . . . As a judge I have seen many dishonest attempts by clever little lawyers to smear and distort the facts. But in all my record as a judge, as head of this committee, I have never seen a man do what Mr. Welch is doing now. . . .

The chairman agreed. He had led in the attempt to separate and dismiss the charges against Carr and he argued with force that the Army had made no case. But it was Carr the witness, not Carr the principal, whose future was before the committee now. As if in recognition of a sense of guilt, the chairman concluded:

> Mundt. For your solace, Mr. Welch, I may say this. . . . Any action that the Senate takes is reversible. If we make an error in voting now to dismiss Mr. Carr as a witness . . . and it develops that you can in fact elicit from the friends of Frank Carr statements with which to indict him that you could not produce by consultation with those who proposed to be against him, then of course we can reverse our position.

Welch might be excused for treating as mockery the thought that Roy Cohn or Joseph McCarthy would pitch in to rebuild his case. McClellan's mouth parted in a thin smile.

> McClellan. I don't want Mr. Welch to get any false hopes that there will be a reversal. This is going to be final and he is going to be eliminated.

McClellan leaned forward. He did not yield an inch in his impartiality and yet at that moment the bond between the two men was deeper than any other in the room. He spoke to Welch alone.

> McClellan. I want to say I agree with you. You say you do not agree with my politics; that is your privilege. But I want to say I agree with you as to the merits of the case. I do not mean that I would vote to sustain it after all the evidence is in but as a lawyer I believe I know [Carr] is still a proper party to this proceeding until all the testimony is in. I agree with you.

He turned then to the dismissal of Hensel and his sense of outrage mounted at the impropriety of the action of the four Republicans.

> McClellan. I want to say I have never before seen a case dismissed where the accusing party was in court and yet refused to withdraw the charges, where those charges made a case if sustained by evidence.
>
> Gentlemen, you are not deceiving the American people, this great jury watching these proceedings. Here are serious, damnable charges made against Mr. Hensel and you have the accusers right here in the room. . . . If they ought to be dismissed then they should be dismissed by those who made the charges stepping up here and publicly withdrawing them.

Then Symington and Jackson were piling on top of the unhappy Mundt. "Will you vote to call Carr as a witness?" Symington demanded. "No," said Mundt, "not unless sworn evidence is made against him." "Mr. Carr has accused the Army of trying to blackmail him. Don't you think we should have the right to question Mr. Carr about that?" shouted Symington. "Not unless it is presented as sworn testimony," said the chairman. In a curious appraisal of Carr's memoranda he referred to them as "newspaper reports." Promptly Jackson pointed out that in sworn testimony Secretary Stevens had called Carr's memoranda lies. Mundt blinked but did not budge.

"Are you ready to vote?" asked Mundt, and Symington answered, "I am not ready!" He cried that the dignity and integrity of the Senate were at stake in the removal of Carr as a witness. Then for one last time Welch spoke.

"I think I can count votes," he remarked, "and I think I observe Mr. Carr disappearing as a principal in this case." He asked that as a witness Carr remain. "I beg of you," he said to the Republicans; "I can take one stab in the heart a day."

But the vote was as good as in. Mr. Welch turned to the one man on the Republican side whose conscience seemed to be waiting for some word of command. "Senator Potter, I couldn't believe, sir, you were going to announce your vote as you have." Potter listened without moving and the Bostonian added, "But I think you have done so." He was very tired. His elbow rested on the witness table; his arm rose and sank with thumb and second finger joined in a delicate circle for emphasis. And slowly it dawned on those present that it was more than Mr. Welch, the skilled lawyer, who was speaking. It was also the lifelong Republican; when he finished, the audience was out of breath and close to tears.

> WELCH. May I say sadly, gentlemen, that it seems strange to me that these Republican lips of mine, Republican for sixty-four years with the single exception of Al Smith whom I admired, that these lips can convince only Democrats, my natural enemies, and that the Republicans whom I love and cherish find my words are dust and ashes.

The vote was taken. Carr and Hensel were removed. Roy Cohn bounced into the witness chair. Welch wandered out into the marble hall, where he stood uncertain. From all over the country telegrams arrived in carloads, many from Republicans, denouncing the action that the Republican majority had taken. John McClellan read them with no enjoyment. As he entered the Caucus Room on the following morning he paused in sadness by a small group of reporters. He said:

> If party advantage were all that mattered, yesterday would be a day for Democrats to rejoice. But the welfare of the country is more important than party, and so it was a day of ignominy and shame.

The Fear of Mrs. Driscoll

Of all the documents presented in the Army-McCarthy hearings the most important and mysterious were the eleven memoranda signed by McCarthy, Cohn, and Carr. They were handed out to the press by Senator McCarthy on the morning after the release of the first Army report and in violation of an agreement with the Republican members of the subcommittee who were not even aware of their existence. Among other reporters, Carleton Kent, chief of the Washington bureau of the *Chicago Sun-Times*, noted in his story the newness of the documents and the curious way in which the Senator guarded them.

The memoranda constituted circumstantial evidence in support of McCarthy's claim that Robert Stevens and John Adams had used blackmail and bribery in attempting to block the subcommittee. In the atmosphere they recreated, the memoranda seemed unassailable and very convincing. At the same time, McCarthy and Cohn showed a curious reluctance to cite them, perhaps because the memoranda contained sharper charges than they were prepared now to defend. It was the Army's view that the memoranda were fraudulent, and many responsible newspapermen agreed.

It was on June 2, the twenty-fourth day of the hearings,

that the memoranda were considered. On that day Roy Cohn testified that they were all dictated to McCarthy's personal secretary, Mrs. Mary Driscoll. So, in his raw manner, Ray Jenkins suddenly called Mrs. Driscoll as a witness. McCarthy justifiably asked for at least a half hour's notice and Jenkins, still raw, granted just thirty minutes. McCarthy went to inform his secretary, and did not return until he brought her to the witness chair.

She was plainly weak with fear. "This young woman," said McCarthy many times in explanation; but she was in fact a grandmother with six years of experience in running his office. Was it the cameras and the floodlamps that unnerved her? Much younger stenographers from the Pentagon had testified without hesitation beneath the blinding lights. Mary Driscoll seemed a strong woman. But now her small chin trembled, her throat seemed parched, and when she moved her lips in answer to Ray Jenkins' first question almost no sound came.

Jenkins was unusually gentle. "Do you recall the dictation of the memos?" he inquired. Mrs. Driscoll shook her head. "I couldn't, I have too much dictation," she whispered. To each question she repeated, "I couldn't."

Had she kept her shorthand notebooks? No. "I never keep shorthand notebooks." Jenkins turned to the file—an old folder with frayed edges, from which the new pages came. His voice for once was soft; hers was almost inaudible.

> JENKINS. Were the copies made after the Army release?
> MRS. DRISCOLL. I think so.
> JENKINS. That particular file now is just identified by the words Investigating Committee.
> MRS. DRISCOLL. That is right.
> JENKINS. Is that all?
> MRS. DRISCOLL. That is all it says.
> JENKINS. How did you know where to go to look for that file, Mrs. Driscoll?
> MRS. DRISCOL. I can't tell you that, Mr. Jenkins.
> JENKINS. . . . I ask you to examine the memoranda to see if you typed them as originals.
> MRS. DRISCOLL. I think, Mr. Jenkins, they may be the originals as typed by me but I can't tell you positively.

There was a breathless silence in the room, a sense among the crowd that strained to hear her thin cracked voice that the McCarthy case was about to break apart. McCarthy, listening intently with his pencil poised, scribbled a note and passed it quickly to her. At her side, Roy Cohn leaned over to whisper advice.

It was Welch's turn, and she moved to face him with a look almost of terror. Holding his glasses high as he rested his elbow on the table, he explained that it was awkward and difficult to cross-examine a lady. He asked, "When did you start working on the file?" After a moment she whispered, "I don't have any recollection."

Then Mr. Welch approached her, like a cat circling a caged canary, looking for an opening in the bars. He possessed proof that the memoranda had been typed on at least three typewriters, and she must have known this. He asked her now on what typewriter the first memorandum was typed.

> MRS. DRISCOLL. I couldn't tell you. I don't know.
> WELCH. You don't know!
> MRS. DRISCOLL. I don't recognize the typing. . . .
> WELCH. The one at your desk is an IBM. Is that right?
> MRS. DRISCOLL. There is an IBM at my desk now.
> WELCH. Was it there then?
> MRS. DRISCOLL. I don't recall. I don't know.

Mr. Welch could not believe what he heard.

> WELCH. Don't you know when you got it?
> MRS. DRISCOLL. No.
> WELCH. You can't tell us whether you've had it a month or two or longer?
> MRS. DRISCOLL. No, Mr. Welch, I can't.
> WELCH. You have no memory at all?
> MRS. DRISCOLL. No. A typewriter is a typewriter and I don't pay any attention to the type of typewriter.

The Army counsel was devastating in his mockery.

> WELCH. You are a paragon of virtue! My secretaries are always kicking about them and wanting a new one. You don't pay any attention to them?

No, Mrs. Driscoll managed to say, she hadn't any idea what kind of typewriter she used.

At that moment Mrs. Driscoll seemed to have no strength left. Joseph McCarthy broke in, ridiculing the Army counsel's questioning as irrelevant and absurd. He couldn't imagine what Welch was interested in. The real issue was brought out as Welch turned on McCarthy.

> WELCH. I'm interested to know whether these memoranda are the real McCoy or not! You know that, don't you!

McCarthy sighed and shrugged his shoulders. That afternoon Ralph Flanders of Vermont was attacking McCarthy on the Senate floor. James Juliana brought the speech to McCarthy in yellow sheets from an Associated Press ticker. He read it, frowning, and seemed to lose interest in the anguish of his secretary. Senator Dirksen came to her aid, and then she turned again in fear to Mr. Welch. He led her to repeat that she had placed all the memoranda in a file that no one else could find. And then he read to her—and twenty million others—the last memorandum of Frank Carr. It was written on March 10, the day that McCarthy learned of the Army report on Schine. It said:

> Senator McCarthy advised Mr. [Fred] Seaton [Assistant Secretary of Defense] that the writer [Carr] was searching the files for memoranda dictated concerning Schine.

Welch looked up at the trembling witness.

> WELCH. Were you startled when Carr dictated that to you?
> MRS. DRISCOLL. No.
> WELCH. Did you say to him, "Mr. Carr, look no further, I've got 'em all here in the slickest little package you ever saw?"
> MRS. DRISCOLL. Hah! Absolutely not!
> WELCH. Did you tell him his search was silly?
> MRS. DRISCOLL. Of course I didn't!
> WELCH. Well, you had them all together, didn't you?
> MRS. DRISCOLL. Maybe I overlooked one.

Her moment of defiance died away and again the witness seemed drained of her will to hold onto the lifeline of her established story. Then, once again, Senator McCarthy broke in. Most men would have been too outraged to sit in silence while a Senate subcommittee considered for more than two hours whether they had faked documents. McCarthy, in contrast, had listened with outward indifference. But something was grinding within him, probably anger at Senator Flanders' use of insinuation and ridicule in his speech. Now, angrily, he interrupted Mr. Welch and demanded an end to the "heckling." Once more the Army counsel made the most of this invitation to be frank.

> WELCH. I cannot conceal from the Senator that I have the deepest suspicion about the genuineness of these memoranda, and having it I must question her.

He turned again to where the witness sat, watching and waiting, almost unable to move.

> WELCH. May I ask you, Mrs. Driscoll, did you ever find a single memorandum to add to this file after Frank Carr dictated that one to you?
> MRS. DRISCOLL. . . . maybe I didn't get them together until afternoon.

So she contradicted her earlier testimony, that the file was prepared long before. This followed an earlier contradiction on the time that she had taken dictation from Roy Cohn. Mrs. Driscoll quivered, but she did not break. At last the Senators drifted away into an inconclusive debate. Then Mrs. Driscoll was released. There was a long sigh from the audience. It was as if everyone present had been treading on very thin ice beneath which swift water ran.

It was a memorable day in the Senate Caucus Room. Great Constitutional issues had been discussed in the hearings, to be recorded only in the dry pages of scholars. Little personal travesties had been committed, and it was these that would be remembered. It was the cropped photograph that brought the meaning of McCarthy home to taxi-drivers. It was Mary Driscoll's inability to recognize her own typing and to explain her own files, her failure to care about her own typewriter and to keep her shorthand books, that women throughout the nation would remember in disbelief.

The Ambivalence of Mr. Cohn

Two fascinating and very different figures moved through the Army-McCarthy hearings. They had the same background, the same appearance, the same name—Roy Marcus Cohn. But apparently they had never met.

There was Roy Cohn, the Young Schemer, whom several witnesses for the Army testified they knew well. He had cried "This means war!" when he was denied entrance to a radar laboratory. He had threatened to expose the Army in its worst light if it denied his demands for preferential treatment for Schine. He had used language "a little lower than a mule-skinner's," and according to John Adams he had forced the dispute between the Army and McCarthy beyond the point of no return.

There was also Roy Cohn, the Young Crusader—a very different individual. He was more like the hero of a Dickens novel—modest, respectful, self-effacing, and kind. The very suggestion that he might be disloyal to his heroes could move this young man to righteous indignation, as when he exclaimed, "Sir! You will never get me to say that Mr. Hoover did anything wrong!"

Those who encountered Cohn before or after his appearances often met a rude boy in a rush. But once the cameras lit up, the respectful and modest image of Cohn's own choosing filled the television screen and only the cynical might conclude that the word "sir" which ended every sentence hid a thinly veiled contempt for every man present save one.

In a somewhat inchoate speech, Senator Symington pleaded that public officials with evidence of wrongdoing should go to their superiors rather than to the McCarthy subcommittee. Senator McCarthy called on the Young Crusader to answer this "diatribe"; Cohn spoke with pride and sorrow of his patriotic little band of fellows, toiling for their country, only to be criticized.

> Cohn. . . . the staff—a handful, a handful, sir, of hardworking boys who work night and day up against probably hundreds and thousands of people who work over in the Army and in other places, this handful of people has brought about the removal from defense plants of Communists.
> They have brought about the removal from government agencies and from the Army of Communists and spies and, sir, it is hard to hear them criticized for having done that job.

How unjust of the Army to drag forth the other Cohn from the dark imaginations of evil men, and to dangle it like a jeering apparition in the face of this gentle boy! The Young Crusader looked at the Young Schemer in total disbelief. He had never seen him. Sometimes, of course, he used words that he wouldn't use on television, but his friends assured him that he cussed much less than most boys his age. Sometimes, too, he got a tiny bit annoyed, and, sir, wouldn't you if people thwarted you in your labors of exposing the Communist menace?

The wicked old wizard, Mr. Welch, conceived a clever plot. It was to turn the Young Crusader into the Young Schemer in front of twenty million witnesses, by sprinkling something on him that would make him mad. It was in the second day of cross-examination that the elderly Bostonian's chance first came. Suddenly he was a crafty and arrogant enemy—probing, jibing, demanding, interrupting, ridiculing, seeking to tear off the armor and display the lace. Once before, at Fort Monmouth, Cohn's enormous ego had been pricked by the routine denial of a simple pass, leaving a spoiled child in a temper tantrum. Now Welch was endeavoring to recreate that scene. If he could make the audience howl enough at the discomfited witness, an awful moment might come at which the violent contours of the Young Schemer might stand forth from the noble outline of the Young Crusader.

Plainly, what Mr. Welch hoped for, others feared. Heads shook in rapid motions of "Yes! Yes!" and "No! No!" Lips moved in whispers and groans. Slips of paper with scribbled advice passed rapidly to the red leather chair which rocked under Welch's sudden fury. McCarthy and Dirksen rode in to break up the attack, and then the ten minutes of torture were up. There was a long sigh of relief in the camp of the crusaders. The two Cohns had passed close by, but they had not met.

On the following morning a mild and contrite Welch apologized to the Young Crusader, who quickly gained the upper hand and held it throughout the day. Nor was there much danger from other quarters. Chairman Mundt made long speeches about Alger Hiss on the witness' behalf; Senator Dirksen served happily as his counsel; Senator McCarthy posed such delightful questions as, "Tell this audience what is the *Daily Worker*?" Senators Potter and Dworshak were harder, but not too hard. On the Democratic side John McClellan and Henry Jackson plodded methodically along in their effort to lay something hard and fast on the steps of the Department of Justice. And while the witness declined, with great skill, to cooperate, he seemed less fearful of this effort than he had been two days before. Senator Symington had a long list of questions on Constitutional issues which, the modest witness at first protested, he was not competent to discuss. But soon it was plain that nothing could restore Mr. Cohn to his usual good spirits more than the opportunity to educate the nation on its Constitution.

After five days of Mr. Cohn's explanations the subcommittee could be sure of only one thing: that it would be hard to pin a perjury charge on Cohn. It was Jenkins who first tried to get a firm answer from the young lawyer. He had beside him a pile of blue volumes of testimony from which sprouted tufts of yellow slips. Fingering the first slip he pointed out that three Army witnesses had testified that at Fort Monmouth on October 20 Cohn had cried, "This is a declaration of war!" Cohn nodded in sad forgiveness. "Did you say that?" demanded Mr. Jenkins. Cohn answered at various times, "I don't recall the exact words I used," "I have no recollection of the words I used," "I do not remember using those words." He even said, "Specifically, to answer you, I do not remember using those words." Mr. Jenkins was terribly insistent. "Well, you don't deny it?" he inquired. "I am pretty close to denying it," answered Cohn. Jenkins, who had been far tougher on the Secretary of the Army, passed on. He next read from testimony that Cohn had said to Army officials, "We will investigate the heck out of you!" Incredulous, he looked up. "Did you say that, Mr. Cohn?" "I don't recall those words, sir," Cohn replied. "You don't deny it, do you?" Jenkins demanded. "Sir," said Cohn, "I come again pretty close to denying that's the type of thing I said. . . ." "You say you were angry?" Jenkins pleaded. "Yes, sir," said Cohn. "But you don't remember what you said?" "I haven't the remotest idea of everything I said," answered the young man whose memory McCarthy justifiably remarked was unsurpassed.

The pattern never varied. "I will ask you," said Jenkins, "whether or not you stated to the Secretary of the Army he had double-crossed Senator McCarthy." Cohn answered, "I don't recall using those words." The puzzled Jenkins continued, "You neither affirm nor deny that statement?" Cohn replied, "The best I can give you . . . if you press me would be a guess." Next Jenkins wanted to know: did Cohn want Schine assigned to the New York area? The fourth try brought forth the sharpest answer, "I can't give you a categorical yes or no." All right, then, said Jenkins, what about John Adams's accounts of the pressures brought by Cohn? "I have no recollection," "quite an exaggerated account," "not accurate," was the most that Cohn would say. Did Cohn and Adams discuss Schine? He couldn't affirm or deny it. Did Cohn say Schine was double-crossed? He was inclined to doubt it. Did Cohn curse Adams on December 17? No, said Cohn, there was just "an animated discussion." Hadn't Lieutenant Blount said that Cohn demanded Schine's leaves? That was for committee work. But committee work was never mentioned! Well, it was assumed. All right, then, did you say on January 14, "Stevens is through"? I don't remember saying that, replied Cohn.

Occasionally, in his poking, Jenkins would poke a hole in the earthworks of Cohn's defense. Then McCarthy would slap a handful of mud on the hole, and the damage would be repaired.

So Jenkins retraced the tracks of Stevens and Adams over four weeks of testimony—and never drew from Cohn a flat denial. The impression left was that the Army witnesses had made an appalling succession of regrettable mistakes. Cohn's only trouble was that the brief of counter-charges he had signed laid a good deal more than error at the Army's door. He refused to admit that the brief contained charges. With some reluctance he reaffirmed its claims. Quietly, almost surreptitiously, Cohn repeated the charge of the brief that Adams had once declared that he would "stop at nothing" to block the subpoenas for members of the Army's Loyalty and Security Screening Board.

It seemed then that only the monitored calls could bring to light or bury the unwelcome image of Cohn that John Adams had conjured up. At noon on June 4 Senator Symington probed into this tender issue. There was at once a cry of pain from McCarthy, and Cohn was back at his side, whispering and looking a little sick. By way of diversion the Senator set off a number of firecrackers in Symington's face.

Where then did the truth lie? The Army accused Cohn of outbursts of temper. He conceded this much. The Army added that the outbursts continued as Cohn demanded privileges for Private Schine. That Cohn denied. The Army maintained that because it treated Private Schine like any other soldier it was punished by the subcommittee in Cohn's desire for revenge. That Cohn denied with vigor. But he did volunteer one interesting story.

At Fort Dix Colonel Earl Ringler, the regimental commander, had objected to special treatment for Private Schine. In turn, according to the sworn testimony of Lieutenant John

Blount, Cohn had told him that he had a long memory and would never forget how Ringler had crossed his friend. Cohn's version of this incident was different but no more pleasant. Schine, he testified, had telephoned to say that his colonel had been heard referring to the McCarthy investigation of Fort Monmouth as a witch hunt.

> COHN. I told Lieutenant Blount about that and it is very possible, sir, that I did say I had a long memory and that I would remember the colonel's name, and I know that I did pass the name along to a member of the staff and ask that a check be made on this particular colonel because he was talking in a pretty peculiar way about Communist investigations.

At that moment the Young Schemer sprang from the shadows, looked the Young Crusader in the face and grinned.

Did they know each other after all? When had they met? The answer, if it was to be found, lay far back in the past, before this June day in the Senate Caucus Room

Roy Cohn was the only child of doting parents. His mother was also his servant, who began picking his napkin off the floor when he was in his high chair, and never stopped. His father had important plans for Roy—part of his dream for his son— and unfortunately he was able to execute them ten years too soon.

Albert Cohn was a gentle and good man. As a major power in the satrapy of Ed Flynn, he was Franklin Roosevelt's first judicial appointment. Within the limits of New York's judicial system his was a distinguished career on the Appellate Court. He laid out a still more distinguished career for his only child.

The child was headstrong, egocentric, aggressive. His father was for him a professional inspiration and a political backer; he was not a companion, a disciplinarian, and a guide. For guidance the boy was sent to Fieldstone, a school run by the Ethical Culture Society. There ethical values were taught first, and the writings of John Dewey were holy writ. But Roy Cohn, his own teacher, left with a highly developed ambition and a puzzling concept of right and wrong.

Roy Cohn was a student at Columbia. He left no outstanding record at law school. He did not work hard, but that was
not the only reason. "Grades in law school," said one of his
classmates, "are determined by each student's approach to his
work. The top students are chosen for the Law Review and
spend hours in editing each number. Yet their high grades continue because their approach is right. In contrast Roy had a
B-minus approach to his work. He just didn't care much about
the law."

His classmates, in fact, saw very little of Roy Cohn. Only
when the time for the moot courts came did they search him
out. Then Roy Cohn was invaluable as the one student who
knew every judge in New York by his first name. There was
not one who would not preside to oblige Albert's son.

The sons of other citizens, when they reached eighteen,
went off to the Second World War. When Roy Cohn's turn
approached, a Bronx Congressman, friendly to his father, put
the young man up for West Point. So he was exempted from the
draft. Cohn's application was rejected on medical grounds. The
standards of West Point did not change over the next three
years. Nor did Cohn's physical disability. But twice more the
Congressman pressed the application.

So at twenty Roy Cohn graduated and went to work in the
office of the U.S. Attorney for Southern New York, John F. X.
McGohey. There, apprenticed to two brilliant prosecutors, he
helped to convict the American Hydrasol Company. There
were no Communists in that case; but there were men who
had concealed German assets. And, involving a violation of the
Trading with the Enemy Act, it raised the same kind of problems as subversion. In that two-year case Roy Cohn learned all
the techniques by which prosecutors gain convictions. But,
lacking experience in life itself, he did not know under what
human conditions they should not be used. He knew every way
to arrive at a given end, and did not always care what the way
might be.

Roy Cohn's interest in the law was personal aggrandize-
ment rather than political change. When prosecuting Communists became the most sensational of pursuits he persuaded

the Assistant District Attorney to grant him a role in the prosecution of the second string leaders of the Communist Party.
There Cohn worked hard and well. His contemporaries enjoyed
time out for good food, but Roy Cohn's only concern was that
the chicken sandwich and bottle of milk should be clean. His
contemporaries went out with girls in the evenings. Cohn
joined the company of older, prominent men. Already they
were grooming the young lawyer. Soon the firm of Curran and
Stim, which he joined, became Curran, Mahoney, Cohn, and
Stim. There, with the Republican State Secretary and the
Democratic Minority Leader in the state senate as his partners,
the 23-year-old Cohn sat in an office that most men might
hope to occupy at sixty-five. He earned large fees from referrals
and other patronage plums, and set equally large fees for set-
tlements in the cases he touched.

At twenty-three Roy Cohn was settled everywhere but
within himself. He knew all but the profound and important
things. He knew how to get theater tickets to the popular
shows. Head waiters scraped as he entered Sardi's and the Stork
Club. Winchell and Lyons picked up the receiver when he
called in with the tip to which there was attached a line of
praise. An influential visitor who could find no room in the
city and phoned Roy Cohn might soon find himself in the unfamiliar luxury of a Ritz suite kept for just such occasions. And
always, the next morning, someone had taken care of the bill.

"Cohn, who testified before the subcommittee, left it with
the impression that he is an extremely bright young man, aggressive in the performance of his duties and probably not free
from the pressures of personal ambition." The words might be
taken from a draft by Mr. Jenkins of his report on the
McCarthy-Army hearings. In fact, they are contained in a report by a subcommittee of the House of Representatives that
investigated the Department of Justice late in 1952. The investigation followed an uproar in which the same charges of bad
faith, double dealing, improper pressures, and disregard for law
were passed back and forth. On one side were the Department
of Justice, the Department of State and the United Nations—
on the other, a New York grand jury and its legal officer, Roy
Cohn.

The grand jury had met for six months to consider minor cases of subversion. Then in March 1952 Roy Cohn was permitted to take to the jury the case of a man whose name he had run across in his files. With his customary energy he built the case until the grand jury had heard nearly one hundred United States employees of the United Nations, of whom almost half invoked the Fifth Amendment.

In the summer of 1952, the grand jury recessed and Roy Cohn, who had gained a personal following among its members, was transferred to Washington. The jurors suspected that he was being "kicked upstairs." Washington officials were told a different story. At the same time the United Nations vigorously protested the grand jury's infringement of its powers. The Department of State joined the UN in this protest. The Department of Justice made no effort to halt Mr. Cohn, and he took this to mean new support. He proceeded to write a draft presentment and gave it to the grand jury to release on its own. Cohn's presentment exceeded the proper bounds of grand jury procedure in punishing individuals by publicity without actually indicting them for a crime. In addition, the Keating subcommittee reported, it was

> ... extraordinary in that it identified witnesses by name and contained direct quotations from the testimony and resorted to the unusual expedient of sending copies to all members of the jury.

On October 7, the jury was convened to consider this draft. On October 8, Cohn was abruptly summoned to Washington for conferences with the department and directed to bring the proposed presentment with him. In the final conference, Attorney General James McGranery called upon his senior advisers to state their views. One was Charles Murray, Assistant Attorney General in charge of the Criminal Division. He told the Keating subcommittee:

> I was strongly against the [Cohn] presentment because of the evils that have been mentioned, the mentioning of names and the revealing in quotations of testimony and statements of refusal to answer. . . . I believe that a federal grand jury has the sole

function to indict or not to indict. ... I believe that when a
Grand Jury is permitted to file a report it ... is being given the
power to destroy the instrumentality that the Constitution was
made to preserve. ... I am against government by hysteria.

Cohn did not think much of these views. In testimony
before the subcommittee, he dismissed his superior, a man of
twenty-five years of practice, as a lawyer with "a District of
Columbia" approach.

The Attorney General turned next to learn the views of the
Assistant Attorney General, Ross Malone, and the U.S. Attorney for Southern New York, Myles Lane. Both men stated that
the Cohn presentment was reckless, improper, and self-
defeating.

The Keating subcommittee hearings continued with
Malone's sworn testimony.

Finally the question came up. ... Who was trying to bring out
that presentment at that particular time in advance of the normal release ... and what was the motivation for it ... ?

The fact was discussed that we were in the middle of a
political campaign.

I opined I believe that it looked like somebody might be
trying to make a political football out of the United Nations
which is not a political issue.

The answer to Malone's question was promptly provided
by Cohn. Malone's sworn testimony continues:

Mr. Cohn delivered a very impassioned statement in support of
issuing the presentment immediately. ... He said: "Well, the
Internal Security Committee is going to start hearings Monday
and if we bring out the thing today, we can beat them to the
headlines."

The Attorney General of the United States did not warm
to this plea. He expressed the view that the presentment was
premature and should not be released.

Cohn was unimpressed. He said, "Well, what if the grand
jury goes ahead and does it anyhow?"

Cohn was in no mind to argue his jury out of issuing his
presentment just because the Attorney General of the United

States was so inclined. But Myles Lane warned the jurors that they might all be sued for the charges it contained. So the presentment was delayed, and the grand jury continued its work. Among the new witnesses called was Adrian Fisher, Legal Adviser of the Department of State. The jurors demanded from him the names of State Department officials who had permitted suspected Communists to be hired by the UN. Mr. Fisher, on instructions from the Secretary of State, stated that the release of the names would be a violation of executive immunity and administrative integrity. The dispute was taken to Judge Edward Weinfeld, and Fisher stated that the Department of Justice supported the State Department's view. Joseph Kelly, foreman of the grand jury, told the Keating subcommittee what followed.

> KELLY. Judge Weinfeld . . . turned to Roy Cohn and said, "You are in a funny spot here. . . . You are arguing against your own department. Do you understand that?"
> Roy Cohn said, "Yes, I do."
> "Do you still want to continue that way?"
> "Yes," Roy Cohn said.

The judge dismissed the grand jury. Its members, resentful, told the judge that Fisher had misrepresented them. They also had apparently been misled as to the significance of the Department of Justice view. Another juror, Joseph Cahill, testified.

> CAHILL. Mr. Cohn on that day said that his only information that the Department of Justice had ruled to the contrary came over the phone; that it was hearsay; that it was not—there is a legal term for it that I do not recall—at any rate all he had was a telephone call that had come to Mr. Lane and Mr. Lane had in turn relayed to him. . . .

Evidently Cohn told the good grocers and housewives that an order, relayed directly to his superior and then to him, could be discounted as "hearsay." The Keating report notes:

> Immediately thereafter Cohn was summoned to Washington and censured by Assistant Attorney General Ross Malone for his defiance and disobedience.

On December 4, 1952, the jury's term expired. As the day approached, a new presentment was prepared. Through a misunderstanding which Cohn blamed on the Department of Justice and the Department blamed on Cohn, the presentment was not even shown to the Attorney General.

On the day of its release the Attorney General telephoned to protest to Cohn that he had not even had a chance to read it although in Mr. Cohn's words it contained "a blast at the State Department." Cohn was asked to hold it up two days. But the McCarran committee, a latecomer, was stealing the headlines, and the grand jurors were fuming. Cohn testified before the Keating subcommittee:

> I told them that . . . I had no intention of telling [the jury] to . . .
> go home and come back another day for no particular reason and
> I further said that this presentment was perfectly fine.

In fact, he told the papers that the investigation which he had led was "the most important investigation ever conducted in the history of the United States." An unnamed informant added that the Department of Justice should be censured for trying to block the release. And so the Keating subcommittee was brought in. It found no evidence of malpractice on the part of the Justice Department. But it did uncover a prophetic story of a young man in an important but sensitive realm— accomplishing some good but at great cost, because of disregard for established procedure and contempt for established authority.

There was no doubt that Roy Cohn expressed the mood of the grand jurors. There was also no doubt that their mood of wayward anger and hostility was substantially shaped by Roy Cohn over ten months. It was a mood careless of injustice. But those who welcomed the results saw a new future for Roy Cohn. George Sokolsky, the Hearst philosopher, followed the work of his young friend with enthusiasm. Joseph McCarthy studied the subcommittee hearings with admiration. Sokolsky helped to bring the two men together and the compact was signed. The youth who had run one reference in a file into a conflict that shook the walls of the Department of Justice aligned himself with one in whose presence alone the walls began to shiver. The story of the grand jury had only to be recreated on a larger scale, sharpened in impact, and heightened in its tragedy by the power and fanaticism of Joseph McCarthy and the unreasoning emotion that raged in Roy Cohn's breast over David Schine, which not even McCarthy could control.

Roy Cohn had no ideological interest in Communism when he asked Irving Saypol to let him help prosecute the second-string Communist leaders. He had little more when he joined Joseph McCarthy as his chief of staff. He was moderate in his political views. He was less concerned with the Communist menace than with his own career. Even after two years of prosecutions, he was not possessed by the fanatic zeal to destroy the enemy that raged in the Wisconsin Senator. Now as always he asked what was in it for Roy Cohn. The answer, he concluded, was power and publicity, at once, and in unparalleled amounts. More patient, his New York backers pleaded with him not to join the invader from the outlands whom politicians of both parties in New York feared. But Roy Cohn believed that his brain and McCarthy's force would be invulnerable. So at twenty-six he became the counsel to a major Senate committee, headed by an ungovernable man.

At first sight it seemed a worthy partnership.

Senator McCarthy had suffered from abominable staff work, relying for assistance chiefly on hangers-on from Wisconsin, a man fired by the FBI, and that shabby crowd of informers who camp around Capitol Hill, often carrying the *Cross and the Flag* in their pockets and reciting to anyone who pays them increasingly lurid versions of their dull careers in the Communist Party thirty years before. As a member of the minority party, Senator McCarthy could get by with these men and with the information thrown his way by his party. Now as chairman of a Senate committee he had to make good his own extravagant claims. He had promised that the exodus he would instigate from Washington following a Republican victory would be the greatest spectacle since St. Patrick drove the

snakes from Ireland. But, unlike St. Patrick, he needed help. It
was a critical moment for the Senator when Roy Cohn volunteered and brought with him his handful of hard-working boys.
From then on they staged the spectacles and wrote the scripts
and McCarthy claimed the front page as his private domain.

In turn, the Senator gave Roy Cohn unheard-of power.
Generals jumped at his command. Heads of departments asked
him for interviews. The Secretary of the Army publicly
apologized for annoying him. He was able to yield three minutes of his time to Senators who wished to be heard. No royal
princes could have staged a more fantastic excursion than the
trip made by Cohn and Schine when, in the spring of 1953, they
toured ten European nations in seventeen days, commanding
the front pages of newspapers, terrorizing government agencies, leaving gasping officials and ruined careers in their wake.

It was Cohn who brought Schine to his castle on Capitol
Hill. It was Schine who brought the castle down by adding one
too many blocks on top of the dizzy structure Cohn had built.
Once before Cohn had gone to extraordinary lengths in secur-
ing a diplomatic passport for a young undergraduate who accompanied him on a trip to Europe. Now he repeated the pattern, with more power—and worse results.

Secretary Stevens testified that "Mr. Cohn was tremendously interested in Mr. Schine." John Adams added that "it was
the subject of Schine that caused the deterioration in an otherwise very friendly relationship." Senator McCarthy joined in
this appraisal in the telephone call of November 7. Almost in
anguish McCarthy said to the Secretary:

> I would like to ask you one personal favor. For God's sake don't
> put Dave in service and assign him back on my committee. . . .
> He is a good boy but there is nothing indispensable about him
> . . . it is one of the few things I have seen [Roy] completely
> unreasonable about. . . . Roy was next to quitting the commit-
> tee. He thought I had gone back on the committee. . . .

It was for Roy's sake, not the subcommittee's, that
McCarthy sought leaves for Private Schine.

McCarthy had an "unbreakable rule," or so he wrote to

Secretary Stevens after Drew Pearson broke the story of Schine's privileges on December 22. It was: "That neither I nor anyone on my behalf shall ever attempt to interfere with or influence the Army in its assignments and promotions."

Cohn knew of this rule. He asked General Walter Bedell Smith, Under Secretary of State, to obtain a commission for his friend in the Central Intelligence Agency. Smith warned of the difficulties but offered to phone the CIA; then, according to Smith's testimony, Cohn demurred.

> SMITH. Mr. Cohn said that I need not do this. The CIA, he said, was too juicy a subject for future investigation and it would not be right to ask them to get Mr. Schine commissioned and then investigate the organization later.

A sound rule—and one which Roy Cohn promptly broke. He broke it with such force that Senator McCarthy fell silent, or supported his demands. They were improper demands, as Cohn and McCarthy surely knew. On this matter alone, Cohn was wholly unconvincing. He first maintained that he had no interest in Schine beyond his committee work; the plea was strange, coming from a close friend. He next asserted that, much as he liked Schine, he never brought pressure to bear on his behalf. Here a half dozen witnesses proved him wrong. Retreating, Cohn argued that it was Schine's contribution to the subcommittee that led him to demand his release from Army routine. McCarthy's own words, of November 7, disputed this claim. Still Cohn insisted that Schine bore a heavy work load before and after his induction. Welch demanded evidence of his work. When Cohn at last produced the evidence, the box was large, the contents pitifully small.

And yet Roy Cohn almost escaped unscathed. He was an excellent witness—eloquent, confident, fast beyond belief. Only on the matter of his friendship with Schine did he falter, staring at the table in front of him.

Cohn was a young man of quick mental resources. He had chosen to use them in the cause of McCarthyism and in the cause of his close friend, who had become a private in the United States Army—thereby stimulating one of the most fantastic hearings in American political history.

Cohn endured with patience the criticisms of himself. Then, as he left the witness chair, an attack developed on his friend. McCarthy had cited a memorandum by Schine as a reason for his employment by the subcommittee; now he produced the text. The Schine plan proved to be a "plan of long range strategy for immediate execution" in the realm of "psychological warfare." It was a jumbled catalogue of gimmicks, professions, and slogans about as meaningful as the classified section of a telephone directory from which it might have been taken. The audience howled as Senator Jackson read it aloud and even McCarthy gave up with a grin when Jackson asked him to explain Schine's proposed use of pin-ups to defeat Communist fire with fire. Cohn was furious. He sent a staff man out for a file marked "Jackson's record." Carrying it like a weapon he headed for the committee table when the session closed. There he caught Robert Kennedy, the 28-year-old counsel for the minority. Newsmen heard him threaten Jackson, and they heard Kennedy tell Cohn to take his threats to the Senator. Cohn answered, "Do you want to fight?" They were separated, and each was asked for his version of the exchange. Kennedy reported without hesitation that Cohn had said, "You'd better tell Jackson we're going to get him on Monday. We're going to bring out stuff on his being favorably inclined to Communism." Cohn refused to speak until he had heard Kennedy's report. Then he gave his own, which reporters wrote was not what they had heard. Jackson announced that this was not the first threat made to the Senators in the course of the hearings.

So the Young Schemer sprang up at the last, and filled the Caucus Room with mocking laughter as the Young Crusader fled down the marble halls.

Great power greatly corrupts; never was Lord Acton's observation more apt. For it was the power of the United States Senate that gave force to the ugly threats of this impudent boy. The absence of countervailing power is also corrupting. And it was the weakness of McCarthy in permitting Cohn's transgression, and of Secretary Stevens in offering his cooperation, that turned Cohn's weakness into a fatal flaw. Looking back on it all, quite a bit could be said in Roy Cohn's defense, if a frank defense were made. It might even be argued with reason that, knowing the deep commitment of Roy Cohn to Private Schine, John Adams did look on it as a lever. It was a poor lever among ordinary men, for the most that Adams could threaten was to treat this private as any other private. But perhaps that was enough to a young man who by then had convinced himself and his friend that they stood above the law.

So Cohn's castle of children's blocks, which Robert Stevens had helped to build, crashed down in the Senate Caucus Room. There, eighteen months after he had joined McCarthy, Roy Cohn was in the dock where he had placed so many others.

In those eighteen months Cohn and Senator McCarthy had been through much together. Cohn at least had suffered on Schine's behalf. A time had come when McCarthy considered firing him. Yet when Dirksen had demanded that Cohn be fired, McCarthy had refused; by then it was too late. Now Cohn and McCarthy were cast together in the Senate Caucus Room, outlawed by their party chiefs, and facing defeat. In a touching moment they swore again their political vows.

> McCARTHY. . . . first, Mr. Cohn, may I say I have been extremely happy to see the comparison between your answers and the answers of Mr. Stevens and Mr. Adams. I've appreciated the way you've answered all questions and not ducked any of them.
>
> I think your performance on the witness stand may be somewhat of a key to why the opposition feels they must get rid of you at all costs.
>
> And I think your performance here has justified the confidence that I had when we induced you to take this job as chief counsel.
>
> COHN. Senator, I deeply appreciate your confidence in me. That means more to me than anything.

Yet Cohn supposed at that moment that the formal partnership could not continue for long. It was his understanding that only Senator Dirksen was prepared to recommend his continuation on the subcommittee which he had helped to bring into disrepute. So at the end of his testimony he asked and gained permission to make what amounted to an farewell adress.

> COHN. My final word, sir, and one which I must make before I leave the stand, is about a man who to me is a great American that is Senator Joe McCarthy.
>   . . . I have never known a man who has less unkindness, less lack of charity in his heart and soul than Senator McCarthy, and I have never known a man who has been more loyal and devoted to his staff and to everybody associated with him in this cause than Senator McCarthy. . . . I think [McCarthy and Carr] have been badly treated in having to sit here when their only crime has been that of doing their level best to protect this nation against the menace of Communist infiltration . . . but their reward comes in the gratitude of the American people.

McCarthy sprang up to grasp Cohn's hand. They smiled at each other as the flash bulbs exploded in batteries.

Roy Cohn had been given all the power and publicity that he had dreamed of. He was by now the best-known citizen of his years. He had defied three Democratic Senators and a great trial lawyer in this hearing. But what did he have left? Where did he stand now in the great career his father had planned?

Judge Cohn was a loyal Democrat to whom party regularity was the first act of political conviction. His son, a Democrat, was part of a political apparatus whose leader called the beloved party "the party of treason."

Judge Cohn was a jurist, held in high professional respect. Roy Cohn was a good trial lawyer. And yet, not even the constant recourse to the one-hundred-and-thirty-Communists-in-defense-plants, who by now were worth as much to McCarthy as Texas millionaires, could prevent close observers from seeing that the polish of Roy Cohn's manner was tarnished by the cause he served. Some phrases seemed brutal but appropriate when spoken by one who had known bitter poverty, and had spent his youth working the Wisconsin soil. The same phrases were far more repulsive mouthed by the sensual lips of a sophisticated and wealthy city youth. Now, like his master, Roy Cohn condemned as spies men never brought to court. He too spoke easily of "Fifth Amendment Communists," thus reducing the Bill of Rights to an epithet and demonstrating his contempt for due process of law. He even coined in passing a new and still more arbitrary epithet—"Fifth Amendment Spy"—so that citation of the Constitutional privilege became evidence of treason. He also held that Senator McCarthy and Roy Cohn were above the law, insisting that they would disregard the law when they disagreed with it, and summoning others to disobey it at their command.

Judge Cohn was a man of honor, to whom it was essential above all that men trust the word of his son. But among all the reporters in the great room, very few trusted Roy Cohn. All through the Memorial Day weekend when others danced, Roy Cohn labored to produce what he swore were the work papers of David Schine. And the reporters concluded that the papers were as interesting as last year's movie reviews.

Judge Albert Cohn had spent a lifetime teaching citizens to respect due process of law, to obey duly constituted authority, and to live in righteousness. Did he now reflect that he had impressed these principles upon thousands of uneducated immigrants and failed in the case of his own adored son? Roy Cohn left the witness chair with a confident smile. But among the debris left by the hearings, the crumpled papers and cigarette butts, there might be found the shattered fragments of an old man's dream.

"Thanks for the Marvelous Cheese"

If John Adams was telling the truth, then some of the worst offenses against the Army were committed over a telephone wire in conversations between himself and Roy Cohn. It was during a telephone conversation in late October that Cohn had threatened to expose the Army in its worst light. It was over the telephone that Cohn had stated on December 9 that "he would teach Mr. Adams what it meant to go over his head." It was over the telephone that Mr. Cohn used "extremely vituperative language" to Mr. Adams on December 11, and over the telephone that the sixty-five long distance calls and local calls without number were made on behalf of Schine.

On the second day of the hearings the Secretary of the Army admitted that he had monitored his calls. Senator McCarthy was enraged. He denounced the monitoring as "the most indecent and dishonest thing I have heard of," "completely indecent and improper," and "indecent and illegal under the laws." For days he brooded openly on the menace of eavesdropping. At the same time he established the sound position that his consent was necessary for the release of the records, and that he would consent only if all calls were released. After five weeks of struggle the Army conceded. And as it turned out, the damaging calls between Adams and Cohn had not been monitored after all.

The first calls were between Secretary Stevens and Mr. Cohn. They revealed an early symbiosis in which the Secretary labored to gain privileges for Mr. Schine and in turn Mr. Cohn protected the Army against public humiliation. In line for humiliation was an inept major general in charge of Army intelligence. Making him look a fool "would have been a lot of fun," said the 27-year-old, who added, "You know I'm an old big game hunter." But Cohn denied himself the pleasure of adding this general's hide and horns to his collection.

Filled with gratitude, the Secretary of the Army went to work for Schine. But Army regulations were rigid on one point—it took at least sixteen weeks of basic training to turn out a soldier. There was just no way out. Regretfully, the Secretary of the Army called Schine.

> I have reviewed the whole situation with Mr. Wilson and it adds up to this. Neither he nor I can see any appropriate way to avoid the basic training. We feel it is almost a must. . . . having done that . . . I think there is an excellent chance that we can pick you up and use you in a way that would be useful to the country and to yourself.

This was the worst of all the calls; spectators who had clung to an identification with the Army side because it opposed McCarthy looked at each other in disgust when this conversation was reported. For this call gave Cohn every right to feel later on that a promise had been broken.

And yet sixteen weeks as a private seemed a long time to David Schine. A week later Cohn mentioned to the Secretary "the matter of our young friend whom we have been talking to you about." He added that Dave and Joe thought that a job in the Central Intelligence Agency would be preferable to the draft. "Do you want me to call Allen Dulles?" said Cohn.

Stevens was pressured, Adams was pounded, Monmouth was torn apart. But before the Secretary of the Army left for the Pacific in January, he called McCarthy to propose one last "little visit." Everything was friendly. He ended with love to Jeanie, the Senator's bride, and thanks to Joe "for that marvelous cheese."

The next call on February 26 was not so friendly. General

Zwicker had balked at giving McCarthy the names of Pentagon officials responsible for the discharge of Major Peress. Stevens, fearful but defiant, called McCarthy to tell him what he had done. "I am going to prevent my officers from going before your committee," he told McCarthy," until you and I have an understanding as to the abuse they are going to get." McCarthy answered:

> Just go ahead and try it, Robert. I am going to kick the brains out of anyone who protects Communists! . . . You just go ahead . . . I will guarantee you that you will live to regret it!

Alarmed, the Secretary called the subcommittee members. The monitored calls revealed a formal and distant Dirksen, a friendly Potter, a cautious McClellan. Mundt, in the wonderfully apt description Stevens gave McClellan, was "highly distressed . . . but noncommittal." Jackson was away. Symington was leaving for Europe and Stevens caught him in New York. "McCarthy . . . really started to beat my brains out," cried the Secretary. "He blew his lid! . . ." "Just keep it all down on paper," Symington replied.

With solemn ceremony, two words were deleted from the Symington transcript. A bored reporter asked McCarthy to find out what they were. In good humor, McCarthy rose, walked round the table and leaned over Jenkins. The reporter searched McCarthy's face for some sign on his return. The Senator shook his head in warning. Much later, when the cameras were looking elsewhere, he scribbled one dreadful word on a scrap of paper and slipped it like a conspirator under the table. The word was "damn."

The Conscience
of Senator Symington

The one fixed idea in McCarthy's mind throughout the hearings was that the Army report was blackmail. To the question of who was blackmailing him, and why, he never had one answer for very long. Nor could his answer be fixed. By contrast the fixed accusation would limit the sense of evil and with it the remedy. But in a world where formless corruption could not be dealt with by the formal law, only a supremely willful man, acting beyond the law, could do the rescue-work of the hour. So McCarthy gave various names to the blackmailers and their work.

In his first version the blackmailers were said to be Secretary Stevens and John Adams. Their motive, as announced by McCarthy, was to stop his investigation of the way they had coddled Communists.

In the second version, which was never brought within range of the kleig lights, the blackmailer was H. Struve Hensel. The motive, as announced by McCarthy, was to halt an investigation of Hensel's wartime activities.

In a third version of the story, McCarthy chose the Communists. He tried, without much success, to imply that they might be found in the Pentagon. He contended, with the aid of huge black photostats, that whatever was said in criticism of

McCarthy was inspired by the *Daily Worker*. On two different days he made untrue statements about Theodore Kaghan, a man of no apparent importance to the case, who was not permitted to testify in reply. Then McCarthy announced that Kaghan was employed by the *New York Post*, a "Communist sheet," and that it was the *Post* that first broke the story of Private Schine.

In the fourth version, the blackmailers were traced, by no choice of McCarthy's, to the White House. They included Presidential Assistant Sherman Adams, Attorney General Herbert Brownell, Assistant Attorney General William Rogers, and others. Senator McCarthy did not divulge their motives. He drew an obscure parallel between Brownell and Attorney General Daugherty, who was heavily involved in the scandals of the Harding administration. He laid the foundations for the wholesale assault on the Eisenhower administration.

Thus McCarthy claimed that the atomic bomb plants, the Central Intelligence Agency, and other departments presided over by the President were rotten with Communists. He held that it was quite useless to give to the leaders of the Eisenhower administration his list of names of Communist traitors in sensitive positions, since no action would follow. And, drawing from a folder marked "Twenty Years of Treason," McCarthy spent one morning of the hearings making a series of speeches on Asian policy. His apparent target was the Truman administration. But he seemed also to be serving notice on the White House that if it fought in Southeast Asia he was ready to condemn it for warmongering, and if it failed to fight and so lost the area he was also ready to condemn it for its appeasement of Communism. So the twenty years of treason became twenty-one.

But 1954 was an election year, in which the President was in trouble enough without McCarthy leading the battle against him. A number of Republican Senators and state chairmen facing hard election contests let it be known that McCarthy would not be welcome in some of his former strongholds.

From all over the nation McCarthy received messages from powerful supporters warning him that he was hurting the

Republican party. He was not yet ready to turn on the President. Nor was he prepared to lose the support of the Republican high command. He understood that the fourth version of his serial, "The Blackmailers," was leading him toward political isolation.

At that moment the telephone calls of Symington and Stevens were released. They came as a windfall. For in Senator McCarthy's fourth version of "The Blackmailers" Secretary Stevens and the other good—if "not too bright"—Republicans were the innocents duped into trying to harm McCarthy by a clever, scheming Democrat who wanted to be President and knew that McCarthy had to be smeared first. This new invention cleared the way for Senator McCarthy to walk arm in arm with his own party leaders again.

In a speech in Appleton, Wisconsin, on Saturday, June 6, McCarthy went through a dry run of his assault on Symington. When the hearings were resumed and the last telephone call read into the record he seized the microphone before him to demand that Clark Clifford be summoned as a witness, and that Symington step down. He ignored the unwelcome fact that Clifford had given no direct advice to Stevens, and that his only indirect advice, on the sole matter of the subpoena, was to be cautious. He further ignored the unwelcome fact that Symington's main call was before the chicken luncheon at which Stevens surrendered to McCarthy in the interests of party harmony. Combining the February 20 call of Stevens to Symington, and the call of March 8 in which Symington's only intention was an unsuccessful effort to see the Army report, McCarthy presented to the nation the totally false idea that it was Symington who had "instituted the charges."

> McCARTHY. We have it proven beyond any peradventure of a doubt that Secretary Stevens was willing to come up here and cooperate with the Committee ... and that ... Senator Symington with Clark Clifford, the chief political adviser of President Truman and I assume the chief political adviser of the man who would be President on the Democratic ticket in 1956, is doing the advising. . . .
> We find that . . . within a day or two the charges were issued

under the Secretary's name charging Mr. Cohn, Mr. Carr, and myself with almost everything except murdering our great-great-grandmothers. . . . For this reason I request that Mr. Clifford be subpoenaed immediately. . . . Mr. Symington should disqualify himself because never before in the history of the Senate as far as I know have we had a man who instituted the charges insist upon sitting as a judge.

To this charge Symington replied at first with a good deal of dignity. He endeavored without much success to disentangle the time sequence of his calls from the snarl created so cleverly by McCarthy. His best moment was his defense of his feeling of concern and alarm that led him to offer his advice in the February 20 call.

> SYMINGTON. Secretary Stevens and General Ridgway, Chief of Staff of the Army, came to see me. Secretary Stevens protested the abuse the Army had received from Senator McCarthy as chairman of this subcommittee. Secretary Stevens said the morale of the United States Army was being severely impaired. . . . It would have been unthinkable for me to disregard this situation. . . . I'm a member of the Senate Armed Services Committee as well as this committee. I've served as Secretary of the Air Force. I have no interest in life that surpasses my great concern for the vitality of our armed forces. I felt that Senator McCarthy's charges that our defense officials were coddling Communists, along with Secretary Stevens' counter-charges, precipitated a great and fundamental danger to the United States.

Reading from a statement which he had written in readiness for the assault, Symington moved up to the battleground of his own choosing, defending tradition against anarchy.

> SYMINGTON. This was no question of politics. It was a question of the loyalty and integrity of the armed forces. . . . For the first time in our history our people have been urged to entertain serious doubts as to the dedication and loyalty of our armed forces, from top to bottom. . . . But the vilification has not stopped with the United States Department of Defense. Millions of Americans have been told by Senator McCarthy that this Republican administration has added a year of treason to our proud history.

. . . I'm a Democrat, but first and foremost I'm an American. It's little comfort to me that these terrible charges are directed against a Republican administration, Republican officials, and our Republican Commander-in-Chief.

It would appear that some of us want to end up in this country with just plain anarchy.

At last McCarthy had an opponent worthy of his strength. To Symington's defense of his position, McCarthy replied with great skill, conceding nothing, adhering to his distortions, returning as always to the attack.

McCARTHY. I may say I was rather amused to hear Senator Symington worrying about the Republicans when he has been conniving secretly to get the top political adviser of the Democrats to try to get the Republicans to commit suicide.

It may seem very clever to Senator Symington that he got Clark Clifford to mislead a fine, naive, not-too-brilliant Republican Secretary of the Army.

But in the end that's going to be bad for his party and the country because the two party system cannot survive if you have the chief political adviser of one calling the shots for the other. If our two party system does not survive our republic cannot survive.

The point was exaggerated, as always. But it was strong. Many organization Democrats felt that Symington had acted improperly as a party man in advising a Republican secretary on how to deal with a member of his own party. And McCarthy had another strong point in insisting that Symington testify under oath on his role.

Symington was reluctant to testify, for he knew that McCarthy had prepared many irrelevant questions about his sources of information among newspaper friends. Yet he needed a counter-position. So he declared two days later that he would testify if McCarthy in turn would take the witness stand on the matter of his own financial affairs. It was not a logical position, for the audience felt that if Symington had information to give he should give it, and not treat it as part of a bargain. But it upset McCarthy, and he reverted to type. He declared now that Symington had "deceived" Stevens and he set forth, in a question to Cohn, a repulsive personal smear.

> MCCARTHY. Mr. Cohn, it develops that an individual here who happens to insist upon being a judge has a background of having dealt with a man, Mr. [William] Sentner, who got five years last week for conspiring to overthrow this government by force and violence.
>
> If it appears that a number of years ago . . . this man Sentner . . . who was a member of the Communist conspiracy called a strike, if it appears that one of the men who asked to be a judge here dealt with that man; that the strike was an attempt to get higher wages for the working man; that they made a deal whereby instead he gave Mr. Sentner a certain amount of money each month out of each man's pay check which reduced their wages and that on that condition the strike was called off, and this man who bragged about being a Communist was part of a study club with one of the judges here . . . and they attended this study club constantly and . . . discussed . . . forming the Communist association . . . would you say that that might possibly give some slight tip to the American people as to why that judge . . . tried so hard and got the chief adviser of the Democratic party to force an end to our investigation of Communists which he has succeeded in doing?

Symington listened with perfect calm. He pointed out that the "study club" was one organized by Protestant Episcopal Bishop Will Scarlett and attended by many Republican businessmen. He added that Sentner had been elected head of the United Electrical Workers, CIO, of Missouri, the union with which he was compelled by law to negotiate. He called the charge of a deal "totally and completely false; just another diversion."

With good humor Symington noted that McCarthy had broadcast all these charges during the 1952 campaign in Missouri. The people, he said, had paid little attention to them then and would pay no more attention to them now.

But if the charges were old, a man who stood up to McCarthy and struck back was something new. With apparent regret Mundt noted that the audience following the hearings rose sharply from that day on.

It seemed at first sight to be a battle between a Republican and a Democrat, but obviously it was not. For Symington was not acting as a Democrat when he accepted the call from Secretary Stevens. Symington, as he said, was not acting then as a party man. He was talking to Bob Stevens, who had been a junior at Yale when he entered there as a freshman. And he was talking about a mortal threat to the armed forces.

For Stuart Symington the armed forces were more important than narrow considerations of party. His grandfather was Major William Stuart Symington of Virginia, who had enlisted in the Richmond militia in 1861. He had ridden at the side of General George Picket at Gettysburg, where he was cited for conspicuous gallantry in that impetuous and costly charge. Symington's uncle was a naval officer. His father-in-law, James Wadsworth, was the leading spokesman of the Republican party on military affairs. Five of his cousins had lost their lives in the Second World War and in Korea. He himself had enlisted as a private in the Army at seventeen; and in turn his son Stuart Jr. at seventeen enlisted as a private in the Army, and his second son James enlisted in the Marine Corps, also at seventeen.

Symington's career was in business, where solidarity transcends party labels. As a businessman cleaning up maladministration, he went to Washington and was confirmed six times by the U.S. Senate for six high offices, by the unanimous vote of Republicans and Democrats. He earned the equal praise of both parties in directing the Surplus Property Board, in heading the National Security Resources Board, and in rehabilitating a shaken Reconstruction Finance Corporation. But it was his post as Secretary of the Air Force, from 1947 to 1950, that meant most to him. It was Symington's belief that the Air Force needed a champion in Congress that led him to run for the Senate over Truman's opposition in 1952.

It was true that McCarthy went to Missouri at the invitation of Symington's opponent James "Petroleum" Kem, to spread his smears about Sentner and the study club. But Symington was not greatly disturbed or concerned. It was the Armed Services Committee that he struggled to join when he came to the Senate. The McCarthy subcommittee to which he was also assigned seemed to him a futile and irritating diversion from his chief interest.

Then in the closing months of 1953, the ferocity with which McCarthy turned on the Pentagon struck in passing Stuart Symington's exposed nerve. As a member of the Armed Services Committee he gauged correctly the disastrous effect upon Army morale produced by McCarthy's attack on General Zwicker. In keeping with his deepest self he told the troubled Stevens, "It is a question of the integrity and fighting morale of the Army and therefore everybody in my opinion who has a concept of what is decent will break their back to help you in any way they can."

So Symington was ranged against McCarthy. Unlike the Wisconsin Senator he did not relish a fight. But he would not retreat from a fight once it began. He was bold and tough and eloquent. And, there were strains in their conflict, deeper than a struggle over military morale. There was a natural antipathy between them, that caused each to bristle as hostile animals bristle on approaching each other.

Joseph McCarthy represented the revolt of the mob, rising in scorn of the well bred. He spoke for a spirit noted a century before by Martin van Buren at a time when mass politics, running at full tide, began to wash over the rocks of aristocratic rule. "Those who have wrought great changes in the world," Van Buren wrote, "never succeeded in gaining over chiefs, but always in exciting the multitude."

Great change was McCarthy's purpose in destroying the established values of the past; exciting the multitude was his method, and he had genius of an evil sort in his pursuit. His attack seemed to be directed at Communists, or fellow travelers—or at liberals, whom many conservatives by 1952 regarded as holders of an alien philosophy. But the truth was that McCarthy, the master of the crowd, was attacking conservatism, the traditional conservatism that cherishes all those previous and now brittle things that make up our heritage. The best opposition to McCarthy was opposition in the name of that heritage. Regrettably the conservatives who should have been the first to defend it against McCarthy's onslaught were so far bewildered by twenty years of opposition that many of them deserted to his side.

Robert Ten Broeck Stevens, the son of the mansion, the product of Andover and Yale, the pillar of private enterprise, the member of the Union League Club, was the man entrusted with the defense of traditional values. Instead, with that political naiveté which is also characteristic of many American businessmen, he threw open the gates and welcomed the invader in.

Tradition was betrayed. Not even in the White House did tradition find a defender. In the stand that had to be made, those in the front ranks would be struck down first. Symington, whom some supposed to be a master politician, knew that. But his heritage made him its defender, moving with courage and grace.

Handsome and eloquent, Symington was well cast in his new role. He was wealthy; but wealth, which led some to worship McCarthy as the Protector of Property, played a minor part in his identification with the aristocratic tradition. Like McCarthy, Symington had known what it was to be poor. But as influences in his life, wealth and poverty alike were far outweighed by a commitment to memories which he had and McCarthy lacked. Some were memories of school and university—of the liberal arts, the right of dissent, the rule of reason. Beyond these were family memories—of lessons in honor, in loyalty, in bravery, in piety, in the duties of privilege, in respect for the past. These were the qualities McCarthy wrapped up in a package of contempt labeled "Sanctimonious Stu.'

When the hearings began, Stuart Symington was a hesitant man. He was haunted by a sense of his own incapacity in a legal dispute. Judiciousness in the person of Senator McClellan sat on his right and spoke in a sepulchral voice. Caution in the person of Senator Jackson sat on his left and spoke always to the point. Their judiciousness and caution alike reflected an earlier training in the law, so that question followed question as if in obedience to an invisible but logical progression toward foreseen ends. By contrast the first words Symington spoke were offered in apology: "I am not a lawyer. . . ."

In his embarrassment Symington employed legal advice. And so he came each morning to the hearings with a list of carefully prepared questions. But they were dry; and once they had been read, he was on his own. He was by nature more of a figurehead than an infighter. Sometimes he was brilliant, more often he missed the point. He added little to the development of the legal argument. But in the drama—and the hearings were predominantly drama—he became what no other would or could become—the protagonist. And soon cartons of telegrams and letters from across the nation were piled on the floor, the desks, the chairs, the filing cabinets of his offices, calling him noble and a leader, or else branding him traitor and wishing him disease and death.

Often, as McCarthy grappled with him, Symington forgot that it was the great ends of society that he was defending, and not the mean issues of McCarthy's choosing. He groped for words as he fought against the man who robbed all words of their meaning, and many times he failed.

With his unerring instinct for the weakness of others, McCarthy played upon Symington's lack of confidence and his sensitivity. He learned to taunt him. He learned how to rip off Symington's dignity and to incite the raw brawl for which Mundt would chide the two men impartially. Frequently McCarthy's method worked. At times, in fact, it looked as though Symington might not survive this battle to be mustered out. Those Democratic regulars who hoped to ride his bandwagon to the White House looked on in dismay as Symington alienated solid blocks of votes. These, they felt, were not the battles for which the people conferred the Presidency as a final citation. Symington knew all this and did not care. His wife had warned him to keep his temper, and trudging back to his office he upbraided himself for not keeping her advice. He scolded himself for being ineffective—beyond that his conscience was his guide. He knew he had compromised his ambition, but his ambition itself was changing. In the smoke and dust of this encounter the image of the White House grew dim. He felt that if he went down and took McCarthy with him, he would have served well.

Symington grasped the simple essence of the conflict between the new elite and the aristocracy of the spirit that he spoke for. "I believe in America," he told McCarthy, "and you do not and that is the great and fundamental difference between us."

As Symington gathered momentum, he also gained in confidence. So toward the end of the hearings he confronted Frank Carr with a series of questions about the security clearances of the subcommittee staff. Symington maintained and Carr agreed that there was danger that a poorly screened staff might gain access to government secrets. At that McCarthy interrupted to accuse Symington of "attempting by innuendo to smear" the staff. Symington politely denied that any inference was intended. He continued to question Carr and again McCarthy intervened. By then a long buzz had announced a Senate roll call, and the gavel had been struck to close the session. Symington stood listening to McCarthy; then, picking up a microphone and facing his accuser, he answered:

> SYMINGTON. In all the years that I have been in government, based on the testimony given to this committee under oath, I think the files of what you call "my staff, my director, my chief-of-staff" are the sloppiest and most dangerously handled files I have ever heard of.

The audience applauded. The chairman struck his gavel again to end the hearings; the Senators rose. Choking with rage and warning the teletypist to remain at his machine, McCarthy shouted that Symington was running away. Quite calmly, Symington buttoned his coat, hoisted his shoulders, and walked off, knowing he had won. Mundt trotted behind him, grinning; the other Senators followed. And as the newspapermen stood around him, laughing and pocketing their notebooks, McCarthy wound down to a lame end, muttering as if to himself, "I guess I'd better go vote."

There were other moments; the most memorable was one

when McCarthy implied cowardice. Symington turned then to confront him.

> SYMINGTON. You said something about being afraid. I want you to know from the bottom of my heart that I'm not afraid of anything about you or anything you've got to say anytime, any place, anywhere.

There were few other men in the home of the brave who could truthfully say that in 1954.

The Reluctance of Mr. Carr

Next to J. Edgar Hoover, Senator McCarthy seemed to admire Frank Carr most. Of his executive director, the Senator said, "Frank Carr is the most outstanding young man I have ever seen with the most outstanding record."

If the Senator spoke the truth, then who other than this most outstanding young man could he wish to testify on his behalf? And yet when his turn arrived on the twenty-first day Frank Carr was gone—banned as a witness from the Senate Caucus Room by Senator McCarthy and his Republican allies. He testified later after public protest, but the question persisted: what lay behind the reluctance of Mr. Carr?

Carr was a young man of thirty-seven who had gone from college through law school simply in order to qualify for employment by the FBI. He joined the FBI in 1942 and rose in eleven years to become supervisor of its security section dealing with Communist subversion in the New York area. He was well regarded in the agency. Perhaps his only complaint was that his salary of about $8600 was not commensurate with his responsibilities, and not adequate to provide for his wife and three children as he approached middle age.

In the spring of 1953 the staff director of the McCarthy committee, Dr. J. B. Matthews, was forced to resign following widespread criticism of a blanket attack he had written on ministers of the Protestant faith. Carr was picked as his successor, and Roy Cohn testified to the tremendous pressures that were necessary to pry him loose from the FBI. Carr's resistance was significant in more ways than one. The FBI may stamp its documents secret; it may lock the sealed envelopes in steel safes whose combinations involve higher mathematics. But of what avail is all this if the man in whose head these secrets are carried picks up his hat from the FBI rack one afternoon and hangs it up the next morning in the office of a Senate subcommittee?

Frank Carr was a valuable addition to the McCarthy apparatus. The chairman and chief counsel lived for publicity; Carr avoided it. McCarthy and Cohn tore through one agency after another, creaming the headlines from a few sensational charges and moving on. Carr stayed behind, digging in his plodding manner for the facts that bored his employers. But hardly had he come to Washington in June 1953 when Roy Cohn led him over to the Pentagon on one of the many excursions on behalf of Schine. He was co-equal with Cohn, and fully entitled to protest the counsel's abuse of his powers. Instead he became a silent partner in the action and so threw away his standing. He seemed now to know this, and to be overcome by it as he sat at McCarthy's side. He studied black photostats of newspaper stories. He reached into five brief cases for papers that Roy Cohn demanded. He drew doodles of an object that resembled an igloo. He mumbled one word, "Yes," on McCarthy's demand. Otherwise he seemed deeply sunk in lethargy, utterly insensitive to the drama that raged around him.

Carr was a principal in these hearings. Grave charges had been made against him which he had not denied. In turn he had made grave charges against Stevens and Adams which, under oath, they branded as lies. In addition, Carr was a central witness. He was the third man present in the conferences of Adams and Cohn. He was the intermediary in January and February when relations between the Army and the subcommittee became strained. And above all Carr was the author of the memoranda which were both the sharpest allegations and the most persuasive evidence on the McCarthy side.

And yet through the long day of May 27 the four Republicans fought to dismiss Carr as a witness. The bitterness of the closing hours could have been avoided if McCarthy and Carr had simply said that the executive director was anxious to testify. Yet they sat silent. If the action of the Senators was strange and reprehensible, the inaction of McCarthy and Carr was even more mystifying. For Carr was the corroborating witness who might make a liar of John Adams and an honorable man of Roy Cohn. Secretary Stevens might smile and shake his head as Cohn and McCarthy told their stories. But if Frank Carr backed up his associates, who could doubt the word of Mr. Hoover's trusted protégé?

An outcry went up in the press when Carr was dismissed as a witness. Two days later Senator McCarthy affirmed that Carr was willing to testify *after all the evidence was in.* So on June 14, when the hearings entered their thirty-third day, Frank Carr at last took his place in the witness chair.

He proved to be the best witness on the McCarthy side— good-natured, calm, and precise. A soporific assistant of Ray Jenkins, Thomas Prewitt, led him through the now familiar story, and he supported and strengthened everything his associates had said. He was so good that in the noon recess this reporter expressed to Carr and to McCarthy his bewilderment at their acceptance of the Dworshak resolution a week before. Both answered that they wished to wind up the hearings. It seemed at the time an unsatisfactory answer, for nothing that the two men could have done could have helped more than Carr's testimony that morning. It became more plausible, however, as the cross-examination began. For in the course of the cross-examination, two shrewd young lawyers, James St. Clair and Senator Jackson, worked back over the testimony with Carr in an efficient, unemotional way. By the time they finished, Carr's contribution to McCarthy's case had shrunk, and McCarthy may have wished that the eleven memoranda had never been released.

First Thomas Prewitt reviewed with Carr the October 2

meeting in the Pentagon which Carr had described in the first of his memoranda. It was an inconclusive meeting and one which Carr could not well remember. His memory faded further as St. Clair pressed him.

Next Prewitt took up the November 6 luncheon in the Pentagon. This was the conference which formed the basis of McCarthy's charge of bribery. And, while the point was missed in the hearings, an interesting contrast showed up between the version of the conference as described by Cohn in his memorandum allegedly written on November 6, and in Frank Carr's testimony.

The Cohn memorandum was the strongest of all the documents on the McCarthy side. The emotionalism of its language sounded far more as if it had been written on March 11 than in the friendly days of November. It stated:

> Mr. Stevens asked that we hold up our public hearings on the Army. . . . He suggested that we go after the Navy, Air Force and Defense Department instead. We said first of all we had no evidence warranting an investigation of these other departments. Adams said not to worry about that because there was plenty of dirt there and they would furnish us the leads. Mr. Stevens thought this was the answer to his problems.

Mr. Carr's version was milder. The Secretary made no request to the subcommittee. Mr. Adams spoke of "information," not of "dirt"; and only with difficulty could Mr. Carr bring himself to say that the Secretary did more than nod his head.

One of the most damaging charges against the Army concerned the events of December 9. Cohn, Adams, and Carr met on that day and Adams drew a map of the United States. His purpose, Adams testified, was to learn whether the subcommittee had been given baseless but embarrasing charges about an Army post. Cohn's memorandum, allegedly written on that day, directly contradicted Adams and greatly hurt him.

> John Adams said today that following up the idea about investigating the Air Force he had gotten specific information for us about an Air Force base where there were a large number of homosexuals. He said that he would trade us that information if

we would tell him what the next Army project was that we would investigate.

The story was improbable. It was not only a grossly disloyal act, if true, but a very poor trade from Adams's point of view. Carr did say that Cohn had mentioned the trade. But he added that he had not heard Adams speak of it.

Carr's own memorandum of December 9 declared that Adams constantly referred to Schine as "our hostage." He added:

I am convinced they will keep right on trying to blackmail us as long as Schine is in the Army.

Now, under close questioning by Senator Jackson, Carr conceded that blackmail was a poor word. "I use words loosely," he said. He further conceded that the Army had never mistreated Schine or discriminated against him, and that the word "hostage" was used "facetiously" by Adams.

> MUNDT. You know John Adams rather well. I know him rather well. He is what you might call sort of a master of a flip phrase, is he not?
> CARR. Yes.
> MUNDT. That is, sometimes the things he says when reduced to print . . . might carry an altogether different meaning . . . is that correct?
> CARR. Yes, sir.

There were many more unpleasant moments for Frank Carr. There was the exchange with John McClellan in which Carr asserted that he had written memoranda about other government officials—but couldn't recall any of them. There was the admission that he wasn't sure if he had ever read the sixth memorandum "From: Senator McCarthy; To: Messrs. Cohn and Carr." And there was the curious fact, brought out by Senator Jackson, that McCarthy had summarized the FBI "letter" to his executive director but never shown it to him. If Carr was to be believed, Senator McCarthy had shown remarkable intuition in not involving his aide in a possible violation of the law.

There was the damaging exchange over the security clearances of Carr's own staff. "All the others . . . have . . . clearance through secret, is that right?" asked Symington. "The other clearances are through secret," Carr answered. It turned out that two staff members had not been cleared at all. Then there was the embarrassment over the loyalty oath signed by Carr's staff members to Roy Cohn which Carr said he had only heard a bit about. There was the further embarrassment over Schine. There was the long distance call to John Adams in South Dakota which Adams swore was about Schine, and which Carr could not remember. There was Carr's own memorandum of December 21 affirming, "I have on many occasions been pretty curt with Dave." "Did you dress Schine down or be curt with him in the presence of the Senator?" inquired Mr. Welch with his finger on Carr's memorandum of December 21. "I may have," Carr replied. On Schine he was trapped and he knew it. If he agreed Schine was important, then he was at fault for not transferring his work load while there was time. If he agreed that Schine was not important to the subcommittee—and obviously he was not—he granted the Army's case. Carr conceded the shocking news that Schine had interviewed witnesses while he was in uniform. He couldn't quite decide about Schine's value. Once he agreed that he was satisfied with the Army's treatment of Schine. But Cohn leaned over to emphasize the McCarthy line that Schine should have had a commission. So Carr changed his testimony and promptly landed in more troubles.

Welch, with his uncanny intuition, poked about among the little inconsistencies of Carr's memoranda and unearthed a number of errors. Instinctively this reporter had wanted to believe Carr and felt that on the memoranda his answers were convincing. But by the second day, the first sharp impact of his testimony had been rubbed away.

One great unsolved question of the hearings was: Where did the public images of the contestants depart from their private images? The best evidence consisted of clues, and the best clue was contained in the final subject of Carr's testimony, the monitored telephone calls between Carr and Adams.

They showed Frank Carr as Adams's counterpart on Capitol Hill—the peacemaker where there could be no peace. He failed, as Adams failed, and now in June he tried to deny to himself the peacemaker's role. But the monitor's echo spoke louder than Carr's small voice. It showed a patient, troubled Carr, very friendly with one he had branded blackmailer and very frank in discussing with this "blackmailer" his troubles with McCarthy, his appraisal of Schine, his concern over the ungovernable temper of Roy Cohn.

John Adams had publicly testified about his concern over Schine's conduct at Dix, his fear of Cohn's attitude, his confusion and Cohn's outburst during the crucial conference of January 14. Now the monitor showed Adams speaking privately to Carr in precisely the same vein.

Carr had publicly testified that on January 14 Adams had deliberately threatened overseas duty and that Cohn had kept his self-control. But on March 5, Adams had privately reminded Carr of his confusion and spoken of Cohn's explosion. He was explaining why he could not tell Cohn of a new assignment for Schine. He said:

> I can't make any commitment, Frank! The reason I can't is you remember the trouble we got in because I spoke before I knew the number of weeks [Schine] would have to stay in Gordon and Roy almost blew the roof off the building!

On March 5, there was no protest from Carr at this appraisal, which he later called false. Adams continued speaking of Schine's past foolishness and growing wisdom.

> I am very pleased Dave is behaving at Gordon the way I was trying to persuade you and Roy he should behave at Dix.

On March 5 Adams dealt further with the subject of Schine and of Cohn's concern for his friend. He said:

> For God's sake don't tell Roy what I am going to tell you! They are considering him for a leadership course.

Carr was pleased. Adams went on:

Don't put anyone in the Army in the way of a commitment. . . .
As I tried to tell Roy sixty-eight times, if he would let the guy be
in the Army things would be a lot better than if he kept haunt-
ing us.

In those March days when McCarthy had learned that the
Army was beginning to give the press the story of Cohn and
Schine, Sokolsky had failed as an intermediary. Carr was the
last hope. Carr denied it in June. But once again the echo intervened. Carr said to Adams on March 2:

I would like very much to get together with you on this so that
we could have a private chat.

And it was Carr who said on March 5:

I want you to come over on other things.

"The other things," Carr testified, were Schine. "I would be
less than frank," he added, "to say that I didn't have an interest
in [Schine] at this point."

Certainly he had an interest—the same interest John
Adams had—in peace. His job, his livelihood, his wife and
children's well-being were at stake!

It was fitting then that the final peace negotiations two
days before the encounter of March 10 occurred between the
two least responsible and most unprotected men. It was Adams
who was stalling by then and Carr who was pleading. He said,
"I take it you are not interested in getting together with me?
. . . I thought I was working with you. . . . I did want to talk to
you. It's up to you, boy . . . this is my last offer, friend."

This is my last offer, friend. Frank Carr was a normal,
decent man. No demons of hatred, ambition, and self-
contempt danced within him. He was happy in his home and
garden in Falls Church. No wonder he pleaded with Adams for
the sake of a settlement, no wonder he sat silent through the
hearings, no wonder he lacked will in defending his case. He
had slaved for eleven years for the FBI while his wife pinched
pennies, and then he had allowed himself against his own better judgment to be dragged into a political charnel house. Now

for all he knew he was on the streets again, thanks to the egotism of a playboy who had never known hunger or stayed at home of an evening to save a dollar. Frank Carr was still a good witness, ready to testify when McCarthy had taken full responsibility for any illegal acts committed by his side, and when all other testimony was in. Within those limits he was loyal to Cohn and McCarthy. But their reluctance to risk his testimony was perhaps no great riddle after all.

The Fanaticism
of Senator McCarthy

It was late on the thirtieth day of the hearings that Joseph McCarthy came to the witness chair. He was flanked as usual by Roy Cohn and Francis Carr. Across the room a large colored map was hoisted onto stands in preparation for a lecture on the Communist Party.

Jenkins had waited long for this proud moment. It was his misfortune that it followed hard after a ghastly hour in which McCarthy had tormented Joseph Welch. In the revulsion that followed, Jenkins' carefully prepared questions, which would have seemed obsequious on the kindest of occasions, became so fawning that even the witness recoiled.

"What has been your interest in Communists, espionage, subversives, poor security risks?" inquired the special counsel. Senator McCarthy affirmed that he was disturbed by them. "Your position on Communism then, I take it, is well known, Senator?" "I think so," said McCarthy with a grin.

> JENKINS. Your viewpoint, you would say, and their viewpoint are diametrically opposed to each other?
> McCARTHY. That is right.
> JENKINS. You are not one of their fair-haired boys?
> McCARTHY. You are right.
> JENKINS. You have never been tendered their nomination

by the Communist Party for the Presidency—is that what you mean?

MCCARTHY. Not yet.

A low groan passed through the audience. Mr. Jenkins asked the Senator to tell the American public "just what the set-up of the Communists is." McCarthy heaved himself up with a sigh and crossed the room to the maps. As he spoke, he rapped upon them with a cane sent from Texas, with a handle carved in the shape of a longhorn steer. The map was brightly colored, and the names and addresses of Communist leaders were listed for each state save Texas, where the local patriotism of the oil men forbade any such slur. Some of these Communist leaders were dead; some others had long since left the Party. One address in the South proved to be the property of a loyal box-holder who protested loudly. But the Senator could hardly be blamed if his material was not up to date. It was a perfectly good lecture whose weakest point was the admission that Communist strength had been halved in the final years of the Truman administration. But the Senator, who needed the Communists as the sharksucker needs the shark, did not allow himself to be comforted by this development.

The implication of Senator McCarthy's argument, unaccompanied by a broader perspective, appeared to be that by cleaning Reds out of Washington the American people could somehow exorcise the mounting dangers in the rice paddies of Indo-China, the villages of Southern India, the slums of Italy and France, the black ghettos of Africa, the schools and factories of Communist China and Russia.

And yet, while McCarthy ignored these mounting dangers, he foresaw nothing but war. "There are many people who think that we can live side by side with Communists," he told Jenkins. And when the counsel asked, "What do you say about that, sir?" he answered:

MCCARTHY. Mr. Jenkins, . . . there is not the remotest possibility of this war which we are in today, and it is a war . . . ending except by victory or by death for this civilization.

The day faded; the hands of the clock wound around. Jenkins became restive.

JENKINS. Senator McCarthy, . . . it is about closing time. . . .
Now, while you have an audience of perhaps twenty or thirty
million Americans . . . I want you to tell . . . what each individual American, man, woman and child can do . . . to do their
bit to liquidate the Communistic Party.

The Senator nodded. First, he said, "They must depend
upon those of us whom they send down here to man the watch-
towers of the nation. . . ." Thus he assumed the whole executive role. Next he warned about teachers in schools, not the
liberals or radicals, he added, but the real subversives. Lastly he
called upon the voters to defeat all candidates for election who
felt (with the President) that we should help allies even if they
traded with China. Well satisfied, the special counsel reached
for a perfect synthesis. What of "the hearthstone of the home"
he inquired; was not that the place "to begin the inculcation
into the minds of the youth of this nation . . . when the minds
are young and pliable and impressionable?" Yes, said the witness, and the counsel went on to bring the Rotarians, the Op-
timists, the Kiwanis, the churches, the kindergartens, schools,
and universities into his expanding vision of a nation where all
citizens would pass through a McCarthy-made mold and be
stamped "loyal."

In the days that followed, Jenkins developed his direct
examination. Then he turned to cross-examination, begging
the Senator's forgiveness. The Senator granted it, and Jenkins
said nothing could make him happier than that. Once again he
traced with McCarthy the familiar story that by now was bor-
ing and tedious. The Senator's testimony was interesting
chiefly in that he also greatly softened his version of the crimes
committed by John Adams and Robert Stevens. For example,
on that old charge in the McCarthy brief, that Stevens and
Adams "offered up the Navy, the Air Force and the defense
establishment as substitute targets" and offered further to provide the "dirt," this exchange took place.

JENKINS. . . . what precisely, Senator, did the Secretary and
Mr. Adams say?
McCARTHY. Again, Mr. Jenkins, I can't give you verbatim
language. But they indicated that they were unhappy about any

concentration on the Army; they indicated that if there was infiltration in the Army there must be in the Navy and Air Corps; and as I recall I heard Mr. Adams offer Mr. Cohn information in regard to the Navy. Just what language he used I don't know.

A strange concession for a man who had cried "Bribery" and "Blackmail"! So the testimony went, with almost every answer stopping short of the clear denial of what Army witnesses had said that could be turned over to the Department of Justice as possible perjury. Welch seemed unable to decide whether he was back in the courtroom trying the legal core of the case, or before the cameras with the job of education only half finished. The Democrats, who had no files to work from, could not do Welch's job. Most important of all, the men around the table were by now nodding in weariness.

So the end of the hearings approached at last, and in the audience the question was voiced: What finally was accomplished by it all? No issues had been resolved, no allegation proved beyond doubt, no verdict established. Perhaps the phrase that would endure as the most accurate appraisal was spoken by Stuart Symington when he said to McCarthy: "The American people have had a look at you for six weeks. . . ."

What had they seen?

McCarthy had shown, first, great physical strength and stamina. He had been more active than all other Senators put together in the hearings. He had gone off each weekend to campaign in Wisconsin. Yet rarely had his eyes closed and his head sunk on his chest in tiredness. He seemed in some obscure way to need the tension that others shunned, to feed on the conflict that exhausted his opponents, to draw nourishment from inflicting punishment and even from being hated and feared.

He had shown great skill and resourcefulness as a showman and a fighter. He had created revulsion against the hearings and then turned it to his own use in demanding a halt to the show. He had driven the inquiry into the swamps and forests of side issues—and then denounced it as a waste of

time. He had missed few opportunities to twist a phrase or turn
a man's own thoughts against himself. When Ray Jenkins asserted that the soldiers at Fort Dix were packed like cattle in
trucks, McCarthy protested in the name of American mother-
hood. When it developed without warning that Private Schine
had been meeting in the evenings with the McCarthy subcommittee staff, McCarthy unhesitatingly launched an attack
on the Army for shadowing the citizens of this free nation. His
enormous charts were paid for by taxes; but when Jenkins produced a two-by-four photostat of Private Schine's telephone
calls, McCarthy swore that he would start a special investigation into the sums poured into charts by the executive branch
of the government.

He had shown charm on occasion; he had even shown
humor. When he tried to ridicule by overstatement the
privileges granted to Private Schine, his eerie snicker was the
only sound in the silence of the Caucus Room. When he offered
to provide some tobacco to replace Mundt's cigar his humor
was pleasant, in the best Kiwanis Club tradition. He showed a
warmth and a desire to be liked, even by his opponents, which
this reporter found almost touching.

Yet all this was the outward and peripheral Joseph McCarthy. Far more important were two revelations of his inner being.

First was McCarthy's freedom from all rules and restraints,
his total disregard for the ancient rule: Judge others as you
would be judged. Typical was his outrage at the "smears"
against his staff even as he introduced smear after smear
against Samuel Reber, Frederick Fisher, Theodore Kaghan,
scores of men with no remote connection to the dispute.

Second was McCarthy's extraordinary power in pursuit of
his immediate purpose; his single-minded concentration on
gaining his objective regardless of the cost to others or to himself; his capacity to return again and again and again to his
original contention and to refuse to yield it or to modify it, no
matter how strongly attacked or how completely demolished it
might be.

Those who watched McCarthy noted these obsessive qualities and tried to assess them in the conventional terms of cynicism and ambition, the emotions of ordinary men. Their efforts were futile, for McCarthy was no ordinary man. He was the product neither of Wisconsin, nor of any other community or communal experience. He was the unique phenomenon that occurs once in a hundred years.

McCarthy is not to be judged by our recognizable past. He is a forerunner and prophet of the American Brotherhood of the Guiltless. Like his brothers, his motivation must stem in part from the knowledge that he is steeped in conventional guilt. He leads the assault upon convention, hurling at society the very accusations which it would level at him. This is the capacity which leaves a nation bewildered as it appraises him by its own standards and symbols—which for him exist only to be abused.

It was Mr. Welch who expressed something of this reaction when he turned to the Senator during an executive session.

> WELCH. Looking at you, Senator McCarthy, you have I think something of a genius for creating confusion . . . creating turmoil in the hearts and minds of this country.

Joseph McCarthy has a genius for creating turmoil in the hearts and minds of this country, and the reason may be that turmoil has long raged in his own mind and heart.

The mind and heart in turmoil were well described by Eric Hoffer in *The True Believer*. "Only the individual who has come to terms with his self," writes Hoffer, "can have a dispassionate attitude toward the world. Once the harmony with the self is upset and a man is impelled to reject, renounce, distrust or forget his self he turns into a highly reactive entity." Hoffer continues:

> The fanatic is perpetually incomplete and insecure. He cannot generate self-assurance out of his individual resources—out of his rejected self—but finds it only by clinging passionately to whatever support he happens to embrace. This passionate attachment is the essense of his blind devotion and religiosity and

he sees in it the source of all virtue and strength. . . . The fanatic is not really a stickler to principles. He embraces a cause not primarily because of its justness and holiness but because of his desperate need for something to hold on to. Often indeed it is his need for passionate attachment which turns every cause he embraces into a holy cause.

The fanatic cannot be weaned away from his cause by an appeal to his reason or moral sense. He fears compromise and cannot be persuaded to qualify the certitude and righteousness of his holy cause. But he finds no difficulty in swinging suddenly and wildly from one holy cause to another. . . .

Though they seem at opposite poles fanatics of all kinds are actually crowded together at one end. . . . They hate each other with the hatreds of brothers. They are as far apart and close together as Saul and Paul.

"The fanatic . . . finds no difficulty in swinging suddenly and wildly from one hold cause to another. . . ." In July 1949, a newcomer arose on the floor of the Senate to make a passionate defense of the belief that all men are innocent until proved guilty by due process of law. He denounced that group of nationalists who would "attempt to call up all the emotions of war and hatred." He scorned those who would "wave the flag and speak of the white crosses over the graves of the American dead." He condemned those who "ask in self-righteous phrases why . . . the government of the United States of America should concern itself with applying decent rules of justice to vicious criminals." He cried:

Mr. President, America came into Europe with clean hands. The people of the world had come to respect not only America's great military and economic power but also to respect and admire her conception of decency and fair play and above all her judicial system which gave to every man no matter how much in the minority his day in court. This vast wealth of good will which had been built up over the years is being dissipated by a few men of little minds who unfortunately, in the eyes of the world, represent the American people.

This enemy of McCarthyism was Joseph McCarthy, speaking in defense of the rights of German soldiers tried and sentenced for the Malmedy massacre.

". . . passionate attachment," says Hoffer, is the essence of the fanatic's "blind devotion." McCarthy was not at first a fanatic in his beliefs. He came late and a stranger to the cause of anti-Communism. His mood, on returning to Wisconsin from Wheeling, West Virginia, where he began his anti-Communist crusade, was one of amazement and delight at the political diamond mine into which he had stumbled. He was not then a believer in any cause but McCarthy. But gradually he came to believe his tirades—or so it seems.

The fanatic is egocentric. And so McCarthy in the hearings saw all issues and conditions in terms of himself. In these hearings, as in other inquiries, witnesses protested that their loyalty should not be judged by the sole standard of whether they supported or opposed McCarthy. To McCarthy there was no other standard and could be none. If the chairman or anyone else turned away as he spoke, McCarthy was enraged; his every point of order was "extremely important." He wanted deeply to be liked by everyone, but he would rather be hated than ignored. His own hatred was directed impartially to men of either party who threatened to take from him the center of the stage.

The fanatic stands above the law and above duly constituted authority. He disdains authority, which supports the society he rejects. He scorns the law as the instrument of the order he is psychologically committed to overthrow. So McCarthy claimed that he, rather than the responsible officials appointed by the President, spoke for the Army. He stated, "I just will not abide by any secrecy directive of anyone."

The fanatic seeks to destroy real and imagined enemies who stand in his way. The fanaticism of McCarthy stood forth in his original brief of counter-charges. The Army brief had attributed to him a minor and rather moderate role. Like one preoccupied with his own persecution, McCarthy struck back. He uncovered "motive" in the supposedly criminal acts of Mr. H. Struve Hensel. Late in the hearings, when his brief had lain for five weeks before the public, he conceded that he had no evidence whatever linking Hensel to the Army report. He had simply read the report, remembered old charges against Hensel, and then "put two and two together." McCarthy had cried that Carr and Cohn had been "smeared." Yet Hensel swore that McCarthy had told him on May 3 that in attacking him he was following the advice an old farmhand, Indian Charlie, gave him: "If one was ever approached by another person in a not completely friendly fashion one should start kicking at the other person as fast as possible below the belt until the other person was rendered helpless."

The fanatic rejects objective truth in dedication to the truth of his own creation. Eric Hoffer quotes the view of Pascal, that self-contempt produces in man "the most unjust and criminal passions imaginable for he conceives a mortal hatred against truth which blames him and convinces him of his faults." McCarthy seemed to have a distaste for the discipline of truth. He said of Symington, for example, "The only time I hear him raise his voice at this table is when we appear to be hurting those that defend Communism." This demonstrably false charge, like the claim that McClellan wished to jail him, was one of McCarthy's big lies. It was indignantly repudiated; but, following the advice of his teacher, McCarthy repeated it over and over and over until in many untrained minds a part of it stuck. He usually did not lie outright, but distorted the facts to leave an impression that was false.

To the fanatic, morality is defined as that which advances his own cause. McCarthy upbraided Symington for using what he called Communist methods. Yet his own methods were flagrantly expedient; H. Struve Hensel swore, and the Senator did not deny, that two of McCarthy's agents falsely told a woman that her daughter had been involved in a hit-and-run accident simply to learn her son-in-law's address.

The fanatics of the extreme left, the Communists, treat morality as a by-product of the capitalist class structure. McCarthy also appeared indifferent to society's code of moral conduct. He seemed insensitive to the suffering he inflicted on others. He was plainly surprised when Welch declined to embrace him on the day after his attack on Frederick Fisher. Only once during the hearings did McCarthy show a glimmer of conscience. "I fear," he said, "I may have done an injustice to

Mr. Hensel and John Adams." But at no other time did he
indicate that there could conceivably be any wrongdoing on his
part.

In McCarthy's world, if he was incapable of immorality his
enemies were not. The attack upon him by Senator Flanders
was "vicious" and "dishonest." The witnesses who criticized
him were "grossly dishonest." The monitoring of telephone
calls (which he himself had practiced) was "the most dishonest
and indecent thing I have heard in years." Over and over he
begged Symington "in common decency, in common honesty"
to testify, as McCarthy had done. He employed these moral
symbols, but ignored much of the content of moral teaching.
But perhaps the use of words like "indecent" and "vicious" rose
also from realms beyond reason. They were the same words
that others might use in condemning McCarthy—that some
part of McCarthy might even use to condemn himself.

Day and night, McCarthy lunged at real and imagined
enemies. Only one was beyond his reach—the enemy within. It
lurked there throughout the hearings, striking swiftly and
withdrawing like the tongue of a snake. And then, late in the
afternoon of June 9, when the hearings were in their thirtieth
day, this internal enemy emerged to inject its venom into the
elderly Mr. Welch until he wept. All present watched in horror
and disbelief. And some newspapers on the following day tried
to reconstruct the scene, pointing out the factual errors in what
McCarthy had said. Nothing could have been more futile. For
the meaning of that event which formed the true climax of the
hearings lay not in what was said but in the manner in which it
was said.

Through the long afternoon of June 9, Welch had labored
to come to grips with the elusive Roy Cohn. His elbow on the
table, his long fingers tracing the furrows on his forehead,
Welch reviewed what Private Schine had done on his many
leaves, leading the discomfited Roy Cohn along a winding trail
of restaurants visited, money spent, and work completed. Then
abruptly he changed.

WELCH. Mr. Cohn, if I told you now that we had a bad

situation at Monmouth, you'd want to cure it by sundown if you could, wouldn't you?

COHN. Yes, sir.

To the left of Mr. Welch sat Senator McCarthy. He had listened, frowning. Now he leaned forward with a grin, preparing to intervene. But Welch did not know that.

WELCH. May I add my small voice, sir, and say whenever you know about a subversive or a Communist or a spy, please hurry! Will you remember these words?

If Mr. Cohn preferred to forget Mr. Welch's words, another turned them to this own ends.

McCARTHY. Mr. Chairman, in view of that question . . .

The chairman turned his moon-face to the table's end. "Have you a point of order?"

McCARTHY. Not exactly, Mr. Chairman, but in view of Mr. Welch's request that the information be given once we know of anyone who might be performing any work for the Communist Party, I think we should tell him that he has in his law firm a young man named Fisher . . . who has been for a number of years a member of an organization which was named, oh years and years ago, as the legal bulwark of the Communist Party. . . .

Mr. Welch had urged the subcommittee counsel to give the names of subversives, Communists, or spies in sensitive agencies to the responsible officials concerned. Frederick Fisher, secretary of the Young Republican League of Newton, Massachusetts, had as a student joined the Lawyers Guild, once broadly based, and now charged with pro-Communist domination. Smiling, licking his dry lips, McCarthy continued.

McCARTHY. I certainly assume that Mr. Welch did not know of this young man at the time he recommended him as the assistant counsel for this committee, but he has such terror and such a great desire to know where anyone is located who may be serving the Communist cause. . . .

How he lingered over the words "terror" and "great," before releasing them! They were spoken in pure hatred.

Why at this moment was McCarthy tearing down his own case? The telephone calls had been a turning point in his favor. Roy Cohn had proved an excellent and persuasive witness. Mr. Welch had conceded that the Army could not hope for complete vindication. The public reaction that had risen against Senator McCarthy had reached its high point and begun to ebb. From now on, if he could control himself and appear as a moderate responsible leader, that might be the final image left on ten million television screens. It would have gone far to obscure earlier impressions of brutality. It might once more have opened the door of welcome to the White House and the Republican high command. With the patronage of a great party behind him, Senator McCarthy could rise to new heights following this trial. Without that patronage he might be left an outlaw.

Why then did McCarthy tear at himself? The kindest answer was suggested by Roy Cohn. In a telephone conversation on September 23, Secretary Stevens had pleaded with Cohn not to stage a public humiliation of Major General Richard Partridge, chief of Army intelligence. Cohn's reply was revealing. "I'm afraid once he gets up there, there will not be too much of a way to stop the thing. . . . You might want a nice gentle fight but once you get in the ring and start taking a couple of pokes it gets under your skin."

Was McCarthy maddened by Welch's taunting of his assistant? It was evident that the Senator had waited a long time for this moment. He had come to hate Welch, not because of any single remark made by the Army counsel, but because he had won the sympathy and admiration of the nation, something that on this stage at least McCarthy wanted for himself alone. He hated Welch further and found it necessary to destroy him because of his spirit of ironic comedy. There was no room in McCarthy's world for such a spirit. For it brings the serious into focus and reveals what is overdrawn and grotesque. It modestly offers perspective, and perspective was the quality most dangerous of all to McCarthyism. In McCarthy's closed world of conformity, comedy and irony were enemies that threatened to expose the dark with a shaft of piercing light.

On June 9 millions were watching who would never forget this scene. And yet McCarthy seemed entirely oblivious of the world around him. Still grinning, he turned and looked sideways at the Bostonian. His voice bore a heavy load of sarcasm.

McCARTHY. Knowing that, Mr. Welch, I just felt that I had a duty to respond to your urgent request. . . . I have hesitated about bringing that up, but I have been rather bored with your phony requests to Mr. Cohn here that he personally get every Communist out of government before sundown. Therefore we will give you the information about the young man in your own organization.

Finally, there came the condescension as the Senator bestowed on Mr. Welch the benefit of the doubt concerning his own participation in treason.

McCARTHY. I am not asking you at this time to explain why you tried to foist him on this committee. Whether you knew he was a member of that Communist organization or not I don't know. I assume you did not, Mr. Welch, because I get the impression that while you are quite an actor, you play for a laugh, I don't think you have any conception of the danger of the Communist Party. I don't think you would ever knowingly aid the Communist cause. I think you are unknowingly aiding it when you try to burlesque this hearing in which we are trying to bring out the facts, however.

Mr. Welch sat, his head in his hands, staring at the table before him, apparently stunned. Once again McCarthy had struck at the jugular, for while Welch cared not a whit what damage was done to him in the course of this case that he had volunteered for, he had carried on his conscience a burden of worry that an encounter with McCarthy might bring some evil on a member of his firm.

Once as McCarthy spoke, Welch formed the mute word "stop." Now he leaned forward to speak.

WELCH. Mr. Chairman, under these circumstances I must have something approaching a personal privilege.

Mundt nodded, distressed, and offered all within his power to confer.

MUNDT. You may have it, sir. It will not be taken out of your time.

Welch started to speak, and as he did so McCarthy turned away. No longer the center of the stage he seemed to have lost all interest in the affair. He ran his tongue along the inside of his mouth as Welch began.

WELCH. Senator McCarthy, I did not know. . . .

McCarthy turned to talk to his assistant, Juliana. Welch paused and asked for his attention. McCarthy turned to him. "I can listen with one ear," he remarked. "This time," said Welch, "I want you to listen with both." And he began again.

WELCH. Senator McCarthy, I think until this moment. . . .

At that McCarthy interrupted again to say loudly to Juliana that he'd better get the news story showing that Fisher was a member of the Lawyers Guild, the citation showing that the Guild was on the proscribed list, and the fact that Welch had recommended him. "I think that should be in the record," he explained.

If he hoped thus to reduce Welch to incoherence he was wrong. "You won't need anything in the record when I have finished telling you this," said the Bostonian. And so he began, and nothing could stanch his eloquence.

WELCH. Until this moment, Senator, I think I never really gauged your cruelty or your recklessness. Fred Fisher is a young man who went to the Harvard Law School and came into my firm and is starting what looks to be a brilliant career with us.

When I decided to work for this committee I asked Jim St. Clair . . . to be my first assistant. I said to Jim, "Pick somebody in the firm who works under you that you would like." He chose Fred Fisher and they came down on an afternoon plane. That night, when we had taken a little stab at trying to see what the case was about, Fred Fisher and Jim St. Clair and I went to dinner together. I then said to these two young men, "Boys, I don't know anything about you except that I have always liked you, but if there is anything funny in the life of either one of you that would hurt anybody in this case you speak up quick."

Fred Fisher said, "Mr. Welch, when I was in law school and

for a period of months thereafter I belonged to the Lawyers Guild. . . ." I said, "Fred, I just don't think I am going to ask you to work on the case. If I do one of these days that will come out and go over national television and it will just hurt like the dickens."

So, Senator, I asked him to go back to Boston. Little did I dream you could be so reckless and so cruel as to do any injury to that lad. It is true he is still with Hale and Dorr. It is true that he will continue to be with Hale and Dorr. It is, I regret to say, equally true that I fear he shall always bear a scar needlessly inflicted by you. If it were in my power to forgive you for your reckless cruelty I would do so. I like to think that I am a gentle man, but your forgiveness will have to come from someone other than me.

"Needlessly inflicted. . . ." So Welch touched on the sadistic essence of the moment. Yet, true to himself, it was forgiveness that was in Welch's mind for the one who had inflicted the wrong.

McCarthy had appeared to be entirely engrossed in reading some paper as the Army counsel spoke. Now he returned to the scene of his ambush, a little defensive and rough. He complained that Welch had no right to speak of cruelty because he had "been baiting Mr. Cohn here for hours." He tried to go once again over Fisher's record. But Welch cut him short.

WELCH. Senator, may we not drop this? We know he belonged to the Lawyers Guild, and Mr. Cohn nods his head at me.

It was true; Cohn was nodding. Had some feeling of compassion and decency stirred in him, some relic of his background and tradition? Welch turned to him.

WELCH. I did you, I think, no personal injury, Mr. Cohn.
COHN. No, sir.
WELCH. I meant to do you no personal injury and if I did I beg your pardon.

Cohn nodded again. The counsel turned back to McCarthy, now staring at his knees.

WELCH. Let us not assassinate this lad further, Senator. You have done enough. Have you no sense of decency, sir? At long last? Have you left no sense of decency?

So the word "decency," long abused, was reclaimed for the English language. And so Welch, in what must have been one of the most terrible moments of his life, was able to distinguish the essential line where decency stopped and indecency began—where prosecution became assassination. Prosecution by due process of law was part of civilized government; assassination belonged in the darkness of primitive man.

There is in man an urge to the primeval, a "longing for the mud," as Frenchmen say. McCarthy said that Welch was pained about the fate of a near-Communist, while he had no pain over the unfounded charges against Frank Carr and—he glanced up at Cohn, who still sat in the witness chair. But the young man was biting his lips and shuddering; unwilling to be cited as a justification of this act, he shook his head. McCarthy began lamely to ask Welch if he had not brought down Fred Fisher as his assistant. But Welch, with quiet scorn, closed out the debate.

> WELCH. Mr. McCarthy, I will not discuss this with you further. You have sat within six feet of me and could have asked me about Fred Fisher. You have brought it out. If there is a God in heaven it will do neither you nor your cause any good. I will not discuss it further. I will not ask Mr. Cohn any more questions. You, Mr. Chairman, may, if you will, call the next witness.

There was a moment of silence. Twice every day the chairman had warned that policemen would turn out anyone in the audience who applauded. Six policemen were standing with their backs to the table staring at the crowd to see to it that the rule was kept. But now everyone in the room began to applaud Mr. Welch, while the gavel lay motionless in the chairman's hand and the policemen made no move. Seated at the end of the table, Senator McCarthy breathed heavily, his face set. For the first time he seemed deserted in the room. Welch rose and passed him on his way to the doors. A woman standing there laid her hand on his arm and burst into tears. The reporters who had joined him on his strolls through the marble halls rose now to accompany him and then left him alone. As the room emptied, Joseph McCarthy looked around for someone to talk to. There were very few who would speak to him; but, finding one, he spread his hands, palms upward, asking, "What did I do?"

Joseph McCarthy was remorseful on the following day— not because he had hurt Fisher, but because he had hurt himself. At times he was fearful. Yet he had nothing to fear from Ray Jenkins.

It was the enemy within that he feared, and with good reason. He explained to a friend that he had felt knots in his throat as Welch spoke, not out of concern for Fisher but because he realized that he had blundered and that Welch had got the better of him at last. Speaking of Robert Stevens, he turned to Shakespeare. The quotation was not exact as he gave it, but no passage could have been more revealing as McCarthy cited it in the hearings. To his wife, Macbeth declared:

> *For mine own good*
> *All causes shall give way: I am in blood*
> *Stepp'd in so far, that, should I wade no more*
> *Returning were as tedious as go o'er.*

Was this in the deeper sense an allusion to himself? Macbeth was noble in origin, haunted by conscience, free of vulgarity, sublime in defeat. McCarthy was none of these, yet they had much in common. The great Shakespearean scholar Bradley said of Macbeth: "He has never . . . accepted as the principle of his own conduct the morality which takes shape in his imaginative fears."

Were there moments when McCarthy doubted and despised himself? Mundt and Dirksen were by his side to assure him that middle-of-the-road Republicans were for him still. Outside the room admirers were waiting to praise him— women to show their adulation, men to shake his hand, nuns to whisper shyly that they were praying for him, children to ask for his autograph. Like other leaders of the masses he made a particular point of appearing tender to children. He smiled. It was true that the forces of freedom were closing around McCarthy, but not yet was Birnam wood come to Dunsinane.

The Curtain Falls

Of all the days of the Army-McCarthy hearings, the thirty-fifth was the most reassuring. The Senators assumed that day would be the last, and every man was conscious of the final impression that would be left on the people of the United States.

Through many days in the Senate Caucus Room, the people had been referred to as the Great Jury—an easy phrase. But on this morning the jury struck a soundless gavel on the committee table and impressed on all present the spirit of fairness and restraint that it expected of its leaders. So a kind of good humor and gentleness flooded into the great room with the morning light, and it was new and strange. Even Senator McCarthy was pressed into the invisible mold. He did imply with a grin that his friend Senator Symington was not the author of the statement that Symington read so ably. But when Symington retorted that McCarthy might hear better if he took the Deputy Junior Senator from Wisconsin out of his ear, everyone joined in the laughter—everyone, that is, except Mr. Cohn.

When Senator Symington made the mistake of referring to the CIA as our world-wide FBI, Senator McCarthy proclaimed this a slur on Mr. Hoover's agency, for the CIA, he said, was infiltrated with Reds. Then he mentioned, as if in evidence, the name of William Bundy, a CIA official whom he had tried in vain to bring before his subcommittee. "Mr. Bundy has . . ." McCarthy began, and the lightning flashed on the horizon. As though he remembered the silent jury, the consequences of his attack on Mr. Fisher, and the fact that this was to be the last day, McCarthy paused for a long minute. "Mr. Bundy has— period," said McCarthy quietly.

But the hearings did not end on that day. On the next morning, the spirit of the thirty-fifth day faded, and the responsibility rested with Chairman Mundt. Evidently he was irritated at the criticism of the "chicken luncheon" in which he had played a part in bringing about Secretary Stevens' acceptance of McCarthy's terms. He referred to that episode as "harmony," contrasting it with the "disharmony" of the hearings. He went on to lay the blame for the whole dispute upon Stuart Symington. "I have no quarrel with the way in which politics is played," he remarked, and in a smooth and rather sleazy manner alleged that Clark Clifford had been motivated by the partisan objectives of the Democratic party in offering advice to a Republican Secretary of the Army. This was a clear endorsement of McCarthy's final contention, an obvious attempt to lay the groundwork for political exploitation of the hearings in later campaigns. Symington protested bitterly, and pointed out that it was the Democrats who had voted to summon Clifford for questioning; Mundt and the Republicans had refused to let him appear. With greater foresight, Joseph Welch asked that a statement from the Secretary be accepted. It came that afternoon and, giving the lie to Mundt's accusation, noted Stevens' amazement that Clifford should be accorded any role at all. Shaking his head in shame for the Senate whose dignity he treasured, John McClellan reprimanded the chairman. Mundt's actions, said McClellan, "testify eloquently to the ineptness, to the lack of capacity of this administration and the Republican party to conduct the affairs of government without turmoil and harangue."

The day wore on as Welch and St. Clair circled McCarthy in the final rounds of cross-examination. They accomplished very little, and at five-thirty, as the light began to fade, the Army counsel paused.

> WELCH. Mr. Chairman, there always comes a time in any lawsuit, no matter how long it is, when some lawyer says those magic words in the courtroom, "I rest!" And those words I now say.

Now, at the conclusion, each actor in turn stepped to the front and spoke his concluding piece. Each speech was characteristic of the man: Potter, simple and troubled; Dworshak, forthright and brief; Dirksen, maudlin and wordy; Jenkins, obvious and gauche; Jackson, direct and intelligent; Symington, generous and concerned. McCarthy as usual was the most purposeful. He announced plans for future investigations of Communism and called on the Democrats to follow where he might lead. Mundt offered, typically, a long, unconvincing rationalization of their failure to meet head-on the great issues involved. John McClellan promptly cut through the fog with bitter truth.

> McCLELLAN. . . . the series of events that . . . made these hearings mandatory will be recognized and long remembered as one of the most disgraceful episodes in the history of our government. . . . Simply to say that this series of events is regrettable is a gross understatement. They are deplorable and unpardonable. There is no valid excuse and justification for this situation having occurred and it will now become our solemn duty to fix the responsibility.

Last of all came Mr. Welch. If his confidence was shaken, his serenity, at heart, was still intact.

> WELCH. I alone came into this room from deep obscurity. I alone will retire to obscurity. As it folds about me softly as I hope it does quickly, the lady who listens, and is called Judith Linden Welch, will hear from me a long sigh of relief. I am sorry that this play had to take place in the fretful lightning and the ominous roll of noises from Indo-China and around the world. It saddens me to think that my life has been lived so largely either in wars or in turmoil. I have already indicated that I could do with a little serenity. I allow myself to hope that soon there will

come a day when there will in this lovely land of ours be more simple laughter.

So "the play" ended. And, it was drama, great drama, in the sense that, for those who witnessed it, great issues seemed to be at stake.

Henry Mencken, in a moment of despair, predicted that our democracy might founder on "the day of fate," when "a master corsair, thoroughly adept at pulling the mob nose" would "throw off his employers and set up in business for himself." Joseph McCarthy, for all his weaknesses, was cast in that mold. He had brought the nation to the verge of a Constitutional crisis when the Hearings opened. By the time that they were over, he seemed shrunken and spent.

Television had enabled the American people to see McCarthy for what he was. But, if it proved itself as a resource for democracy, it was only because a few good men were seen in action on the screen. It was not their intention at first, to stand and fight, but, they did. To those, like Everett Dirksen, who clad themselves once again in the mantle of moderation, when the battle was won, they could say, as Henry the Fourth said to a tardy general: *"Hang yourself, brave Crillon. We fought at Arques, and you were not there."*

This First Edition
designed by George Mattingly
edited & set in Georg Trump's Trump Mediaeval
by Robert Sibley of Abracadabra
with mechanicals by Alan Bernheimer
printed & bound in the United States
by McNaughton & Gunn Lithographers
Autumn 1979